Samplers, Sewing
&
Simplicity
in
Quaker Ireland

Clodagh Grubb

Samplers, Sewing and Simplicity in Quaker Ireland

Clodagh Grubb

Published by

The Historical Committee of the Religious Society of Friends in Ireland

© Clodagh Grubb, 2020.

ISBN 978-1-9161092-1-6

The production of this book has been greatly aided by sponsorship from
J. & L. Grubb Ltd. (Cashel Blue cheese) and the Robert and Kezia Stanley Chapman Trust.

Typeset and Printed in Ireland by Central Press Bray Limited, Bray, Co. Wicklow.

Acknowledgments and thanks to

Ackworth school;   Allen, Clive and Jo;   Allott, Norman;   Buchanan, Kate and Steve;
Badman, Judith;   Baker, Tom;   Castagner, Rosemary Sinton;   Chittick, Merida;   Clarke, Eithne;
Clifton Brown, Petronelle;   Corrigan, Mario;   Chester Beaty Library;   Douglas, Shirley and Glynn;
Feller, Elizabeth and Micheal;   Fennell, Lesley and James;   Ferguson, Lydia Shackleton;
Finkel, M. and daughter;   Flanagan, Elaine;   Gibbon, John and Carol;   Goodbody, Michael;
Goodbody, Wendy;   Grafton Academy of Dress Design;   Greenhow, Desna;   Grubb, John;
Grubb, Louis;   Grubb, Nicholas and Barbara;   Grubb, Patrick;   Hamilton, Sophie;   Harrison, Ciara;
Hill, Venetia;   Jacob, Brigid and Philip;   Johnson, Joan and Roger;   Keogh, Jenny;   Lamb, Peter;
Lehane, Rachel;   Marr, Susanne;   Moriarty, Christopher;   Murphy, Etain;   Nuttall, Jenny;
Nuzum, Christopher;   O'Brien, Valerie;   O'Dea, Catherine;   Pearson, Irwin and Roy;
Perry, Pleasaunce;   Pim, Malcolm;   Scallan, Eithne;   Shackleton, Jonathan;   Rowe, Veronica;
Tarrant, Naomi;   Victoria and Albert Museum study room for textiles;   Ward, Alex;
Wardell, Olive;   Wigham, Jonathan.

Special thanks are due to my husband John McCormick for photography and general editing and to
Tim Jackson for copy-editing.

The majority of the illustrations are from the Friends Historical Library Dublin (indicated as FHLD in
captions) or from individuals (indicated as Private collection). Diagrams and sketches are by the author.

Other illustrations are courtesy of:

Local Studies, Genealogy and Archives, Kildare Library Services (KLS)

National Museum of Ireland, Collins Barracks (NMI).

Irish Linen Centre and Lisburn Museum (Lisburn).

The Mount School, York (The Mount).

Newtown School, Waterford (Newtown).

Swarthmore College, Pennsylvania (Swarthmore).

Glorney Foundation (Glorney).

Conflict Textiles - CAIN.

TABLE OF CONTENTS

Introduction

Samplers, Sewing & Simplicity in Quaker Ireland

Throughout the world, embroidery has been used for centuries to adorn fabric. It has been both executed and worn by men and women at all levels of society. Standards for workers, whether professional or amateur, could be amazingly high. In the Middle Ages rich cloths, silks, tapestries and embroideries were vital symbols of wealth and status. Highly portable, they could accompany a prelate, king or nobleman on their journeying. Monarchs such as Francis I of France or Henry VIII of England used magnificently embroidered attire as a way of emphasising their power, and pieces of fine embroidery might also be presented as gifts. The feudal aristocracy made great use of heraldic banners as a way of identifying themselves and their followers. A much-reduced version of that today is the embroidered badge on a school or team blazer.

Needlework executed by Quaker women in Ireland in the eighteenth and nineteenth centuries provides the central focus of this book and there is a particular emphasis on the sampler. The word *sampler* derives from the Latin *exemplum*, meaning an example. Originally it was like a personal note-book, a strip of linen a woman kept in her pocket with her sewing kit. If she saw an interesting design, motif or stitch, she might take out her needle to record it for possible future use for embroidery on furnishings or dress.

In older houses framed samplers have sometimes hung on the walls for over a hundred years and deteriorated from exposure to light. Lettering in some cases has become so faded as to be almost invisible. There are cases where once the sampler has been removed from its frame the letters or text can be read on the mounting board, rather like the negative of a photograph. Many samplers have never been framed, but simply rolled up and placed in a drawer, and may therefore be in a better state of preservation. Where wool has been used either for the base or for the execution of letters or designs, moths have sometimes taken their toll. Until more recent years, samplers tended to be regarded as vaguely decorative objects, sometimes carrying an association with an earlier generation of a family. Today the situation has changed and an interesting sampler in good condition can fetch a price well over a thousand euros. They have become collectors' pieces, and are also regarded as being of significance in the study of genealogy. An incomplete list of pupils at Mountmellick school was produced for the centenary in 1886, but a study of existing samplers has already revealed the names of a further twenty students. This has given the sampler a value additional to its purely aesthetic or artistic one. With a growing interest in material culture the sampler has come to take its place amongst other objects that help us understand the everyday life of past generations.

---

[1] The classic study of the sampler is Averil Colby's *Samplers*, but this does not specifically refer to Quaker work. Betty Ring's *Girlhood Embroidery - American Samplers and pictorial Needlework, 1650-1850* looks at the schools and teachers of the East Coast, and one of her most interesting findings is the proportionately large number of samplers of Quaker provenance. Naomi Tarrant in her recent and invaluable study of Scottish samplers, *Remember Now Thy Creator – Scottish girls' samplers 1700-1872*, looks at such work against a background of Presbyterianism. There are many parallels with the Irish Quaker situation, most notably in the emphasis on the education of girls, where the main aim was that of making them sufficiently literate to read the Bible and providing them with practical skills, particularly spinning, knitting and sewing. Carol Humphrey's *Sampled Lives* (2017), based on the extensive collections in the Fitzwilliam Museum, Cambridge, includes a specific chapter on early Quaker work. Her *Quaker School Girl Samplers from Ackworth* (2006) looks at the school and at some of the girls who produced the work. Micheál and Elizabeth Feller's *The Needlework Collection* (2010 and 2012) shows an understanding of the contexts in which some of the Irish samplers in the collection were produced and also has a perceptive section on Quaker examples.

A study of the sampler immediately opens up a much greater field, since it is a form of needlework that must be placed in the context of even more ephemeral work executed at a time when the sewing machine did not yet exist. When women referred to their 'work', this generally meant sewing, and many samplers carry the information that the piece was 'worked', or sometimes 'wrought' by a particular person. A number of samplers have survived until today, whereas a shirt or a pillow case could have ended up as a cleaning rag. To understand more fully the centrality of needlework, it has been necessary to examine the broader area of a woman's activities in the past. In the eighteenth and nineteenth centuries girls received training in different forms of sewing, and when they went to school this could take as much as three hours of class time every day. The needle was both a basic way of earning a living, and a requirement for the housewife, whether looking after a modest household or running a large establishment. Consequently, the economic and social background of the girls is a factor that will be taken into consideration in the present study.

A major reason behind the writing of this book was an awareness that, with the exception of Heather Crawfords' valuable study, *Needlework Samplers of Northern Ireland – Patterns and History*, there is no book on Irish samplers.[1] Her focus is on pieces made by nineteenth-century schoolgirls and over half is devoted to working drawings of patterns employed. Many of her examples are held in the Ulster Folk and Transport Museum.

Excellent small collections of Irish samplers are held in both the National Museum of Ireland (NMI) and the Friends Historical Library Dublin (FHLD), and a number also remain in private hands, often with descendants of the families of the original makers. NMI has some sixty-three samplers, of which fourteen are of Quaker origin. FHLD holds about seventy pieces, in addition to other examples of needlework and dress-making coming from Quaker families. Research for the present book was initially prompted by two samplers from the 1790s which had remained with the author's family and have now been given to FHLD.

The sampler did not exist as a one-off phenomenon, and the aim of this book is to establish a clearer idea of the context in which such work was produced in Quaker Ireland.

As the greater part of needlework was carried out by women, it has proved necessary to examine their general situation in the context of the household. In Ireland the best descriptions are in Mary Leadbeater's letters and her *Annals of Ballitore* (a significant Quaker town in the eighteenth century). Mary's own sister-in-law, Lydia Shackleton, was a direct descendant of Margaret Fell, a key figure in the establishment of Quakerism in the 1650s and 1660s. By sheer chance, an account book for Swarthmoor, her home in Kendal, managed to survive and this rare example of seventeenth-century household records gives an understanding of the domestic background of many of the early Quakers in both Britain and Ireland. Kept by Margaret's daughter Sarah, these accounts provide an exceptionally full idea of the running of a house at that period and of the different responsibilities of the housewife.[2]

At a time when many children received no schooling at all, Quakers, with their belief that all children, both rich and poor, should be properly prepared for work, whether in the home or outside, attached great importance to education, a field in which they later came to hold an important place in Ireland. From the beginning they emphasised the equality of the sexes and felt it was important for all girls to have an education. The first Quaker Committee school in Ireland was set up for girls in Edenderry in 1764 and this was followed in 1786 by Mountmellick, a co-educational boarding school. In England Ackworth, also co-educational, dates from 1779, and Sarah Grubb's account of that school provided a blueprint for a Quaker Committee school. At such schools, together with literacy and other academic subjects, an accent was placed on practical skills which, in the case of girls, involved a very thorough training in different forms of dress-making and needlework. The cashbook accounts for the pupils' clothing at Mountmellick school in the 1790s provide much information about the clothing itself and all the materials purchased for this.

[2]   A valuable account that has been drawn on for the nineteenth century, although not a Quaker one, is the writing of Elizabeth Smith (neé Grant) who arrived in Ireland in 1830 and lived for over fifty years in Baltyboys, Co Kildare, a relatively short distance from the Quaker village of Ballitore. The mansion which her husband inherited had been partially destroyed in 1798 and the badly neglected 1,200-acre estate was in a ruinous condition. Elizabeth painstakingly spent years putting the place together on a very tight budget, and this is recorded in part of her memoirs, more recently published as a separate volume, *The Highland lady in Ireland* (1991).

Clothing and costume in the days before the advent of the sewing machine required a great deal of hand labour. Tailors generally made up coats and breeches, but otherwise almost everything from men's shirts to knitted stockings might be made at home. In the case of Friends, the enormous emphasis on simplicity and plainness has to be taken into account, but the widespread myth of the 'grey' Quaker has no basis.

In everyday living, the making and maintenance of the household textiles formed an important part of women's work. In particular there was everything relating to beds and bedding which, besides blankets and sheets, included the feather beds and curtains. Even the textiles might be woven and hem-stitched at home, with further skills drawn upon for the embroidery of cushions and upholstery.

The sampler itself is best known as a form of embroidery. On examining a wide range of different samplers, mostly worked in Ireland, it became clear that there is no fixed idea of a Quaker sampler. What we have are a number of pieces known to have been executed by Quakers, frequently in the context of the schools, but not necessarily as a teaching exercise. The main aim of needlework was practical and utilitarian, but it could also be a creative form of expression and its decorative value was often not far away. The finest samplers go far beyond any utilitarian idea of learning stitches, but the variety and combinations, as well as the actual skill in handling the needle, produce immensely satisfying results. A closer study reveals that most of the motifs and stitches used derive from a much wider and older European tradition.

Irish Quaker samplers are amazingly varied and a number offer clues that indicate their provenance. Thanks to the precision of Quaker record-keeping, which goes back to the seventeenth century, it is often possible to identify the makers of samplers, their age and the contexts in which the work was carried out. Quaker provenance may also be indicated by specific details, such as the manner in which dates are given, as 'third month' rather than 'March'. In other cases, it is more a question of the use and arrangement of motifs and lettering, and sometimes the choice of colours.

Apart from the samplers, other related forms of needlework ranging from stumpwork to Mountmellick whitework and from quilting to forms of Dresden whitework and lace were executed by Quaker women. Many became expert in the use of these other techniques which further expanded the range of skills which they had acquired.

Needlework, like many pre-industrial activities, had lost much of its necessary function by the later nineteenth century. By the twentieth century, sewing had often come to be regarded as an insignificant activity practised by women who had nothing better to do, and sometimes, by extension, as an indication of the inferior status of women in British and Irish society (see for example Rozsika Parker *The subversive Stitch*).

Nowadays a girl is usually educated for work outside the home. She may eat in a canteen, buy her food pre-prepared or even as a complete frozen meal. With running hot and cold water and electricity, housework is easy. Usually clothes are bought readymade, as are the household textiles, and sewing skills are no longer absolutely necessary. The modern woman has a career, earns money and so is part of the consumer society.

CHAPTER ONE

QUAKERISM IN IRELAND

Quakers today are a small but significant part of Irish society, heavily involved in concerns from ecology to education and from prisons to the promotion of peace in difficult situations both at home and abroad. In historical terms they found themselves, as dissenters, placed in a similar category to Roman Catholics, Presbyterians and Methodists, none of whom could enjoy full civic rights before the nineteenth century. Consequently, they formed a tightly-knit group that developed many strategies to ensure survival, one of the most important of these being education, where practical skills leading to employment were combined with a more academic curriculum. Mutual support within the group was specially important in the early years and members who had fallen on hard times might receive assistance. Meetings often organised help with schooling and books, with arranging an apprenticeship and paying the fee, or finding a small dowry for a girl. In cases of serious hardship they might provide loans ranging from money to bedding in very cold winter weather, tools, or even the 'Quaker cow' to provide milk.[1] Quakers became known for their probity, and this in turn proved valuable for their business dealings.

George Fox and the emergence of Quakerism

Under Henry VIII the Anglican church had become the established church in England, and conformity to it had political as well as spiritual implications. Many were dissatisfied, feeling that under Henry, and later Queen Elizabeth I, the Reformation did not develop much beyond establishing the use of English rather than Latin for worship and placing the monarch in the position previously held by the pope. Elsewhere in Europe, scholars, spiritual reformers and mystics of the sixteenth and seventeenth centuries, especially in the German-speaking lands, thought the Light (the Holy Spirit) was in everyone, even the 'heathen'. They perceived the true church as a communion and fellowship of spiritual persons, without any need for ceremonies or sacraments. In England, initially influenced by continental thinkers and the spread of printing, real spiritual reform developed.[2]

The wide availability of the Bible in the vernacular as well as Latin allowed for direct access to the scriptures, and during the puritan period in the seventeenth century gave rise to a great number of inspired writers, thinkers and preachers who believed that man could have direct access to God without the mediation of the clergy.[3] John Bunyan, author of *The Pilgrim's Progress* (1678), the second best-selling book after the Bible for over 200 years, was such a preacher, and for his pains had to spend a considerable period in prison. It was possible at the time for an itinerant preacher to stand up in a church and preach, but attacks on the established church were not necessarily tolerated, especially if they questioned the authority of the priest and, by extension, of the monarch. Such heretical ideas could be perceived as potentially treasonable and on occasion led the imprisonment of early Friends.

---

1 Grubb, 2018, p.52, p.79.
2 The various strands, from the Dutch Anabaptists and Mennonites to the Cambridge Humanists, and a number of mystics and poets, such as Thomas Traherne, Francis Rous or Sir Henry Vane, all combined, despite persecution, to develop puritan thinking both among the clergy and the laity. Giles Randal at Oxford preached that the scriptures must be transcended and must be spiritually discerned and experienced. In his preface to *Theologica Germanica* (1648) he pleads for freedom and variety in religious thought and life.
3 The Geneva Bible (1560), used by the Calvinists (with John Knox as one of the translators) was the most widely available version of the Bible in the later sixteenth and early seventeenth centuries. It was the first bible to have numbered verses and to be produced in a smaller format. The extensive marginal notes sometimes questioned authority when it was felt to be misused, and this was one of the reasons for the publication under Elizabeth of the Bishops' Bible and subsequently the important Authorised Version promoted by King James I.

Puritans felt that the Church of England needed purification, including getting rid of superfluous ceremonies. Growing up as the son of a weaver and church warden, in the village of Fenny Drayton in Leicestershire, George Fox (1624-91), was a member of the established church in an area where the priest and the leading family, the Purefoys, had strong puritan leanings. He absorbed and developed these ideas, but went further. He saw the Scriptures as vitally important, and essential for him was the idea that worship should be in silence and that people should wait for God to inspire them (the Inner Light). He believed that the Inner Light corresponded to a belief that there is that of God in everyone and that direct access to the divine removed any need for an intermediary such as a priest. All people are equal in the sight of God and each person, male or female without distinction, if they felt called upon by the Spirit during a religious meeting, might stand up and minister.

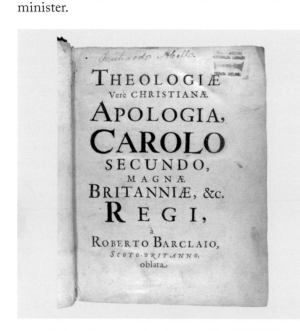

Robert Barclay Apologia 1676 (FHLD)

Fox's preaching started to take effect around 1652, and gradually groups initially calling themselves Friends of the Truth came together for worship. The term Quaker originated as a derisive nickname employed by Justice Bennet of Derby, before whom George Fox appeared in 1651. The early Quakers were from many walks of life. Robert Barclay (1648-1690), who, in 1676, published his defence of Quakerism in Latin, *Theologiæ Vere Christianæ Apologia*, and translated it into English two years later, belonged to a noble

Scottish family closely related to the Stuart kings. Others were landowners, shopkeepers, artisans and servants. For all of them their way of life would be modified by religious belief.

George Fox suffered several periods of imprisonment and was also beaten up, but he could draw huge crowds, sometimes numbering in the thousands. As he travelled round England, he would receive accommodation from people sympathetic to his ideas, many of whom were members of the local gentry. In 1652 he came for the first time to Swarthmoor (later 'Swarthmore'), a great house in the north country and the home of Thomas Fell, a distinguished puritan judge, a former MP in Cromwell's Parliament and vice-chancellor of the duchy of Lancaster. Fox spoke to all the household in the Great Hall, and many were convinced of the truth of the Inner Light from God in all mankind. Fell himself never became a Quaker, but he allowed his home to be used for meetings for worship, and, until his death in 1658, his protection was very valuable in that time of religious and political turmoil. As an important lawyer, Fell was often away for weeks on circuit, During his absences his wife Margaret (1614-1702), herself an heiress, whom he had married when she was 17, took charge of Swarthmoor which became the centre of the emerging Quaker movement.[4] Women, like the men, would often set out in pairs on long journeys ministering like Fox. Margaret provided hospitality for the 'Valiant Sixty' Friends who could stay at Swarthmoor for healing and renewal after travels, persecution and prison. She also wrote one of the most important tracts in the context of its period: *Women's speaking justified, proved and allowed of by the Scriptures, all such as speak by the spirit and power of the Lord Jesus* (1666). This marvellous piece pleads for the recognition of the spiritual equality of man and woman, as in the early church. It attacks those who deny the right of women to speak in church, illustrating the arguments with Old and New Testament stories and quotations, including many from Saint Paul.

With the restoration of Charles II in 1660 royal power was limited but there was still a climate of suspicion, with fears of revolt. George Fox and many other Friends were unjustly imprisoned. Margaret Fell rode over two hundred miles to London, handed a letter to the king and reminded him and his brothers about their promises to respect

---

4   Fell died in 1658 and in 1669 Margaret married George Fox.

the consciences of their people. A Declaration drawn up by her, and subscribed to by thirteen of the leading Friends including George Fox, was put into the king's hand. This document was the first public statement of what would become the Quaker Peace Testimony:

We are a people that follow after those things that make for peace, love and unity: it is our desire that others' feet may walk the same and we do deny and bear our testimony against all strife and wars and contentions [...] Treason, treachery and false dealing we do utterly deny [...] and all our desire is your good and peace and love and unity.[5]

In 1664 Margaret herself was arrested and tried. As she would neither swear an oath in court nor stop holding meetings for worship in Swarthmoor, she was imprisoned in Lancaster castle for four years. At this time Britain was far from being the sole country where only one religion was tolerated. Huguenots were persecuted in France, Waldensians in Italy, while the Inquisition burnt heretics in Spain. The notion that religious conformity and loyalty to the crown went hand in hand was widespread at the time in Europe. In England the Oath of Supremacy stated that the king was the head of the Church. Those of the other religious denominations who could not take this oath were deemed to be disloyal. Friends were regularly imprisoned during the seventeenth century. Whilst a prisoner in the Tower of London in 1670, William Penn (1644-1718), who would go on to establish the Quaker colony of Pennsylvania, wrote his essay on *Liberty of Conscience* in which he firmly made the point that religious dissenters are not political subversives.

The Scottish Parliament in 1567 had declared the Reformed Church of Scotland to be the only Church within its realm. Based on the Calvinist model of a congregational church, it had no bishops but was governed by a body or presbytery (hence 'Presbyterian'). The staunchly protestant King James VI of Scotland who inherited the English throne as James I in 1603, wanted to keep the old episcopal structure so that he could control the Church, and his son, Charles I, tried to impose uniformity of worship in both realms in 1638. The Presbyterian Scots believed that a subject must disobey the lawful ruler if he unlawfully insists on things such as 'idolatrous mass' instead of 'true religion', and were prepared to go as far as armed resistance. This was a 'godly revolution' and the next year thousands signed the National Covenant against popery and despotism. [6] The Covenanters raised an army which then occupied the north of England, thus initiating the 'Bishops' War' which lasted from 1639-41 and in 1644 the Covenanters helped the Puritans defeat the Royalists (Cavaliers) at Marston Moor, the decisive battle that led to the end of the Civil War and ultimately to the execution of the king in 1649.

The Irish situation

After the Anglo-Norman invasion in 1169 Ireland was nominally under the English crown. By the sixteenth century a small area around Dublin (the Pale) had the English language and legal system but much of the country continued with the Brehon laws and Irish customs. Under feudal law the land of England, Wales and Ireland belonged to the king, but, in Ireland, according to Gaelic law, land had belonged to each tribe. The powerful chieftains disliked Tudor attempts to control them and frequently rebelled, which resulted in the confiscation of their lands. Between the mid-sixteenth century and the mid-seventeenth planters were given the opportunity to lease these lands. Under Queen Mary these would have been Catholic English but subsequent Plantations of 'New English' were Protestant settlers loyal to the crown, and in Ulster the main group was Scots Presbyterian,.

After Henry VIII, with the brief interlude of the reign of Queen Mary I (1553-1558), the official religion in Britain and Ireland was the Protestant Church of England. However, the vast majority of the Irish population, including former Anglo-Normans, remained Roman Catholic, and, in addition, were Gaelic rather than English speakers. For them Church of England services, being in English, meant nothing.

---

5   The peace testimony has remained one of the pillars of Quakerism until today. It has inspired such movements as the Friends Ambulance Unit which started in an attempt to alleviate suffering caused by the Franco-Prussian War of 1870 and continued through both World Wars, helping wounded soldiers and the local civilian populations. Post-war reconstruction was another major activity and this led to the award of the Nobel peace prize in 1947. Today Quakers are also heavily involved in reconciliation and continue valuable work in Northern Ireland as well as internationally.

6   See Sefton, 1993, p.21.

The Counter-Reformation, largely led by the Franciscan Brothers and the Jesuits, had resulted in a movement of spiritual renewal within the Irish Catholic Church. The Jesuits were perceived by the English as the militant wing of the Church and, given the claim of Catholic Spain to the English throne through the marriage of Philip II to Mary, this increased fear of a possible invasion. By 1639 Thomas Wentworth earl of Strafford, the king's Deputy, had imposed the Thirty-Nine Articles of the Anglican faith on the Protestant church, reaffirmed the place of the episcopacy, and reinstated the collection of tithes, a compulsory tax, to support the Anglican clergy. Catholics, Presbyterians, and Puritans united against this and Strafford, having been recalled to London, was condemned to death by the Puritan-controlled Long Parliament.[7]

In the seventeenth century the Irish wanted their parliament unfettered by Poynings' law of 1494 which stated that no acts could be passed by the Irish Parliament without the approval of the King, whereas all acts passed by the English parliament could be binding on Ireland. The Catholic Confederation met in Kilkenny from 1642 with the aim of obtaining full civil and religious rights for the Catholic population. Hostile to the puritan parliament, they were supporters of Charles I, their motto being 'For God, for king, for Ireland united'. Unfortunately, the papal legate seized this opportunity for political interference and scuppered the Ormond Peace Treaty of 1646 between the various factions by excommunicating those Gaelic Irish and Old English who supported it, and consequently the ongoing state of warfare continued.

An uprising in Ulster had resulted in the murders of a number of Protestant settlers. In Portadown in 1641 about 100 men, women and children were thrown from the bridge, drowned and died in the 'Bloody Massacre' which became part of North of Ireland mythology. In Cashel on New Year's Day 1642 there was a massacre of Protestants, and in 1647 the Catholic congregation barricaded within the cathedral on the Rock of Cashel was slaughtered by Lord Inchiquin's troops in retribution.[8] The Puritans, having defeated the Royalists in England, turned to Ireland. where Cromwell sacked the Royalist-held towns of Drogheda and Wexford, indiscriminately killing men, women and children in revenge for the 'Bloody Massacre'. These events also remain in folk memory even today, and the name of Cromwell, held in respect in England, still remains in total odium in Ireland.

With the ending of the war in Ireland in 1652 the Puritan English Parliament had passed the Cromwellian Act of Settlement, whereby papists deemed to be rebels forfeited their lands and were sent across the Shannon to much smaller estates. Many of the Catholic aristocracy, known as the 'Wild Geese', went abroad and became officers and generals throughout Europe, but the poorer people remained and provided a labour force for the new settlers. Some settlers, known as 'Adventurers' received land in return for financing the army. The rest were Puritan soldiers, and a grant of land was a way to pay them without making demands on the exchequer. This also served the policy of making Ireland into a Protestant colony. The first Quakers in Ireland found themselves in the anomalous situation of being a minority, not in a Protestant country but in a Catholic one. In his book *The English in Ireland* (London 1872) James Froude speaks of the violent persecution of Quakers by Catholics in the south of Ireland, but this cannot be substantiated by any Quaker document.[9]

Barbarous as were the attempts by some Catholic Irish to regain their land from the settlers, it would seem the reports were deliberately exaggerated by settlers who hoped to get help from the English government. Even George Fox in England had received what Isabel Grubb termed 'grossly biased accounts [...] about the war between the Irish people and the English invaders.'[10]

---

[7] The Long Parliament wanted a limited democracy and were at loggerheads with Charles who, with his belief in the Divine Right of kings, saw himself as the absolute monarch of both Great Britain and Ireland, but was ready to sacrifice Strafford who had been one of his most loyal and able supporters.

[8] See Butler, 2006, p.43.

[9] Barbaric behaviour was not peculiar to the Irish or Cromwellians in Ireland. In mainland Europe in 1631 the Protestant Swedish king had brutally sacked Frankfurt, but in May of that year the Imperial army took Magdeburg with even greater brutality. Of nearly 40,000 souls within the city on the eve of the siege, nearly three-quarters died and most of the houses were burnt.

[10] Harrison, 2018, p.11.

The first Irish Quakers

After eleven years of war, hunger and plague, the country was in a ruinous state and half of the population had died. Highly religious and self-disciplined, the new settlers had to embark on reconstruction. The Cromwellian soldiers, being a mixture of gentry, farmers and tradesmen, had many skills. A number now embraced Quakerism and became pacifists. They would not fight, but helped those on both sides. Almost none of them were killed, though their houses could be burned and their goods and livestock stolen or requisitioned by the various armies who seldom offered any compensation.

In Ireland the first Quaker Meeting was 'settled' in 1654 at Lurgan by William Edmundson, a carpenter and ex-Puritan soldier, who had come there as a shopkeeper. After two years he moved south to a small farm at Rosenallis, near Mountmellick which would go on to become one of Ireland's major Quaker centres.

One of the best pictures of the situation of the small farmer or shopkeeper is provided by Edmundson's *Journal*. Highly respected by all who knew him, he had to face arrest and loss and destruction of goods and property, and his life was in danger more than once. Not only did he have to cope with Jacobite and Williamite armies, but also with marauding bands of Rapparees. In England the Civil War had lasted a relatively short time, but unrest continued in Ireland for most of the second half of the seventeenth century. The devastated state of the country forced the first generations of Quakers in Ireland to develop a degree of resilience and an ability to cope that was different from that of English Quakers, able to evolve in a more peaceful environment.

In England the Puritan parliament and others decided on the Restoration of Charles II in 1660, but the powers of the king were more limited. With the background of the Thirty Years War in Europe the fear of the Catholic countries, especially Spain and France, meant the Catholics, who were not the majority, were mistrusted in England. Ireland presented a situation in which the majority population was Catholic, and this led to further unease. Charles's brother James, who came to the throne in 1685, had been married to the Protestant Anne Hyde (1637-1671), by whom

he had two daughters (later the queens Mary and Anne). By 1685 James was a Catholic and his attempts to restore full civic rights to Catholics led to confrontation with the parliament. This came to a head in 1689 when he married the Italian Mary of Modena and she produced a male heir. Fears of a Catholic take-over led to the 'Glorious Revolution' of 1689 (so-called because no blood was spilt in England). Parliament offered the crown to James' daughter Mary and her protestant husband William of Orange (whose mother, Mary Stuart, was a sister of James).

In Ireland the consequences of the 'Glorious Revolution' were disastrous. Dynastic change in England was part of a much larger European war between Louis XIV of France and a Grand Alliance of other powers. In Ireland, Dutch, German, Danish, English, French and Irish soldiers trampled over the land for three years, and the country's own internal conflicts added chaos and confusion to the general letting of blood. The Battle of the Boyne (1690) was won by William of Orange and James fled. His departure from Ireland was helped by the Quaker, Francis Randall, who fed him, lent him a horse, told him not to ride with his pistols cocked, and sent him on his way to Waterford harbour where he found the ship to take him to France.

After the Battle of the Boyne, James' Irish and French forces retreated west to hold Limerick and Athlone. From the writings of Mary Leadbeater and Isabel Grubb we have an interesting account of the experience of a Quaker family in Limerick during the siege.[11] Joan Rooke, an heiress, had lived all her life in a house with fine furniture. Soldiers were billeted on her and one day she heard them planning to intimidate her family and plunder the house. They talked in Irish, unaware that she understood them. Calmly she listened until they had finished, and then astounded them by declaring in fluent Irish that she would inform their officer of their purpose, if she perceived any attempt to execute it. This alarmed them and they behaved better. This anecdote is a reminder that many Quakers learned to speak Irish, thus placing them on a much better footing with their Catholic Irish-speaking neighbours.

The siege conditions meant that food was in very short supply and Joan had to guard the household

[11] See Grubb, 1932, p.49.

provisions, even sitting in the kitchen to watch the pot cooking, lest the aroma of the boiling meat would tempt the hungry men. One day a cannon-ball came through the wall and dashed to pieces the seat she had just quitted beside the fire. Soon cannon-balls had visited almost every room. Flames engulfed a nearby house, but a timely outburst of rain saved her home. George, her husband, as a Quaker, could visit and succour the English prisoners in the gaol. Disease was spreading in the heat and by the end of August 1690, it was even hotter. King William's army were attacking with great fury but without success. The rain returned and their ammunition ran out, so they drew off from the city. In the following spring George got a pass from the governor to leave Limerick. The Rookes melted down their silver plates into wedges that could be carried. Joan hid some gold pieces in the heels of her shoes and more were stitched into their clothes, especially her quilted petticoats. Taking their baby son, the two little girls and what could be carried on the horses, they left with an Irish countryman who was willing to undertake the risk of guiding them across the wild region between the part held by the Irish and that already conquered by the English. Bandit gangs roamed and the way was very difficult but the guide was honest. When they reached Cashel they rewarded him well, and years afterwards were able to help him in his old age. Two years later they sold their property in Limerick and this enabled them to follow a business in Dublin.

An Irish Quaker identity

While researching, it became increasingly clear to me that there were intangible but evident differences between Quakers in Ireland and those in England. Ethnically the first Friends in Ireland were of the same stock as English Friends, but unlike them they were immigrants into another land ravaged by war, and they had to cope with this. The Irish were mostly Roman Catholic with Gaelic as the main language outside the towns, and Ireland itself was regarded as a colony by London.[12] Presbyterian Scots had been settled in the north and Anglican Protestant English in the midlands. All brought their own ways of doing things, but to survive they had to adapt to local conditions.

By the early eighteenth century the overall number of Quakers in Ireland has been put at somewhere between 6,000 and 9,000. However, many Friends left Ireland in the first decades because of deadness of trade and serious crop failures, and numbers slowly declined in the following years.

In 1722 William Sewell published *The History of the Rise, Increase, and Progress, of the Christian People Called Quakers*. Previously, in 1700, The National Meeting in Ireland had asked a Cork Quaker, Thomas Wight, to write the first history of Friends in Ireland, *A History of the Rise and Progress of the People called Quakers in Ireland from the Year 1653 to 1700*. By this time a separate Irish Quaker identity had begun to emerge. Dr John Rutty, who was asked to complete Wight's account up to 1750, noted 'diverse occurrences have happened peculiar to Ireland, both before the year 1700 when Thomas Wight finished his account, and thro' a series of years to come to the present time.'[13]

A.C. Myers in his study of Irish immigrants into Pennsylvania between 1650 and 1750 also noted the difference between Irish Quaker immigrants and English ones. Both James Jenkins (1753-1831) from England in the 1770s and Margaret Boyle Harvey, arriving from America in 1809, were also struck by various differences when they came to Ireland. In England, at the Mount School (York), Rebecca Constable, a Scottish girl who later became a teacher there, commented:

During the whole of my tarriance at school I much enjoyed and valued association with the Irish girls. There was something so bright and cheerful and witty about them and so much genuine kindness in their disposition, that these qualities had a very beneficial influence in the school.[14]

The difference noted by Rebecca Constable also seems to express itself in the samplers made in the Irish Quaker schools, as these are much more exuberant in choice of lettering and colour than those made at Ackworth and other official Friends schools in England.

---

[12] Grubb, 1927, p.14.

[13] Thomas Wight (1640-1724), the son of a Protestant clergyman in Cork, was 'convinced of the Truth' (i.e. became a Quaker) as a result of hearing Francis Howgill speak at a Meeting in Bandon in 1655. Dr. John Rutty (1697-1775) was an English Quaker who came to Dublin after studying medicine in Leiden.

[14] Sturge and Clark, 1931, p.51.

The London Quaker apprentice James Jenkins was employed by Mary Stokes who took him to Clonmel in 1771 when she married Robert Dudley, in whose ironmongery he then found work. Very happy here, he comments on the difference between English hospitality and Irish:

An Englishman receives his guest, tells him he is welcome, and when they sit down to dinner, hopes he will make a good meal: and there generally begins and ends his attention – Mistress doth the rest. In Ireland, the Master of the house performs what are called the 'honours of the table.' He deems the company of his guest as a favour conferred upon him, and (in return) helps him to his good cheer and by courteous attention, and sprightly converse, perpetually strives to make his visitor happy.[15]

Catherine Marie O'Sullivan in her *Hospitality in Medieval Ireland* speaks of the obligations under Brehon law which included the custom of providing food, lodging, drink and entertainment for visitors. Irish hospitality was commented on favourably even in the characteristically jaundiced writings of English observers such as Richard Stanihurst who concedes that 'the Irish are without doubt the most hospitable of men', while John Dymmok in *A Treatice of Ireland* (1599) stated that they were 'great [with regard to] hospitallitye [...] and a kinde harted [people].'[16]

This tradition for generous hospitality seems to have been adopted by the Quaker settlers. Richard Shackleton (1726-1792) was seldom without company, and often provided accommodation for numbers of visitors travelling to various Friends' meetings. He probably did not always realise the extra amount of work involved for the women. Big tables were set up to accommodate extra side dishes. In everyday life the corner-cupboard had a small leaf which was let down at dinner time and this was sufficient for a sideboard.[17] Betsy Shackleton's aunt Sally's reminiscences let us see behind the scenes:

Sheets, bolster-cases, and pillow-cases had to be aired; fires had to be made; beef steaks and mutton chops had to be dressed; geese, ducks, and chickens had to be killed; big tables had to be laid out; head, foot and side dishes to be provided. Sometimes company arrived on washing day, or a wet drying day. This was inexpressibly teasing and 'hampering'.[18]

'Friends in Ireland seem to live like princes of the earth [...] with the abundance of their tables,' was the comment in 1798 by William Savery (1750-1804), a Quaker from Philadelphia.[19] When he was in Clonmel he breakfasted at Sarah Pim Grubb's home. Years earlier, when her father had moved the Pim family to London, the young Sarah Pim's impression of the English was in complete contrast to what was normal for her in Ireland: 'They have not the Hospitality about them that the Irish have.'[20] Her son-in-law, John Barclay Clibborn, in his will, expressed the wish that the family home be 'kept in the simplicity and with the hospitality which marked its character for generations.'[21]

What visitors to Ireland did not always realise was that as guests they must be given the best. After they were gone the family might live frugally on the leftovers, and, if poor, on very short rations.

The economic situation in Ireland

Poyning's Law meant that economically as well as politically Ireland was controlled by the English Parliament. In 1666 the jealousy of English cattle-breeders led to a ban on the profitable export of Irish live-stock to England. The woollen industry was then encouraged by the Irish Board of Trade, but was crushed in 1699 by legislation prohibiting the export of Irish manufactured woollen goods anywhere except to England, where heavy duties prevented them competing with the English woollen industry.

England limited the wool trade from Ireland, but promoted the linen industry which became very successful in Ulster with its Presbyterian ethos

15 Frost, 1984, p.59.
16 O'Sullivan, 2004, p.12
17 Corrigan, 2009, p.282.
18 Corrigan, 2009, p.287.
19 Savery 1844, p. 267, 269.
20 FHLD, Letters 13, 14, Box 1 e, Fennell collection.
21 Ahern, 2009, p.217.

of hard work. Here a number of Quakers developed large enterprises. Irish commercial business and the few manufactures that were feasible under the legal restraints from the British government were mainly in the hands of Dissenters: Presbyterians, Huguenots and Quakers.

In 1824 a mill for spinning of Irish flax into linen began to operate in Belfast using new technology. A major figure in the linen industry was John Grubb Richardson of Moyallon who in 1846 decided to build a model village for his workers at Bessbrook, Co Down. This was like one created at Portlaw, Waterford, in 1825 by the Quaker David Malcolmson, along similar lines to that of Robert Owen at New Lanark in 1800, and anticipated the Cadbury village of Bournville, developed at the end of the nineteenth century. Malcolmson, initially a flour miller in Clonmel, built his cotton mills at Portlaw and the model village for his workers included housing, schools and even a Roman Catholic church.

Quaker success in business was partly the indirect result of honesty and integrity which sprang from an insistence on truth in all matters. A fair and fixed price was established in contrast to the more usual practice of bargaining. Combined with hard work and an emphasis on plain living, these factors could result in some Friends building up considerable capital.

Grain milling became a very important industrial activity in Ireland in the eighteenth century and much of the flour was exported to feed England's rapidly growing population. In Ireland most of the processes had been mechanised by 1750, and were worked by water power. Capital was now needed to build larger mills and it was often Friends who had the money which allowed them to do so. Grain mills in Ireland were amongst the first to expand vertically with extra storeys for the processing plant and for additional storage. In 1768, although not owned by Quakers, the largest water-powered flour mill in Europe was built at Slane on the Boyne river.[22]

The flour mill foreshadowed the multi-storied textile mill. In the 1780s the town of Mountmellick, on the River Owenass, expanded with the setting-up of large-scale manufacturing based initially on cotton and woollen production, a business in which Quakers were central players. In 1837 it was estimated that there were about 4,000 workers employed in the various mills.[23] John Bewley had some 200 looms in his cotton factory and employed about 400 people daily. The thread was supplied by Mungo Bewley, listed as a Linen and Cotton Manufacturer, who had a cotton spinning mill in Mountrath. In addition to his mill in Mountmellick, John Bewley seems to have owned a textile printing works near Blessington, Co. Wicklow.[24] Cotton cloth was a luxury in the 1780's but by 1820 had become one of the cheapest and commonest materials for clothing.

Also in Mountmellick, William (d.1818) and Joshua (d. 1815) Beale, both coming from an early Quaker landowning family with business interests, moved into cotton manufacture. William's son Joseph continued this activity, along with prosperous concerns in the woollen, brewing and flour-milling industries in and around Mountmellick. These lasted until the Potato Famine of 1845-8 when, combined with other economic problems, the Beales' business collapsed and they had to emigrate to Australia.[25] The story of the Beale family reflects the decline of Mountmellick from being one of the more prosperous towns in Britain and Ireland to becoming what today could be called an economic blackspot.

In nineteenth-century Ireland poverty increased radically. Between 1801 and 1817 the cost of the lengthy Napoleonic wars increased the British national debt by 50 per cent but that of Ireland by 250 per cent. The revenue of the expanding English economy could meet most of its liabilities, but Ireland had to raise loans, mainly from England, to pay off its liabilities. Further money was drained out by absentee landlords, many of whom had moved to London following the so-called Act of Union in 1801. Rack-renting and unjust land laws made for inefficiency and evictions. The endemic poverty and stagnation of the country in

---

22 In the early nineteenth century Slane Mills was converted into a flax mill, and in the early twentieth century became a cotton mill.

23 O'Keefe, p.20.

24 Ibid, p.21.

25 Ibid, see pp.20-26, pp.31-5. Quite recently a map sampler was found by a Beale descendant in Australia who has returned it to Mountmellick, where it is now proudly displayed.

the nineteenth century was a contributory cause to the appalling effects of the Potato Famine. In 1848 Jonathan Pim (1806-1885), a major figure in Irish business, was one of the secretaries of the Central Relief Committee during the Famine and published *The Conditions and Prospects of Ireland and the evils arising from the present distribution of landed property with Suggestions for a remedy*.[26] As well as land reform, he noted the extent to which Irish trade was constantly restricted by the British government, whether with Britain herself or with foreign countries, and pointed out that 'Ireland was treated as a colony to be governed for the benefit of her powerful neighbour, not for her own.'[27]

Even after the Act of Union, which transferred the legislature from Dublin to Westminster, Irish industry that offered competition to English was suppressed or placed at a disadvantage by means of taxes. As well as lacking the capital for large-scale industrial development, Ireland had insufficient coal and iron for the new power-driven machines. Consequently, Irish industries found themselves too small to compete with the newer factories of Britain, where the cotton mills of Lancashire dominated in exporting textiles, as did the Yorkshire woollen industry.[28]

Quakers, having developed strong traditions in trade, became particularly active in industrial and mercantile activities in nineteenth-century Ireland. The Jacobs moved from making hard-tack for sailing ships in the 1850s to the manufacture of table biscuits in Dublin and Liverpool. The Goodbodys, at first grain-millers, added the making of bags for flour, initially out of flax and later expanded into sacks for other uses made of jute imported from India. Families such as the Malcolmsons, Pims and Bewleys were involved in shipping. The Malcolmsons built ships and a member of the Beale family in Cork paid for the coal for the Sirius, the first ship to cross the

Pim's Department Store, 1856. Irish Builder, 1 November, 1869.

[26] Copies were sent to MPs, including Sir Robert Peel.
[27] Pim, 1848, p.32. From the copy in FHLD which belonged to Sir Robert Peel.
[28] See Beckett, 1966, pp.289-291.

Atlantic entirely under steam (1837). The Pims, Alexanders and Perrys financed the Dublin to Kingstown railway (1834), the first commuter train in the world.

The diverse interests of some of the more prosperous Quaker families are illustrated by members of the Pim family. Thomas Pim (1771-1855), son of a tanner in Mountmellick, became apprentice to a linen-draper in Dublin. After this he began trading as a merchant and was joined by his younger brother Jonathan (1778-1841). Before long they were involved in the import and export business with New York, Liverpool and the West Indies. They exported linen and poplin and imported cotton wool which they supplied to Irish manufacturers.[29]

They acquired a cotton spinning enterprise at Greenmount Mill, Harold's Cross. 100 power looms were installed in 1834 and improved cottages were built for the workers. Their three ships plied between Dublin, New York, Barbados and England. Amongst the goods transported were linen and poplin for export, whilst sugar was brought back on the return journey. Cotton was now the most important raw material imported from America, while cotton yarns and Manchester goods (textiles) now came from England. Together with his son Jonathan, whose involvement in Famine relief has already been mentioned, Thomas Pim followed the new trend for large department stores. Thomas died in 1855 and in 1856 Jonathan opened Pim Bros Drapers, a huge emporium in a building designed by Sandham Symes in South Great Georges Street, Dublin, and this continued in business until the 1970s.[30] Quaker association with department stores can also be found with Newsomes in Cork (1883) and is yet another example of the move from manufacturing to trading and business.

---

[29] Shaun Boylan 'Thomas Pim' in *The Dictionary of Irish Biography*, Cambridge University Press, 2019.

[30] Besides a large furnishing and carpet department there was a specialist interest in poplin. (See Wigham, 1992, p.90.) Access to public office had been extremely difficult for any dissenters before the abolition of the Oath of Supremacy in 1829, but by the mid-nineteenth century Friends such as John Bright, the radical and liberal politician, were able to become MPs. Jonathan Pim, was invited to stand for the liberal party in Dublin in 1865. He was elected an MP and served in this capacity until 1874.

CHAPTER TWO

FROM DOMESTICITY TO UNIVERSITY

The Household

In the past, being the mistress of the house was an extremely important job. While 'lord' in old English meant literally 'keeper of the loaf' and by extension master of the house, his wife was the 'lady' (literally, loaf-kneader), and consequently the female head of a household. In Gaelic the wife is, *ban an tigh* (the woman of the house), and very formidable some of them were! The word 'spinster' (late Middle English) meant a woman who spins, especially as a regular occupation, but later it became the legal definition of an unmarried woman and, as the origins of the word were lost, it ironically acquired negative overtones. In contrast to this, the word 'distaff' came to signify female authority, or the female branch of a family. According to the 1969 Shorter Oxford Dictionary definition, a 'housewife' is the mistress of the house who manages it with skill and thrift. This requires a considerable degree of practical knowledge and planning, as well as management of people and budgets.

There is a list from 1725 relating to the women's work among the Quakers of Pennsylvania which mentions the spinning of flax and wool, weaving, knitting, candle-making and soap-making, dairying, including cheese and butter making, and poultry and gardening. Such matters as child-rearing, cooking, sewing and washing are not mentioned, but obviously taken as understood. By and large everyday things happening in the home tend not to be recorded and much knowledge was handed down orally. In the past even family cookery recipes were often learnt in the kitchen by observing and helping the older women.

A visual record of everyday domestic life in an Irish Quaker household in the late eighteenth century comes from an unexpected source. In March 1768, Mary Shackleton (later Leadbeater, 1758-1826) was sick with the 'ague'. Her older brother Abraham Shackleton told her stories and gave her a little drawing book. This contains amusing sketches by Abraham illustrating his

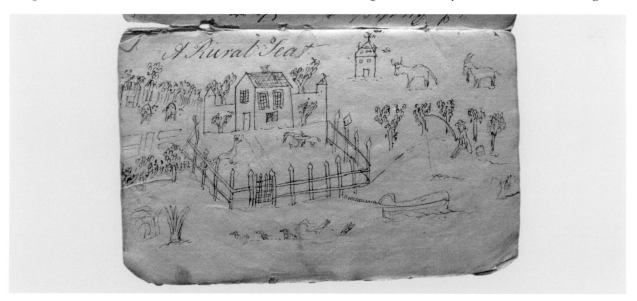

Abraham Shackleton sketch, 1768, "A rural seat" (KLS)

Abraham Shackleton sketch, 1768, living-room scene. (KLS)

stories and depicting aspects of everyday life of the time. There is a composite picture of a 'rural seat' which shows things associated with the running of a middle-class household – fishing, gardening, bee-keeping, poultry, orchard, dove-cot (pigeons for the table), cow, goat – and even peacocks.

An interior view of a house shows a living room with a woman seated at a cloth-covered table laid with cups and saucers. From her left a man approaches with a kettle he has taken from the fireplace behind him (where a pair of bellows is also depicted). On the other side is a man seated at what appears to be a bookcase, and in the corner is a chair with a 'sugan' or straw rope seat made in the Irish manner.

Another drawing is of a kitchen with a woman using a dash churn to make butter, a two-tier hen coop, and on the extreme left a fold-out table. The fireplace includes a built-in English-style bread oven. On the mantle-piece there are candlesticks, a clock and a clevy holding a spit. An iron pot on a swing-out crane hangs over the fire, and on one side there is a long handled frying pan. The contents of this kitchen are fairly typical of Irish country kitchens and broadly similar to what is mentioned in two earlier Quaker inventories. In 1694, the Dublin weaver, John Johnston, possessed a brass fish-pan, 4 brass candlesticks, 2 iron pots, 3 spits and a dripping pan, a ladle, a spice box, 6 porringers and an assortment of pewter dishes and earthenware. In 1705 the kitchen of the less affluent Wexford weaver

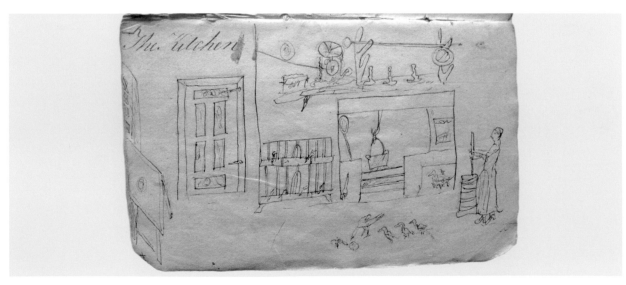

Abraham Shackleton sketch, 1768, "The Kitchen". (KLS)

William Willin contained 2 brass candlesticks, 3 iron pots with a crane, 1 spit, a cheese-press with dairy bowls and some pewter-ware.

In 1796 the pregnant Mary Leadbeater sent for her eighteen-year-old niece Anne Grubb to help with the churning and butter-making, and the washing, mangling and ironing. This was heavy work involving the fetching of buckets of water, fresh from a spring, to wash the butter, and the maintenance of fires for heating the water and the irons to do the laundry. Freed from these chores, Mary used the time to sew the clothes for the new baby, and she specifically mentions finishing the tenth shirt.

Glass laundry-smoother. 14.5cms high, 14cms diameter. (Private collection)

It was not uncommon for children and young people to be sent to live with relatives, as this made it easier to cope with sickness or other situations that might arise.[31] Quaker women often had to travel in the Ministry, sometimes for quite long periods, and this was possible because of the more flexible family structures of the time. In 1788 Mary Dudley left a ten-week-old baby in Clonmel when she embarked on an extensive European tour through Holland, Germany and France. Some years later, Sarah Lynes Grubb, when she felt called to minister in England, left a niece to help look

after her children who remained with her husband John in Clonmel.

Vital information for the purpose of the present study is provided by household accounts, diaries, letters, memoirs and biographies of Irish, English and Scottish women. Much can also be derived from the novels and writings of Mary Leadbeater, Maria Edgeworth, Jane Austen, the Brontës and others. Though not all were Quakers, their everyday lives would have been similar in many respects, and common to all of them was an excellent education. Such women were extremely busy, some managing great houses and their estates, and others more modest establishments. Their activities ranged from looking after a farm and a post-office to running a very successful school, and even writing books that are still best-sellers. Many were avid letter-writers, and their correspondence might relate to family matters or to discussion of more spiritual concerns. In addition, most of them are known to have had the ability to do both plain and fancy sewing.

In Ireland the writings and letters of Mary Leadbeater help with a picture of middle-class Quaker domestic life. Her *Annals of Ballitore* (based on her diaries and first published in 1862) furnish a rich picture of life at the time, including the 1798 rebellion, and together with her correspondence, give an excellent insight into the running of a Quaker household. Her *Cottage Dialogues among the Irish Peasantry* (1811) were published with a view to helping the impoverished country people use their resources to maximum advantage and are full of advice on everyday living. The preface was written by Maria Edgeworth, author of *Castle Rackrent* (1800), with whom she corresponded regularly, and who, with her father arranged the publication.[32] Leadbeater wanted to call her book *Cabin Dialogues*, but it was recognised that for the English reader the word 'cabin' had only a more nautical association. For the English edition Maria Edgeworth also provided a glossary and notes, in which a number of Hiberno-English terms and customs are explained. In Ireland a larger and cheap edition was designed and produced for schools.[33]

---

[31] When Mary Leadbeater's father Richard Shackleton was the master of Ballitore school, it sometimes arose that the whole house was filled with the boarders and, on such occasions, one or the other of the two younger girls was sent to live with their grandmother and aunt.

[32] Maria Edgeworth herself was very well read and her *Castle Rackrent* was admired by Jane Austen and Walter Scott; in addition to this she was a capable assistant to her father who was an enthusiastic admirer of Jean-Jacques Rousseau and an enlightened landlord working for the improvement of the poor peasantry in Ireland.

[33] Leadbeater, 1862, vol. II, p.191.

Textiles

Very little has been written about the education of girls in earlier times. Most treatises on the education of the upper classes in England from the thirteenth century onwards were about boys. A significant exception to this is Vincent of Beauvais who in his *De eruditione filiorum nobilium* added ten chapters on the upbringing of girls, arguing that they should be carefully guarded, and follow a curriculum of reading, writing, prayer and the scriptures, good behaviour (modesty, humility and silence) and the arts of sewing and weaving. Additionally, they should be prepared for marriage and told how to deal with a husband, mother-in-law, children and domestics.[34]

The production of textiles was a very important part of the housewife's responsibility from time immemorial. By 750 B.C. women in Ireland were spinning and weaving sheep's wool, and textiles from two different sites in Antrim and Tyrone show that these skills were highly developed with both tabby and twill weaves being known by the late Bronze age.[35]

In Homer's *Odyssey*, thought to have been composed around 800 B.C., cloth was both an essential covering and a status symbol. Helen of Troy with her golden spindle draws forth fine-spun yarn from deep blue wool, as she questions her husband about Prince Telemachus. Later she presents the departing prince with the precious gift of a most richly decorated robe, embroidered by her own hands. Meanwhile, his mother, Penelope, waits for news of her husband, Ulysses, who has left her in charge of Ithaca until his eventual return. Beleaguered by opportunist suitors, she keeps them at bay, telling them that she will re-marry once the weaving of a winding-sheet is complete, but each night she unpicks the previous day's work on the grounds that it is not fine enough.

Spinning and weaving occur frequently in European folk tales, such as those collected by the brothers Grimm. The poor girl in *Rumpelstiltskin* is given the task of spinning straw into gold. The princess in *Briar Rose* (Sleeping Beauty) pricks her finger on a spindle, and in *All-kinds-of-fur*, the dresses woven for the princess are so fine that they can fit into a walnut.

At his death in 1467, Philip the Good, Duke of Burgundy, said to be the richest man of his age, left to his son, an exceptionally fine collection of precious textiles, including eighty-six sets of tapestries. Technically and artistically they set standards which for the most part have never been surpassed. In addition to the many professional weavers at the time, many high-born ladies were very skilled also. A picture in a late fifteenth-century Flemish manuscript depicts such ladies working at upright looms and weaving tapestries with scenes from stories.[36]

In 1615, barely thirty years before George Fox began to preach, Gervase Markham published *The English Huswife, Containing the Inward and Outward Virtues Which Ought to Be in a Complete Woman*. In it he describes the activities of the rural housewife including her skill in

> Physic [medicine], chirogery [surgery], cookery, extraction of oils, banqueting stuff, ordering of great feasts, preserving all sorts of wines, conceited secret distillation of perfumes, ordering of wool, hemp, or flax, making cloth and dy[e]ing; the knowledge of dairies, the office of malting of oats, their excellent uses in families, of brewing and baking, and all other things belonging to a household.[37]

This study is about Quaker women's sewing and textiles and the context in which they were produced. The Household Account Book (cashbook) of Sarah Fell for Swarthmoor Hall is one of four significant account books of women from the seventeenth century still existing in Britain.[38] It is invaluable for the picture it gives of the running of a large (Quaker) household, and amongst other things

---

[34] See Orme, 1984, p.107

[35] Dunlevy, 1989, pp.15-16.

[36] Reproduced in Ginsburg, 1991, p.33.

[37] Quoted by Christina Hardyment in Whatman, 1956, p.6.

[38] Three other seventeenth-century books of accounts (not by Quakers) are by the wives of Scottish border lairds: Dame Margaret Nicholson, Grisell Horne and her daughter Lady Grisell Baillie.

a Wool carding; wool combs. b Spindle, whorl and distaff; Dutch spinning wheel.

provides considerable information relating to textiles, most of which would be relevant to Irish Quaker households at the time.

In her account book Sarah Fell includes payments to women for pulling hemp and shearing sheep. After the wool was cleaned it was ready for the carding brushes between which it was brushed till it formed a soft fleecy roll ready for spinning. This could be done by quite young children. The alternative to carding was combing, a more difficult process that involved using metal-toothed combs heated over charcoal. The short fibres would be combed out for woollen thread and then the long fibres combed into straight parallel lines and spun into worsted. Wool had to be carded and combed in preparation for spinning, whether with a distaff and spindle or a spinning wheel.

Abraham Shackleton sketch, 1768, "An old gentlewoman teaching her daughter to spin". This depicts the 'great' wheel not the smaller Dutch one. (KLS)

The Swarthmoor account books mention that spindles and whorls costing twopence were bought for the servants on 18 December, 1673. As well as being cheap, these had the advantage of being very portable. They could be used while herding animals or when visiting a neighbour. At Swarthmoor Margaret Fell is described as spinning joyfully. She was probably using a 'Dutch' wheel, as the accounts also mention a wheel of this type being bought for her daughter Rachel in 1678.[39] Also known as a 'Saxony' or 'Scotch' wheel, this was worked by a treadle and was best for spinning yarns from long fibres, such as linen or worsted. It was fast but cost a lot more than the great wheel which was the usual choice for woollen yarn. An amusing picture of an old gentlewoman teaching her daughter to spin using a great wheel can be seen in the Abraham Shackleton sketchbook. Both this and the Dutch wheel continued in use in Ireland into the twentieth century.

In Ireland it was women and children who spun the hemp, flax or wool into yarn, but by the eighteenth century most of the weaving was done by the men. Woollen cloth was usually fulled, which involved pounding the cloth in a tucking mill to shrink and cleanse it. In the village of Ballitore, one of the houses retains the name of 'Fuller's Court', reminding us of the business originally carried out there.

Sewing and knitting

Bed-linen, towels, napkins and tablecloths required hemming and this work would be done by most women, even the well-to-do, who would have been assisted by relatives and maids. Making the men's shirts, together with the petticoats and shifts, was also the women's province. Margaret Fell's daughters either paid seamstresses for this or did such work themselves, and there are various references to threads, pins and needles, specially got for each of them. Needles were handmade at the time, and not unduly cheap. Margaret Fell and her daughters loved colour, so cloth and garments were sent to Kendal to the dyer, who would have used vegetable dyes, obtained locally or imported from Holland.

In the Swarthmoor cashbook payments are noted for the knitting and also re-footing of stockings, another activity that could be done outside while herding animals, or at home in the evening. Knitting was practised at every social level.[40]

In 1661, Henry Fell visited Malta where two Quaker women, Katherine Evans and Sarah Cheevers had been imprisoned by the Inquisition for giving out tracts. They were condemned to remain in prison until they died or converted. In fact, they remained there for over three years. Fell's letter tells how a Captain Harris tried to help them: 'They were knitting and he saw them have bread and water allowed them. He saith he did believe they were much in want, though they said they were pretty well and contented and wished him not to trouble himself for them.'[41] In all probability the sale of their knitwear helped pay for their food.

Knitting is one of the subjects mentioned by Mary Leadbeater in both the *Annals of Ballitore* and the *Cottage dialogues*:

> Ally Johnson, an old inhabitant of Ballybarney, having lost her sight, was allowed a shilling a week by Melusina Trench, and was led to me once a month to receive it. Her benefactress suggested knitting, and I got wool spun, and taught her to knit petticoats.[42]

Mary Leadbeater's niece, Betsy Shackleton, writing about her childhood in Ballitore in the 1790s, recalls Molly Haughton whom she describes as 'a very neat, industrious, economical body', adding that 'it was a pleasure to visit her for a gossip in her parlour where she sat at her knitting'.

Schooling

For Quakers schooling was essential for both boys and girls. The development of education in Ireland in the years after the Battle of the Boyne was very different from that of Protestant England. In Ireland the majority of the population was Catholic

---

[39] At Ackworth, the English Friends' co-educational school, the girls, besides reading, writing and arithmetic, devoted a great deal of time to spinning, sewing and knitting which were important curriculum subjects. Spinning was dropped in 1817, as the old wheels were now worn out and factory-spun thread had become widely available.

[40] We know that Marie Antoinette, queen of France, knitted stockings for her son in prison. At her trial the women who were paid to clamour for her execution were the *tricoteuses*, poor women who earned their living knitting stockings. When sitting around the guillotine they were simply continuing their work whilst they watched one of the more popular spectacles of the day. (See Fraser, 2002, p.505.)

[41] Ross, 1949, p.395

[42] Corrigan, 2009, p.181.

and for those not of the Established (Anglican) Church access to education and many of the professions remained difficult until the nineteenth century. Roman Catholics often had direct trade links with the continent, whither many Catholic students would go to study for the priesthood or for the medical profession. The *Act to restrain foreign education* was passed in 1695, with the aim of limiting contact between Irish Catholics and their continental allies.[43] A folk memory of the Armada meant that the English were obsessed with the fear that Spain, or even Catholic France, might gain a foothold in Ireland and this led to schoolmasters of the 'popish religion' being forbidden to teach, and if caught being liable to very severe penalties.

Sometimes Protestant masters allowed Catholics to teach in their schools, but most important of all were the underground schools, generally known as 'hedge schools', as they were often conducted hidden in a field beneath the sunny side of the hedge. Their location changed from day to day,

and a pupil would keep watch as sentinel. Later, as the law was not so strictly enforced, they might meet in barns. Paid a pittance by the mostly poverty-stricken parents, these Roman Catholic schoolmasters ranged in quality from the indifferent to the outstanding.[44] Latin and Greek were taught in the best hedge schools. An extremely wide range of books was used, including Quaker ones such as Lindley Murray's books on English grammar and literature, and the schoolmaster John Gough's *Practical Arithmetick in Four Books*, first published in Dublin in 1767, which ran through at least sixteen editions, remaining in use for more than a hundred years. Gough's work was also entitled *Arithmetic both in theory and practice adapted to the commerce of Ireland as well as of Great Britain*. The inclusion of commercial mathematics was of importance to Catholics as well as to Friends, and the book was much used in the hedge schools, where it was generally referred to as a 'Gough'.

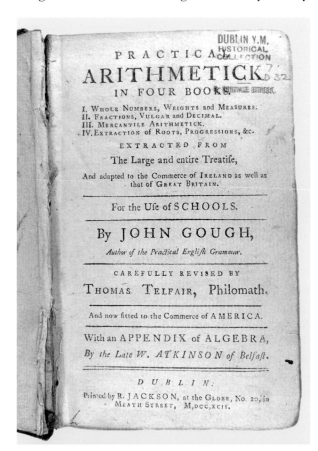

Title page of 1792 edition of
John Gough's *Arithmetick*. (FHLD)

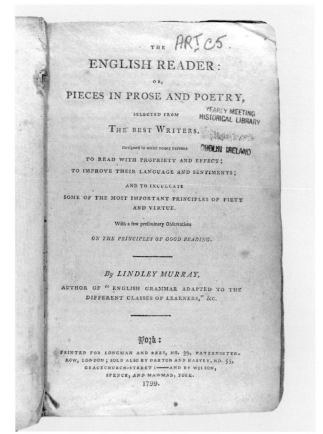

Title page of 1799 edition of
Lindley Murrays *English Reader*. (FHLD)

43 McManus, 2002, p.15.
44 Ibid, p.16.

Mathematics cypher book of Alliss /Allice Patten
(1739), who may have been taught privately
by a tutor.. (FHLD)
Note the mix of a page on measurement with
decorative calligraphy and the picture of a bird.

Learning might begin at home, provided by a family member, a servant or even a governess. From the late seventeenth century onwards Quaker day-schools of varying quality, mostly with a single master, started in Mountmellick, Dublin, Clonmel, Waterford, Edenderry and other places. Often these were held in the meeting house. Latin was useful in coping with legal documents, whilst arithmetic was needed for business. Reading and writing were essential for everyday life, for the recording of the minutes of Friends' business meetings, the writing of letters and pamphlets and particularly for perusing the Scriptures.

In some cases, girls received instruction from a tutor employed for their brothers, but many were taught at a 'dame school'. Dame schools were small privately-run places usually in the mistress' home with one or more teachers. The quality ranged from the most basic, consisting of reading, writing and needlework, to a few schools with a slightly wider curriculum. The mistress was not necessarily a Friend, and there could be children of various denominations. Subjects might be costed separately. For example, a Cork schoolmistress in 1709 got three shillings for 'readers' and four for 'sampler children'.[46] Presumably the extra charge was to cover the cost of materials. The early schools were dependant on a single teacher who might or might not be well qualified, and was usually poorly paid. The ad hoc nature of this arrangement made for a patchy standard of learning.

A specially interesting document in FHLD is an arithmetic copybook belonging to Aliss (Alice) Patten and dated 1739 when she may have been about fourteen years of age.[45] The range of practical mathematics and exercises in this book covers essentially matters of direct practical use in trade: addition, multiplication, subtraction, division, addition of money, apothecaries' weights, addition of wine measures, measurement of length, measurement of land, etc. An example of a practical exercise is the division of £2760, 17s and 6d equally between 274 men (Aliss worked out the answer as £10,1s and 6d.). It is particularly interesting to see the importance of such training for a girl who might later become involved in the family business.

Ballitore School (1726-1836)
The Ducketts, affluent Friends in Carlow, brought over the Yorkshire Quaker Abraham Shackleton (1696-1771) as a tutor and then in 1726 encouraged him to set up a boys' boarding school at Ballitore, a small town that they had developed on their land. Taking about sixty boarders, this was a private, fee-paying, Quaker-run, liberal and non-sectarian school, which attracted boys from all parts far and near, even the West Indies, France and Norway, as well as from wealthy Irish families. Shackleton's brother's advice to him on setting up was that good management was essential, and he advocated patience, a good choice of texts and an avoidance of heavy loads of memorising, which he felt dulls the mind.[47] Latin and Greek were regarded as a

---

45 The Patten family were friends of John Wesley and later Aliss' sister Eliza married into the Bennis family of Limerick who became Friends.
46 Cork Men's Meeting Eleventh-month 1709. Grubb, ed. Harrison, 2018, p.86.
47 Brannigan, 1982, pp.204, 209.

Ballitore School, early twentieth-century postcard. (FHLD)

part of the core curriculum, but English literature, French, mathematics, book-keeping, history and geography, including the drawing of maps, were also taught and science was explored. Abraham's son Richard went on to study Hebrew in Trinity College Dublin. As a Quaker he could not be formally awarded a degree, but this was of little importance to him and after university he returned to teach at Ballitore.

Richard's grand-daughter Betsy remembered her father showing them experiments with the air pump, the electrifying machine, the *camera obscura*, a solar microscope and a telescope. Lectures on the globe bored her but the magic lantern was 'inexpressibly amusing'. The boys had their own little gardens. The boys' birdcages hung up and down the dining hall where there were two long tables. In the evening it was lighted by six candles and the boys read or did what they pleased, with Betsy's father sitting there and talking with some of them.[48]

Ann White, who spent a year at the Quaker Mount School in York in 1835, indicated in

her letters home that the standard of scientific experimentation and thinking at Bootham School was not as high as in Ballitore.[49] The geometry book of thirteen-year-old Thomas Pim, a pupil at Ballitore in 1784, provides an excellent idea of the level of the teaching.[50] Apart from basic measurements and calculation of length, area and angles the exercises also run to trigonometry and logarithms. Much more down to earth are specific exercises relating to roofing and mason's work under which heading are placed tiling, walling and chimney work. Preparation for a career in business was also important for pupils of Ballitore and remnants of another exercise book belonging to Thomas Pim, indicate that shorthand was being taught with this aim in view. Thomas, like many schoolchildren of the time, happily embellished his school books with exercises in calligraphy and decorative scrolls.

Having passed through Ballitore, Quaker boys might go on into businesses, or, like Richard Brocklesby (Ballitore1734-42), study medicine at Edinburgh and Leiden. Non-Quaker boys went on to university or into the army. Some became

---

[48] Corrigan, 2009, p.299.
[49] Sturge, 1835, p.42. Anne was the daughter of James White, from Cork who studied at Ballitore and subsequently became headmaster. Her mother, Mary Pike, married him in 1818.
[50] FHLD, Mss box 87.

very famous like Napper Tandy, a leader of the United Irishmen, the Catholic Cardinal Paul Cullen and the great parliamentarian Edmund Burke. The latter remained a great friend of Richard Shackleton and of his daughter, Mary Leadbeater, corresponding frequently until his death. Whenever Richard Shackleton was in London, Burke would invite some of the more interesting people of the day to meet him.[51] On one of these occasions Mary enjoyed meeting Sir Joshua Reynolds and the poet George Crabbe. Amongst her other acquaintances were the Le Fanu family of Dunlavin, who were part of an interesting and intelligent circle of people which included a niece of Richard Brinsley Sheridan and Everina, the sister of Mary Wollstonecraft.[52] Mary Leadbeater admired the latter's *Vindication of the Rights of Woman* (1792), in which it is argued that women are not naturally inferior to men, but only appear to be so because of a lack of education. Mary Leadbeater and the other Shackleton girls, unlike most girls at the time, were given the same wide education as the boys and this was coupled with the acquisition of the necessary skills for running a house.

All Friends' children, regardless of economic status, were expected to have a basic education. This was often followed by an apprenticeship. Boys might also work on family farms or in family businesses, and girls would learn all the skills needed as a housewife, a seamstress or a domestic servant. A major Quaker concern was that no young people should be allowed to be idle or lack training, especially in cases where families had fallen on hard times or children had been orphaned.

In 1701, Middlesex Quarterly Meeting acquired the old Clerkenwell Workhouse in London. After a few years, this ceased to take in old people and continued as a co-educational school for very poor Quakers. Here children could learn trades leading to apprenticeships. To help finance the community, the children were also trained to produce saleable articles, such as shirts and shifts sewn by the girls.[53]

In 1779, Sarah Lynes, whose father had had a good job as a block and mast maker in Wapping docks but had died when she was six years old, was sent to Clerkenwell. Sarah endured 'sore privations' at school, and was often punished. Having already been taught to read by an older sister, she noted that the school with its emphasis on practical instruction 'had few books, the Bible, and one or two Journals of Friends'.[54] At the age of fourteen Sarah left to work as a governess in Clonmel, Ireland, for the widowed Sarah Pim Grubb, who had to take on the management of her husband's extensive mills. Later, her beloved mother being poorly, Sarah stayed a while with her in her humble dwelling in London. Here too she was able to support herself by assisting in a school and taking in needlework.[55] In 1803 she married John Grubb, a cousin of Sarah Pim Grubb's husband, who accompanied her from Clonmel to England where she continued as a Minister.

Committee schools under Quarterly or Yearly Meetings

The right education for all, male or female, well-to-do or in 'low circumstances', was felt to be essential for both practical and religious reasons. In 1763 the Half-Yearly Meeting in Ireland put forward a recommendation that boarding schools should be set up that would ensure a 'guarded education'.[56] 'Guarded' in this sense meant protected from the bad influences of the world. A draft plan for a 'General Boarding School for the Select Education of Friends Daughters' was produced, with indications that there should be Committees able to raise the finance necessary and oversee the 'rightness':

> Expect 800-1000 pounds for subscription. Most of which to buy House (& to furnish it) in a healthy place near to a Friends Meeting. Remainder of money to be placed at interest - to educate children of Friends in low circumstances, as many of which as convenient to be placed as Apprentices to the Mistress, who is to give them suitable education, employ them as Servants in

51 Corrigan, 2009, p.109, p.78.
52 Ibid, pp.xxiv, 174, 191.
53 Braithwaite, 1919, p.571, pp.584-7. Clerkenwell continued as Saffron Walden Quaker school and finally closed in 2017. Prior to Clerkenwell, but as an Anglican charity, King's Hospital was founded in 1670 for the aged and infirm of Dublin, and their children. Lacking enough funds, after 1680 it was only able to continue the boys' school, which rapidly rose to 170 pupils. Many were supported by voluntary contributions, including ten by the Erasmus Smith foundation and the Corporation of Merchants paid for a further ten boys to be instructed specifically in Navigation.
54 Grubb, 1848, p.2.
55 Ibid, Letter 24/7/1799.
56 FHLD, Grubb coll. Mss box 56, folder 5, S121.

the House or Assistants in the school, according to their capacities […] others to be boarded with nearby Friends.

Mistress of school to have a reasonable gratuity. Each province has a right to send an equal number of girls. They should seek out & give preference to Girls who discover a Genius for such Accomplishments as may qualify them for that undertaking [of governess in a school or private family]. [57]

Edenderry, a midlands town with a strong community of Quakers, was chosen for the first Friends' National Female Boarding School. The National Committee (all Male) included Abraham Shackleton of Ballitore school and Dr. John Rutty, a learned physician and author of books on Natural History and Mineral Springs, who often took the children of John Gough's school out for botanical rambles in the countryside round Dublin. [58] Other members of the Committee were Samuel Neale (1729-92), from Cork, a powerful minister who travelled in Europe and America and was highly regarded as a person of discernment and a great help to others especially the young, and Joseph Grubb (1710-82) from Clonmel, the father of Robert Grubb (1743-97), who would marry Sarah Tuke of York, and share her interest in education.

Ebenezer Mellor, of a well-to-do Manchester family, and his wife Margaret, born at Swarthmoor and a great-grand-daughter of Margaret Fell, came to take charge of the new school in 1764. It would seem that some pupils paid full fees while girls in low circumstances were subsidised. A document of 1769 gives a further picture of the school:

Ebenezer and Margaret Mellor having renewed their agreement with the Committee to conduct the National Female Boarding School at Edenderry, Select, hope Friends will encourage their undertaking by sending their Children thereto, of whose Morals and Education the greatest care will be taken and particular Attention paid to the Directions of the parents in the Branches they choose to have them taught by their obliged Friends,

Ebenezer and Margaret Mellor.

Terms
One Guinea Entrance.
Board and Education £13 per annum.
And those who choose Tea to pay for it as usual
Also to pay for Washing white Gowns,
Petticoats and White Stockings.
Edenderry 5 mo 3ᵈ [i.e. 3 May, 1769]. [59]

Tea was heavily taxed by the English government, and this was a luxury for which some girls paid a supplement. [60] They each had to bring their own teacup, as the ordinary drinking vessels in the school were beakers of turned wood or coarse pottery. The closure of the school after about ten years may have been a consequence of Margaret's death. A boys' school had also been considered to be essential, but did not materialise then.

In 1764 a bequest of £1,000 was left to found a school for Friends in Lisburn. John Gough, who was a very able schoolmaster, took charge of it under the executors till his death in 1791. In 1794 it became the Ulster Quarterly Meeting Committee School, variously known as Prospect Hill or Friends' School Lisburn.

Other schools set up under Quarterly Meeting Committees were Mountmellick and Newtown. Mountmellick, established in 1786 in the midlands and taking both boys and girls, opened initially for Friends in low circumstances. However, within a short time it was felt beneficial to all to accept the better-off also, but they had to pay full fees.

In 1796 Munster Quarterly Meeting at Clonmel, decided to establish a co-educational Provincial School for the children of Friends and, recognising that parents' incomes might vary, a sliding scale of fees was operated. They bought the very fine Newtown House, recently built by Thomas Wyse in Waterford. [61] The setting-up of

---

[57] Ibid.
[58] Grubb, 1927, p.88.
[59] Copy of a document formerly in the possession of Daniel Alesbury of Edenderry. FHLD, Mss. Box 56, S 123.
[60] The tax on tea had become an important source of revenue for the British government. The Americans refused to pay this tax in 1773 and this led to 'The Boston Tea Party' where they threw the tea into the harbour. The Quakers of Philadelphia simply sent the tea back.
[61] The Wyses were an old and wealthy Roman Catholic family. Thomas Wyse's son, Sir Thomas Wyse, married Napoleon's impossible and expensive niece, Letitia Buonaparte.

the school was carried out in a remarkably short time. After a week of committee meetings, a number of decisions were made ranging from beds and bedding, food and fuel to removing most of the decorative features of the house, such as fireplaces, so as to make it suitably plain. Newtown Boarding School opened in 1798 with 50 pupils (twenty-five of each sex). A library was set up from donations of spare books from meetings and Friends, while the local committee had the brief of procuring bibles and choosing school books, and were instructed to buy 50 copies of Lindley Murray's *Grammar* at the best price.

At these three schools, children were accepted at eight and could attend up to the age of fifteen. There was a basic curriculum with Latin and French only becoming available at Newtown in the 1830's, and at an extra charge. Book keeping was learnt by the boys, but there is scant written information about the girls.

Leinster and Munster Friends had raised considerable funds in 1793-4 to subsidise schooling for poor Ulster Quakers. Money from the fund was allocated for apprentice fees if students needed them. Most of the poor friends in Ulster were engaged in farming and linen weaving, where no apprentice fees were necessary. Girls who had spent two or more years at Lisburn, might be apprenticed to the trades of mantua maker (dress maker), milliner or shopkeeper, or could go into domestic service. It was found that girls from Friends School, Lisburn, who were better-educated compared to their neighbours, were often snapped up in marriage by non-Quakers (and disowned as a result). Assistance was given to young men and women of good conduct who had 'married agreeably according to the good order of our Society.' Apart from apprenticeships and marriage grants, a single female could get an interest free loan which had to be paid back only if she left Friends.[62]

In 1836 in the north of Ireland Ulster Friends opened Brookfield Agricultural School which continued until 1922. Brookfield was for the children of those who were disowned but continued to attend Meetings. Most of these families were also very poor and needy. Basic elementary school subjects were taught, with practical farming and its management for the boys, and household management, including butter-making, dress-making and knitting for the girls.[63]

One difficulty for this study has been the paucity of records of what the girls did in school. Occasional recollections and odd references turn up, and, of course, there are the carefully stitched samplers which provide material evidence. The best contemporary account of a Friends' Committee School refers to Ackworth School in Pontefract, Yorkshire, which was set up in 1779, fifteen years after Edenderry. Written by Sarah Tuke Grubb (1756-1790), this account became a point of reference for the setting up of Newtown and also of the American school, Westtown. The Friend in America to whom Sarah Grubb wrote was almost certainly Rebecca Jones (1739-1818) with whom she travelled in Ministry between 1785 and 1788. Rebecca was on the committee that founded Westtown, the first official American Friends' school, which opened near Philadelphia in 1799. Together with George Dillwyn (another member of the committee) she had visited schools run by Quakers in both Ireland and England after their visit to London Yearly Meeting in 1784. In July1785, Rebecca Jones and George and Sarah Dillwyn joined Sarah Grubb to visit Ballitore school.[64]

Leather-covered travelling trunk belonging to Mary White c.1775. 61cms x 25cms. (FHLD)

62 FHLD, PB 20 A, no.96.
63 Jackson, 2005, pp.130-3. Sampler of 1865 in FHLD.
64 Grubb, 1792, p.92. Rebecca was struck by the non-denominational nature of the school: 'amongst about fifty boys, mostly not members of our Society. This was a time of great favor.' (Jones, 1849, p.111.)

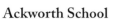

Ackworth School

In 1777 London Yearly Meeting agreed to the setting up of boarding schools for children 'not in affluence' and approved the project of buying the disused Foundling Hospital at Ackworth. The splendid building of the Hospital had only been finished in 1765, but had closed in 1773. John Fothergill, doctor and botanist, and David Barclay, a banker, who were both from London, together with William Tuke, father of Sarah Grubb and a very successful tea merchant in York, had convinced London Yearly Meeting, and the place was bought for £7,000 in 1778. Ackworth School opened one year later.

Sarah Grubb's *Account of Ackworth School addressed to a Friend in America* (1786) provides a description of the organisation of the school.[65] There were 300 pupils, of which 180 were boys and 120 were girls. Board, education, clothing and incidentals cost eight guineas per annum, with an additional deposit to allow for one penny a week as pocket money. The school was under the care of two committees, each of 28 members, one in London and the other in the Ackworth area. They met once a month, checked everything and planned. Copies of the minutes of each committee were exchanged. The progress of the children was inspected; the female side was done by women Friends. The boys had four or five masters, each with his own specific skill, such as reading, writing or arithmetic. The children passed from one teacher to another, except the little ones who stayed under one master. There were some apprentices, together with ten or twelve senior boys who were chosen as monitors. At least four mistresses were employed to teach the girls sewing, knitting, spinning flax, reading, and English grammar, whilst writing and arithmetic were initially taught by one of the masters till they were able to get a female teacher capable of instructing in these subjects. Everything was organised in quiet order for both boys and girls:

> A wise attention is paid in the girls' schools [classrooms] to quietude and regularity; each is to know her own business, and the time for applying for instruction about her work [sewing] &c. There are two or three apprentices for whom there is a considerable sphere of action, in assisting the mistresses, as there are many more articles of care amongst the girls than the boys; such as large stocks of goods to be made up into wearing apparel, cutting up work, teaching various branches of the executive part [making-up], and dealing out haberdasheries to the children [...this] preserves the mistresses from too oppressive a load of anxiety about smaller matters.[...]They also have monitors.
>
> The reading mistress has seldom more than one class in her school [classroom] at a time, which consists of six or eight, and they read paragraph by paragraph, all standing so remote from her, as to render a proper exertion of their voices necessary, by which they are inured to read audibly.
>
> The mistress or assistant teacher, to whom is committed the care of spinning, attends to that employ only a few hours a day; the rest of her time being taken up with mending the children's linen, especially that of the little ones, and instructing five or six girls at a time in that art, having them, and that kind of work, in a room wholly set at liberty for the purpose. The eldest girls take it in turns, one or two at a time, to assist the mantua-maker, who is supplied with plenty of work. They also take it in turns to work with the laundress every week, in washing, and getting up small linen, and in waiting at the housekeeper's table [...] Two of the girls are weekly appointed to sweep the lodging rooms every day [...] Their apparel in general, and especially such as passes through the washings, is marked with the initials of their names, and the number of their bill of admittance.
>
> The girls are provided with work by the institution, and for their improvement, finer needle-work is taken in for hire than the family [school] can furnish them with; and when that falls short, child-bed linen is sometimes made to sell, in which superfluous work is guarded against [no decorative or unnecessary stitching or pleating].[66]

By the early 1780s Sarah Tuke's 'excellent stepmother' Esther Tuke had come to a realisation of the need for girls to receive a longer education, of a higher standard than Ackworth could provide,

---

[65] Grubb, 1792, pp.249-70.
[66] Ibid, pp.259-60.

so that they would be better able to take their part more fully as active members of the Society of Friends. Nine women Friends, four of whom had been in the delegation to ask for proper recognition of the Women's Yearly Meeting in 1784, decided to open such a school.[67] Their husbands, though not part of the executive, fully supported this venture and attended their yearly committee meeting, held when the Spring Quarterly Meeting was at York.

A prospectus was issued:

> Proposed BOARDING SCHOOL for
> GIRLS at YORK
>
> By Esther Tuke, Martha Routh, Mary Proud, Elizabeth Hoyland, Ann North, Sarah Priestman, Tabitha Middleton, Sarah Grubb, Sarah Swanwick.
>
> To open 1/1/1785 under immediate supervision of Esther Tuke, and occasionally of others of the aforesaid Friends. Suitable teachers to be provided for instructing the Children in useful Needlework, Knitting, the English Language, Writing, and Arithmetic.[68]

In January 1785, Esther and William found a suitable house in York, and here this private school for girls opened under the charge of Esther. *An Account of York School* was found amongst Sarah Grubb's papers and this too may have been composed for Rebecca Jones. In it she expresses the aim of providing a guarded education, and of receiving girls of any age or description:

> Simplicity of manners, and a religious improvement of the minds of youth, were the principal objects in view of the friends who established this school; and therefore whatever has a tendency to obstruct this work, is cautioned against, and such apparel as the children bring with them, if deemed inconsistent with the plainness which truth leads into, is not allowed during their residence here; nor such

literary publications as unprofitably elate the mind and give a disrelish for the purity of gospel truths; but a knowledge of useful history and geography, as additional branches of learning to those of reading, writing, arithmetic, and the English grammar, are by no means disapproved. And whilst a careful attention is paid to the improvement of the children in necessary needle-work and knitting, all that is thought merely ornamental, is uniformly discouraged.[69]

Clonmel Boarding School

When she came to Ireland Sarah Grubb's concern was to start a school like York for Irish girls. She and her husband Robert Grubb had for some time been pondering the propriety of opening a boarding school at Clonmel for the religious care and education of female youth. Their motives were purely idealistic but both obviously had good management skills. Robert was a wealthy mill-owner who had built and operated two large flour mills. Sarah, though only thirty years old, had already had experience in the planning and organisation of York School, and had been Clerk of the Women's Yearly Meeting in London in 1786.[70] She sought advice from other Friends. In an undated letter to Samuel Neale she writes of:

> opening a boarding school for girls at Clonmel something like this at York as to the plan of education [...] It might be right to take with us three or four young women from these parts who may be qualified for teaching for leavening the house and business not doubting but Ireland may after that furnish us in every respect suitable persons for every department.

One problem she had to face was that of finding young women well enough educated to be able to teach at a more advanced level. She also had fears of having a negative impact on the Provincial school at Mountmellick, but these were needless.[71] Clonmel Boarding School, often known simply as

---

[67] Rebecca Jones commented on this idea: 'Proposals are on foot for another boarding school for girls only, intended for the accommodation of 40 or 50 girls, to be established at York, under the particular inspection of Esther Tuke, who is truly a mother in Israel------I am inclined to think it will be of great use and benefit to the female part of society. Indeed, in a general way, Friends here seem more attentive to their daughters' education than in some parts of our country [America]. They are mostly good pen-women, and read with propriety.' (Jones, 1849, p.82).

[68] Sturge, 1931, p,4.

[69] Grubb, 1792, pp.277-279.

[70] Ibid, p.133.

[71] Later, in 1842, Lizzy Greeves, aged thirteen, was ready for more advanced teaching. Her family from Armagh, were comfortably off and able to afford extra schooling. Her aunt wrote 'Lizzy Greeves is still at school in Waterford and is likely to remain for sometime longer; and leaving there, she is to be sent to a school in England or to Suir Island to be finished.' (Jackson, 2011, p.246.)

Suir Island from its location, was conceived for the further education of girls who might have received their initial instruction elsewhere. She writes:

> My dear R.G. has kindly [...] made ample preparation for a boarding school for girls, and has built a comfortable addition to our present dwelling; which stands upon an island, in a navigable river called the Suir.[72]

Set in a beautiful location, Suir Island offered education of a very high quality. It was not the only Irish private Quaker school which took girls till about eighteen. In Mountmellick, Anne Shannon's boarding school offered instruction to girls between the ages of fourteen and eighteen and lasted from 1787 to 1826. Anne Shannon herself was a Quaker and her school was highly regarded, but the pupils were not exclusively Quaker.[73] This and other similar schools usually had a mixture of Anglicans, Catholics and Friends and therefore could not give the guarded education which kept Quaker children separated from the influences of the 'world's people'. A surviving account from 1791 for an Elizabeth Hogg, a pupil of Anne Shannon, mentions board and tuition for six months as amounting to 9 pounds, 2 shillings, with a number of extra charges including money for a writing master and geography, a 'Fair Geography' (7 pence), a ciphering (arithmetic) book and a copy of Entick's spelling dictionary. Sewing equipment and silks are listed in detail, and we also learn of a payment for dental treatment. In addition, there was a charge of 5 shillings for breakfast tea and 6 shillings for a gallon of port wine (presumably for medical purposes).[74]

The education at Suir Island was described as excellent by Mrs Greer (formerly Sarah Strangman), a pupil in the 1820s. For forty girls there were two mistresses, an English governess, who was a first-rate scholar herself, and five young women, referred to by Mrs Greer as half teachers, half pupils. She also commented on the fact that the students always had the very best plain fare and that there was a well-stocked garden behind the school. Coming from Mrs Greer, who was often incredibly critical and unkind, this was high praise.

When Sarah Grubb opened the School in 1787, fees were 25 guineas per year with instruction in French, German, the principles of geometry and natural philosophy, astronomy and English literature, drawing, keeping accounts, deportment, household duties, scripture and needlework.[75] The main objective was the provision of a superior education for better-off Quaker girls, but they also had to be proficient in plain sewing and mending. One of the interesting things is this combination of the spiritual, book-learning and housewifery.

Charitable Schools

Robert Grubb was on the original board of the non-denominational Clonmel Charitable School which was set up in 1789 by a number of wealthy citizens concerned by the lack of any education for the poor in the town.[76] He also arranged for the school to receive a small annual income from his estate, and this continued until its closure in 1863. The Clonmel Charitable School opened in the old meeting house (a new bigger one had been built) to educate boys and girls 'whose parents are not of ability to bear the expense'. The Superintendent was Anne Grubb (1759-1818), who continued in this capacity at the girls' school after the Roman Catholic priests opened their own Charity School for boys in 1804. By 1826 there were 93 Roman Catholic girls and 7 Protestants.[77] According to the annual reports, the important subjects of sewing and knitting were taught to a high standard. Evidence of this is provided by a number of tiny samplers made by the pupils, together with a Teacher's book of examples that still survive today.[78]

In his diary of 1798, when he visited Clonmel, William Savery wrote 'Visited a public Charity School [...] it is held in Friends' old Meeting-house [...] 150 poor Ragged children, boys and girls, apart are taught Reading, writing, Knitting and sewing, - the Boys nearly all without shoe or stocking and a greater part of the girls.'[79]

---

[72] Grubb, 1792, p.186.
[73] O'Keefe, n.d., p.42.
[74] FHLD, Portfolio 46, Supplemental Richardson Letters, Folder 15, no.142. Elizabeth Hogg, born in 1779 to James and Mary (Greer) Hogg, was the youngest of thirteen children, many of whom had died before reaching the age of five. The Ann Shannon account referred to here was sent to John Cullimore of Ross (Wexford), her aunt's husband. Elizabeth died in 1797.
[75] Ahern, 2012, p.139.
[76] FHLD, Mss. box 52 S.C. 4&5.
[77] See Ahern, 2009, pp.114-116.
[78] FHLD, sampler cabinet.
[79] Savery, 1844, p.268.

Clonmel Charitable School samplers. (FHLD)

The Dublin Free School in St. Catherine's parish opened in 1798. The committee included a number of Quakers and a specially active member of it was Samuel Bewley (1764-1837). Like Clonmel it was non-denominational. Savery's comment in this case was: 'about 80 boys and girls - they appeared ragged and many without shoes or stockings, yet kept in pretty order.'[80] Later up to a thousand scholars would attend daily.[81] Such a large number of pupils was possible because of the good discipline and organisation which were part of the Lancastrian method that was employed.

The Lancastrian method.

Joseph Lancaster (1778-1838) came from a London Quaker family. In 1797, after working as an assistant in several schools, he started to teach very poor children in a room on his father's premises. Overwhelmed with numbers he rented a bigger space, and by 1801 had had to move with his 350 pupils to a large room in Borough Road, Southwark.[82] Unable to afford assistants, he devised a monitorial system. A number of the older children were trained to be helpers (monitors) to guide the other pupils and for this they received 1d per day. In a school with 300 children the cost of teaching a child for a year amounted to seven shillings.

All the pupils (maybe 1,000) were in one room, which was arranged so that a teacher in a raised area could oversee them. Quiet discipline and constant occupation obliged the children to concentrate:

> The teacher should be only a silent spectator and overseer. The less the pupils hear the voice of the teacher, the better they will obey him. The disturbance in a school is usually proportional to the noise that the teacher himself makes; punishment of the pupils and exhaustion of teacher are interdependent.[83]

The children were divided into small groups, each consisting of about ten scholars, with a monitor who was responsible for the progress of the group in studies and orderliness, neatness and good behaviour. Some groups stood in a semi-circle, learning tables, spelling or reading aloud, while others sat at desks and worked on slates, and when given the order 'Slates up!' they all produced their slates for writing. For example, when the monitor read out a single word, the children spelled it and wrote it down on a slate. Then at a certain moment all groups changed occupation. The Bible was used as the main text for reading, but without comment, and arithmetic involved a mixture of oral and slate work, as pupils did not have their own books. Needlework was taught along the same lines with groups performing such exercises as threading needles or being drilled in the use of the thimble at the age of four or five.

The Lancastrian system took off and was supported by many, including the King and the nobility. In his model village of New Lanark Robert Owen set up a school based on this method which became known as the 'Royal Lancasterian System of Education' in 1808, and in 1813 was re-named the 'British and Foreign School Society for the Education of the Poor'. Unsurprisingly, the Established Church objected to it for being non-denominational and set up its own schools in England and Wales using a similar system developed independently by Andrew Bell (1753-1832) working in Madras. Called 'National Schools' these were designed to indoctrinate the children in the established faith.

In Ireland a number of Lancastrian schools were established, while at the same time this system spread across the world, being taken up particularly in South America and Africa. Around 1806 a day school was opened in Ballitore under Thomas Doyle, who had received instruction in Dublin in Joseph Lancaster's method. This was followed by a girls' school with a mistress in the next house. Fees, according to ability to pay, ranged from 2d to 6d per week.[84] Considerable interest was aroused by this method of education and Mary Leadbeater mentions that a delegation headed by the Duke of Leinster was appointed by the Farming Society of Co. Kildare to visit the Lancastrian schools in Ballitore.[85]

---

[80] Ibid, p.259.
[81] Kingsmill Moore, 1904, pp.8-9.
[82] Parkes, 2011, p.19.
[83] Jorns, 1931, pp.122-3.
[84] See Corrigan, 2009, pp.178, 183, 191, 199.
[85] Ibid, p.183.

These schools were non-sectarian, unlike the Charter Schools set up by the Established Church with a serious proselytising intent. They were carefully supervised on a very regular basis and this was another factor that contributed to their success. In the case of the girls' school in Ballitore, a list of female visitors in 1811 has survived. There are fourteen names, all Friends, and these rotated so that one visited the school each week: Hannah Davis, Fanny Bewley, Elizabeth Barrington, Mary Leadbeater, Mary Farmer, Jane Thomas, Sarah Shackleton, Deborah Leadbeater, Sarah Butler, Mary Chandlee, Mary Pike, Elizabeth Leadbeater, Sarah Leadbeater and Mary Shackleton.[86]

A proposal was drawn up for subscriptions to create a premium fund for the school: 'Subscriptions of money, donations of materials of clothing such as wool, flax, yarn, stuff, linen, etc. to be sent to Mary Leadbeater'.[87] Materials collected were to be used for the sewing classes since most of the poorer girls would have had no opportunity to acquire the necessary skills.

In London, Joseph Lancaster's sister, now in charge of the Female Borough Road School, Southwark, had a carefully graded system of Needlework to enable the monitors to impart the skills the children needed. To make this easier for the teacher an instruction board for needlework with twelve examples of plain sewing and a small alphabet sampler was produced.[88] In the *Manual of the System of Teaching Reading, Writing, Arithmetic, and Needle Work in the Elementary Schools of The British and Foreign School Society* (1816) the programmed learning of needlework was further developed.

Kildare Place

Joseph Lancaster's Borough Road Schools came to be a model for Irish primary schools. A group of philanthropic Dublin businessmen, including Samuel Bewley, met in December 1811 to found the 'Society for Promoting the Education of the Poor in Ireland' (later popularly known as the 'Kildare Place Society'). A report of 1812 had estimated the number of schools in Ireland at 4,600 with 200,000 pupils. By 1825, excluding Sunday Schools, there were over 10,000 schools with about 500,000 pupils. Bewley stated: 'It cannot be doubted that the Society was a main agency in producing this increase and therefore did promote The Education of The Poor in Ireland.'

The aim was to provide non-denominational elementary education for the poor in Ireland. School-houses, equipment, books and trained teachers needed to be found. Samuel Bewley brought Joseph Lancaster to this first meeting and it was decided his methods would work well and be very cost-effective. The latter's monitorial system was adopted, being well-ordered, cheap and efficient. Extremely good but humane discipline, together with excellent organization made it possible to teach very large numbers. John Veevers, who had been taught by Lancaster and was recommended by him, came to Dublin to take charge of training, initially in a room rented from the 'School Street Society'. In 1819 a purpose-built model School with separate class rooms for boys and girls was opened in Kildare Place, Dublin.[89] Teaching included serious sewing to very young girls.

In 1816 a representative of the Kildare place Society, after an examination of the teaching of needlework in English and Scottish schools, found their standards to be poor. So, the Society decided to publish its own manual basing it on Miss Lancaster's plan. This was later entitled *Simple Directions of Needlework and Cutting out; intended for the Use of National Female Schools of Ireland* and ran through a number of editions during the century, becoming a basic textbook for all Irish primary education.

Carefully programmed, it started with the basics of plain sewing and garment construction, then came knitting, and finally, for the top classes, lace and embroidery. This was a complete syllabus for a comprehensive course in sewing, knitting and whitework. It was also possible with both the 1816 and subsequent editions to buy small examples of needlework, made by the pupils, to accompany the directions.[90]

---

[86] FHLD, Portfolio 5A, no.7.
[87] FHLD, Portfolio 5A, no12.
[88] An instruction board for Needlework done there in 1819, still with all its small specimens of plain sewing attached, was shown in Witney, 1997.
[89] See Parkes, 2011, pp.19-20. In 1825 Samuel Bewley wrote his observations on the 14th Report of the Commissioners of Education Inquiry. A copy of Bewley is in the Dublin City University archive.
[90] Tarrant, 2014, p.51.

CONTENTS.

NEEDLE-WORK.

Simple directions in needle-work and cutting out – List of contents (first page, 1853 edition). (Private collection)

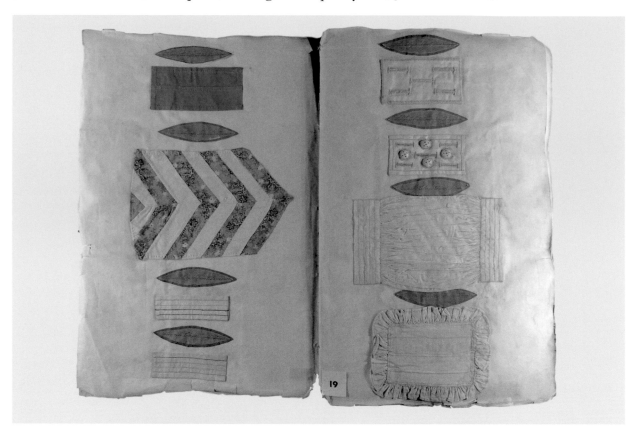

Mary Armstrong folio, Kildare Place, 1827. Plain sewing. (FHLD)

Mary Armstrong Folio, Kildare Place, 1827.
Whitework including Ayrshire embroidery and Limerick lace. (FHLD)

In 1824, before taking charge of the new women's department in Dublin, a governess, Jane Edkins, was sent to see women's training establishments in England and then spent three very informative months at Borough Road. The student teachers entering Kildare Place had to have a high standard of needlework besides a knowledge of reading, writing, arithmetic and scripture.[91] Each female trainee made a folio book in which she mounted specimens of all the needlework exercises performed, from basic hemming right through all the techniques needed to make an actual shirt or frock. Knitting, straw plaiting for hat making, and whitework embroidery follow these. Five such folio books still exist, dated between 1829 and 1832.[92]

A sixth folio book of needlework specimens with the name, Mary Armstrong, is held in the FHLD collections. It came from the Clonmel Charitable school where, one may assume, she was employed as a teacher. Mary had entered the Kildare Place seminary at the age of 23 on 15 November 1826 and completed the course on 7 March 1827. Like the majority of the girls there, she was recorded as a Protestant. Before this she had been teaching at Werburgh School, Dublin, and had been recommended by the Revd. M.L. Short. Mary Armstrong was in one of the first intakes of female students and the exercises and their order are the same as those in the other folios and in the later printed Dublin manuals.

Although she was clearly in possession of the appropriate techniques, her folio book, unlike the slightly later ones, does not include any garments such as a shirt or a frock. She has miniature examples of long mittens in cloth and further specimens of knitting - gloves, mittens, a shawl, stockings and slippers. One particularly interesting article is a cap employing the technique of 'Scotch knitting', a very old and firm method using only one needle. In addition to all this, Mary also has some examples of Ayrshire whitework, lace and embroidery for upholstery which she worked in worsted.

The Kildare Place Schools were the models for the Irish National schools established by the

Mary Armstrong folio, Kildare Place, 1827. Knitting. (FHLD)

government in 1831. Their needlework manuals were the best available in Ireland and Britain for much of the nineteenth century. An 1853 edition runs to over 100 pages. Published in Dublin it was also sold abroad in Montreal, Halifax and Nova Scotia as well as London, Liverpool and Edinburgh. The instructions are printed on white paper and these are followed by specimens of an extraordinarily high standard executed by the pupils and mounted on green paper.

In Ireland, unlike Britain, formal needlework classes could last until the eighth or sometimes the ninth year.[93] With very few factories, the need for skills of this nature was even greater than in her more industrialised neighbour. Mary Leadbeater's stories in her *Cottage Dialogues* (1811) were written to show the advantages of acquiring practical skills and knowledge. They were not designed specifically for Quakers, but for the huge number of girls living in poverty at the time.

---

[91] Parkes, 2011, pp. 29-32.

[92] Those of I. Henderson (1829), Margaret Alexander (1831) and Mary Fisher have been moved with the Kildare Place Society and the Church of Ireland Training College archives to Dublin City University Library. Those of Dorothy Tyrrell (1832) and Christiana Norwood (1831) are mentioned in Tarrant, 2014.

[93] Crawford, 1989, p.1.

One way of earning money for the poor around 1800 was straw plaiting. Some Kildare Place Teachers' Books show samples of three different plaits: Rustic, Dunstable and Tuscan which were taught in Twelfth Class. Such work could be done at home in the evening or while minding old people or the sick, and was also suitable for blind people. The making of straw hats expanded in Ireland when supplies from Italy were cut off during the Napoleonic wars. Betsy Shackleton, having learnt to plait straw, taught the art to several poor children, and introduced a little manufacture. She also assembled her plaiters twice a week and taught them reading, writing and ciphering (arithmetic).[94] Mary Leadbeater wrote that straw plaiting:

> needs about 3 months careful training [...] importance of smooth, close, and clean work [...] before getting up speed. Molly Carney earns 1 shilling a day, but Becky Timmins earns only 3d. a day because her work is scarcely fit to make up.[95]

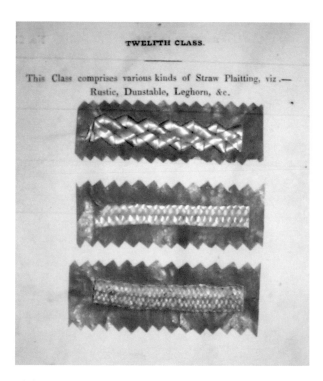

Types of straw plaiting in early undated edition of *Simple directions in needle-work and cutting out.* (Private collection)

In response to the appalling economic situation of Ireland in the 1820's, a number of ladies and nuns explored and introduced different lacemaking techniques and fine work, and Limerick, Youghal and Carrickmacross each developed its own distinctive type. All of these found a ready market abroad. Lace-making was included in the curriculum of Kildare Place, and Mary Armstrong's folio book shows a specimen of what is now called 'Limerick lace'. Using Nottingham machine net as the base with the design in needle-run or tambour work, Limerick lace, as a commercial industry, was started in 1829 by an Englishman, Charles Walker, who realised the advantage of the supply of cheap labour available in Ireland.

Irish Quaker girls and schooling

Many girls at this time received a very sketchy academic education, with possibly some music and drawing as accomplishments as well as the usual needlework. Exceptionally, some girls might be taught or encouraged by their fathers who had studied at university. The first, and, in many cases only, education that a girl might receive was often at a dame school, and, after this, Quaker girls might attend Friends' Committee Schools.

For girls like the Shackletons a high standard of sewing was not incompatible with a good education in the classics and literature. Two nieces of Mary Leadbeater, Betsy (1783-1843) and Margaret (1793-1816), daughters of Abraham Shackleton junior, attended Molly Webster's dame school, but after this received an exceptional education, being privileged to study with the boys in Ballitore under their father. Margaret 'possessing a classical taste, and having a judicious instructor in her affectionate father, she made considerable proficiency in the Latin language. She often chose this reading in preference to English authors.'[96] 'She also enjoyed with keen relish the writings of Pascal in French, and the finer passages of Burns and Cowper.'[97] Her reading helped her to endure the four years of illness before she died at the age of 23. The quality of her stitching can be seen in a token of love sampler given to her cousin Elizabeth Leadbeater.

---

[94] Corrigan, 2009, p.176. In the North of Ireland Jane and Susannah Greeves wrote to their sister Anne O'Brien: 'Susan is home from Newry and making straw bonnets—she can make them very neatly' (letter of 3/3/1819 in Jackson, 2011, p.10).
[95] Leadbeater, 1811, p.215.
[96] Corrigan, p.193.
[97] Ibid, 2009, p.258.

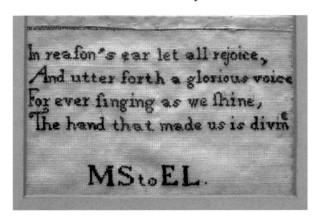

Margaret Shackleton sampler – MS to EL.
c. 1804, 7.5cms x 10cms. (FHLD)

Both girls enjoyed their early learning and Betsy gives us a vivid picture of Molly Webster, the village school-mistress who was also a healer and often had 'cruiskeens' (pots) of herbs simmering away to make infusions, poultices and salves. She taught them their alphabet and to read, employing virtually no punishment but fun, good humour and wonderful stories. Betsy writes:

> We loved our school, but it was the patience, the perseverance, which taught us to read [...] A number of impressions of seals hung in a frame at her back. She sat near a window. Many books lay in the window-seat. I believe a Bible was one of them - *The Universal Spelling Book*, *The Pennsylvanian Spelling Book*[98], *Reading Made Easy*, and no doubt many of the little books which were then given to good children, such as *Cinderella*, *Sinbad the Sailor*, *Tom Thumb*, *The House that Jack Built*, etc. Bags of old samplers hung near her. A bed was in one corner of the room, and a large box of apples at the foot of the bed; for her husband, Joss Webster, dealt in apples besides being a wool-comber. A chest of drawers stood near the bed, and I think they generally lay more or less open, for the hen laid in one of them, and the cat kittened in the other. I believe I never thought of this being untidy, but, on the contrary, a very great perfection; and indeed, only what I could wish, if I had a house and a chest of drawers. I thought the mistress happy to have such tame hens and cats.[99]

The Websters were not well off, and the Shackletons employed their daughter Lucy as a servant. Their house most probably had only one other room besides the kitchen, in which they both lived and worked. Betsy also spoke warmly of the way in which Molly Webster trained the girls in sewing, and of the various stitches she learnt:

> She was no less expert in teaching girls to work. I remember contemplating her powers while she was settling my work, with a feeling I could not describe. She appeared to me to be a sort of creator. She led us through all the gradations of hemming, and sewing, and running and felling, and stitching, till we were fit to work a sampler. That was the highest of our ambitions, except it might be to work flowers upon a pocket. We soon learned the marking stitch; then to make letters; then little stiff sprigs; then great flaunting flowers such as never grew. The mistress knew the various stitches which an accomplished girl ought to learn - double cross stitch, hem stitch, queen stitch, Irish stitch, chain stitch, oilet (eyelet) holes, &c.

Women's pockets in the past were shaped bags about 18 inches (45cms) long, hung on a belt, worn over the petticoat and accessed through side slits in the skirt. In the eighteenth century, pockets often

Working flowers upon a pocket.

<hr />

98 *The Pennsylvania Spelling-book, or Youth's Friendly Instructor and Monitor : On an Easy Plan, for Exciting the Attention, and Facilitating the Instruction of Children and Others, in Spelling and Reading* by the Quaker Anthony Benezet was published in Philadelphia in 1776.

99 Corrigan, 2009, p.272.

had flowers embroidered on them. We know that Mary Leadbeater, as a young child, worked a shell pattern in green worsted thread on her pockets.[100]

Betsy Shackleton also relates: The mistress sometimes amused us even in school with wonderful stories. If she saw us biting off our threads, she would tell us of a beautiful young girl who did so. At length she became very ill, and grew worse and worse till she died, was opened, and a large ball of thread was found in her stomach. This story made an indelible impression.[101]

One hopes that after this they all cut their threads properly with a scissors! Another of Molly Webster's stories was to frighten the girls from sighing, whilst others described the terrible consequences that followed stealing and lying.

Our knowledge of Irish schools relates mainly to Mountmellick, from which some committee lists of rules and clothing survive.[102] At Mountmellick, rising time was 6 o'clock in summer and 7 o'clock in winter, as was normal for most people in the days before electric light. After a Bible reading, spelling was done by all the boys and most of the girls, except those appointed for the week to carry out household chores such as sweeping. Breakfast at 8 o'clock, consisting of potatoes, porridge or bread with milk to drink, was followed by school. In 1816 while all studied spelling, reading, grammar, writing, arithmetic and catechism, the girls had two or more hours of instruction in plain sewing and knitting, with less time spent on the academic subjects. Spinning and sewing had always been most important skills for girls, who would have started as soon as they could hold a needle and now had needlework classes from 9.30 to noon each day. With regular and constant practice, they achieved a high degree of manual competence and coordination not unlike that of a musician or an athlete.

Clothing at school
Every child entering a school was expected to bring clothing according to the list specified by the committee. As travel was difficult and expensive,

To be sent with each Girl.

One woollen coat or cloak.
One bonnet.
Two pair of stays or bodices.
Two gowns, if summer, whole coloured calico; if winter, stuff.
One wrapper.
Two stuff skirts.
Two flannel petticoats.
Two pair of coloured pockets.
Four new shifts, *linen.*
Two night shifts, *linen.*
Two neck handkerchiefs or pillareens.
Four pocket handkerchiefs.
Six tuckers.
Four night caps.
Four pair worsted stockings, *or*
Four pair thread or cotton stockings,
One warm shawl for winter.
Two pair shoes.
Four check bibs.
Two pair of gloves.

It is requested that pieces of stuff and calico may be sent for mending the clothes, also worsted and cotton to match the stockings.
Each child is also to bring an ivory and a pocket comb, and a comb brush; and each girl a pair of scissars.
The Stockings sent, to be new and runned.
It is desired that an account in writing, be given of the clothing, &c. sent with each child to the School.
Those who shall have the care of providing clothing, for children about to be sent to the School, are requested to be particular, that it may be such as shall be consistent with our Christian profession.

Mountmellick Boarding school.
Clothes list for girls 1816. (FHLD)

pupils boarded for up to five years with no holidays. Consequently, the mending, maintenance and making of clothing was important. From the lists of clothes each child needed for school it is possible to get some idea of what the girls learnt to make. Material for mending was specified on the school clothes list and they were also taught darning and patching.

Elizabeth Hogg, who was born in1782, lost her father before she was ten.[103] Monthly Meeting accounts for 1792 indicate that at that date four guineas were to be paid by a John Gatchell, for the support of her mother, Anne Hogg and family, and to permit Elizabeth to be admitted to the school, and the following year John Gatchell was to pay for her continuance there. Fabric was sold to her out of stock so that she might make up new garments, as those she had brought from home were either completely worn out or outgrown. These she would have made up in sewing class after cutting out the

---

[100] Ibid, p.46.
[101] Ibid, p.271-272.
[102] The list is published by Michael Quane in *Journal of the Royal Society of Antiquaries of Ireland*, vol.89, part I, 1959.
[103] Elizabeth was a daughter of Joseph and Anne (née Jellico) who were married in Mountmellick in 1773. She was almost certainly the maker of a sampler dated 1790, which suggests that she was already at the school before 1792, but the death of her father might have made her continuance there questionable.

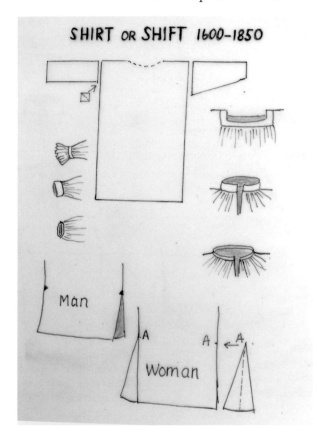

SHIRT or SHIFT 1600-1850

Man

Woman

Basic Pattern for a Shirt or Shift.

fabric with as little waste as possible and keeping the spare bits for patching. She would also have learnt about the different fabrics, what weight of thread and which type of needle to use.

In Newtown school Margaret Abell, the teacher, took care of the girls, assisting them in mending. This included darning and possibly re-footing their stockings, and 'doing up' their small clothes. On Fourth Day (Wednesday) afternoon she assisted them in making the boys' shirts. The housekeeper, Susanna Robinson, bought the materials. Most garments were made in the school but one of the many local tailors would have been used for the making of the girls' coats as well as the boys' coats and breeches.[104] As at Mountmellick, where the charges for leather and stitching are recorded in the clothing cashbook, shoes would have been repaired by the cobbler.

The Mountmellick Pupils' Clothing Cashbook for the years 1794-7 has survived and serves to give us a good idea of the needlework done by the girls. The school held stocks of fabrics, threads of different weights, various types of needles, pins

and other haberdashery. When a pupil needed a new garment, careful measurements were taken and the required amount of material noted in the cashbook. Fabric cost a lot at this period, with much of it hand-woven from hand-spun thread. To avoid any wastage, the measurements were of an extreme degree of precision.

The cashbook gives the exact amount and type of fabric used to make each shirt or petticoat, night cap, bonnet and gloves, etc. Bolts of cloth were bought and kept in stock. Fabrics in stock on 1/ 5/1794 were the following and the price is per yard:

    39 yds. Linen @ 12d
    4 yds. Linen @ 1s.2d
    12 yds. Grey Linen @7d
    3 Muslin Handkerchiefs 5s.6d
    6 Muslin Handkerchiefs 9s.6d
    Neck handkerchiefs 2 14s 6d
    11 yds. Corduroy @ 2s.10d
    38½ yds. Chequer @ 11d
    18½ yds. Fustian @1s.5d
    21½ yds. Cloth @ 3s.0d
    10 yds. Linsey @ 11d
    8½ yds. Broadstuff @ 11½d
    5yds. Camblette @ 8½d

The list also includes: 'Tapes 3 dozen bobbins @ [illegible], Tapes 5 [illegible], 2 pairs Garters @ 8d, 11 pairs Pattens @ 10d each and 8 papers of Pins.'

Threads of various weights, including tailors' thread, indicate the importance of the correct type of thread for the different weights of fabric. Lists in Mountmellick in 1794 mention a variety of gauges used in the schoolroom, including No.7, No.10, No.12, No.16 and No.18.

Usually a bonnet and gloves required one yard of material, often calico. Pairs of pockets used about a yard, although Eliza Hogg's pockets needed only $^7/_8$ of a yard of fustian. Esther Shaw's two nightcaps took $^3/_8$ of a yard of linen. For a petticoat Eliza was given $3^{13}/_{16}$ yards of stuff, while Mary Stacey, obviously a much bigger girl, received $4^5/_8$ yards of stuff and Sarah Alexander needed 4½ yards of stuff for her petticoat, and 14 oz of worsted wool to knit two pairs of stockings was also listed to her account.

[104] Wigham, 1998, p.18.

Between March 1794 and October 1795, the fabric issued to Elizabeth Flanagan provides a remarkably complete picture of the quantities and type of fabric required to dress a schoolgirl. A pair of garters has no special indication, but was probably cut off a long strip. Her tucker used $^7/_{64}$ yard of lawn, the bonnet $^7/_{12}$ yards of nankin (a strong cotton cloth of a yellowish buff colour, often used for men's trousers) and the gloves $^3/_8$ yard of the same fabric. A day cap needed $^5/_{32}$ yard of lawn and $^1/_{24}$ yard of cambric. $^{13}/_{24}$ yard of fustian made a pair of pockets. The stays were made up from ½ yard of 'ticken' (ticking), ½ yard of linen and 1 ounce of tailor's thread plus other thread [illegible], 2 $^3/_8$ yards of chequer was allowed for the slip, 4 yards of [illegible] for the petticoat.

Elizabeth Flanagan's coat required 10$^1/_8$ yards of 'cambletee' (camlet) in 7 breadths. The breadths refer to the width of the fabric. The yardage of fabric sometimes appears excessive, but this reflects the use of a narrow loom. In March 1795 Elizabeth Hogg got 8 yds of camblette for a coat of 6 breadths. Both coats were obviously unlined as the only extra fabric is $^7/_8$ yard of linen for Elizabeth Flanagan and one yard for Elizabeth Hogg. In each case the making required two skeins of thread. No buttons are listed, but women's coats were also fastened by ties at this period.[105]

Elizabeth's cap of lawn and cambric would have been for daywear, as was the tucker, a yoke of fine fabric inserted as a fill-in to a bodice with a low neckline. Other girls would have large muslin handkerchiefs to cover the shoulders. In Lisburn the tuckers were of muslin, very neat and ornamental, being drawn in with a string run through the upper edge. On Seventh Day (Saturday), according to a former pupil, Mary Creeth (1792-1883), there were no lessons but they had to see their clothes were in order, and tack their clean tuckers to their dresses. Worn winter and summer, the dresses were of dark colour stuff with short sleeves and a low neck. Over these, for going to meeting in summer, the girls wore white Vandykes of thick muslin, or a white muslin handkerchief crossed in front. In winter they put on little cloaks. They also had gloves of slate-coloured muslin which reached above their elbows; these were made in sewing class, as were their little bonnets of the same material.[106]

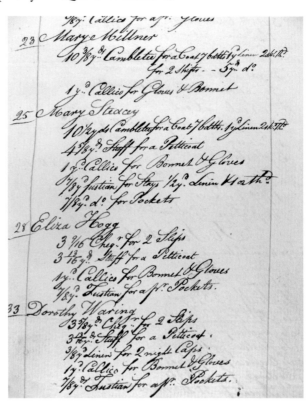

Mountmellick pupils' Cashbook entry,1795.
(FHLD)

All schools included stays (corsets) in the list of clothing for girls. The Mountmellick cashbook mentions Sarah Alexander having to have her stays altered at a cost of 3 shillings and 3d, a lot of money, but still much less than purchasing a new pair. A description from the early 19th century gives a fair idea of the process of construction which would have been used in the 1790's, though the cut would have been different.[107] The basic materials were a strong cloth such as ticking or fustian, and in one case the Mountmellick cashbook also mentions a yard of Wilton drugget, while linen was often used for the lining. Strong sewing silk, called stay-silk, was used for the best corsets, and strong waxed cotton thread for the common ones, which were often made out of jean, a robust and heavy twilled cotton cloth. The needles used for making stays were known as 'betweens'. Back-stitch was used for seams, including the gussets which were made for the bones (whalebone appears in the Mountmellick cashbook). Button-hole stitch was used for finishing some of the edges, and making the 'oilet' holes through which the laces to tighten the corset were threaded.

---

[105] The Victoria and Albert Museum also has women's long and short jackets of this period closed in front by hooks and eyes.
[106] Creeth, 1921, p.49.
[107] Waugh, 1954, p.155-156.

The schoolroom lists of orders at Mountmellick also include tape and braids, knitting needles, 1 doz. thimbles, 700 needles and 300 darning needles. In 1799 Westtown School in Pennsylvania instructed parents of girls to include scissors, thread-case, thimble and work-bag, plus some plain sewing and knitting, with their things. Mountmellick seems initially to have supplied such items, but those pupils who later went on to use their sewing skills to earn a living as milliners, dressmakers or ladies' maids would have had to provide their own needles, scissors and thimbles. In Sheffield, steel scissors had begun to be produced on a large scale in the 1760s and were becoming commonly used household tools. They had a sheath to prevent the sharp points making holes in the pocket, workbag or 'huswife', which was a roll-up fabric pocket-case for sewing equipment and thread Needles were handmade from steel wire, with water power used to speed up some of the processes, which included heating, rolling, piercing, pointing and sharpening, hardening and polishing. They were kept carefully in a cylindrical wooden needle-case, or a needle book with wool flannel leaves. These flannel leaves were often incorporated into a huswife and Quaker girls sometimes embroidered this with flowers and patterns.[108]

Thimbles, usually made of metal such as brass, copper or steel, protected the finger when pushing the needle through fabric.[109] Some of the girls at Clonmel School had silver thimbles, and this was recorded when they were stolen.[110] In the early nineteenth century the Infants class of five to six year-olds at the Irish National schools was taught thimble drill, the correct technique for putting on a thimble in four simple movements.[111]

The practical application of acquired skills
In many cases girls made baby clothes in class and these were sold. They executed commissions to a professional standard and the money raised helped to support the school. The sewing skills learnt at school gave some girls a possible way to earn a living, and for poorer girls provided an opportunity to gain employment in domestic service. Such was the case of Elizabeth Flanagan, who found work as a servant in Waterford.

Jane Hudson, the daughter of a dressmaker, went from Ballitore to Mountmellick in 1793.

While at Mountmellick School she learned to work neatly with small stitches, a different technique from her mother's rapid mantua-making flourishes. Married to John Atkinson and widowed early, she was left with 'three nice little children', who were all well brought up by her. They lived with old Nelly (her mother), and according to Betsy Shackleton, 'were employed in mantua-making, quilt-making, spinning, knitting, and doing everything that could be wanting in such a little family'. Ellen Atkinson, probably one of Jane's daughters, later became the mistress of the Lancastrian school in Ballitore, where her needlework skills would have been essential. Jane's sister Molly made patch-work quilts and was also a great spinner.[112]

Another outlet for sewing skills was the making of stays. After the 1760s, with the introduction of lighter stays, women had become increasingly involved in the stay-making business. Susanna Greeves, in a letter from Dungannon, writes in March 1819: 'Peggy Roberts is carrying on the stay making business as usual.'[113] Then in May she writes, 'We have got another stay maker in town. [...] I believe she gets a good deal of work. They make Gowns & dress caps for Ladys.' Susanna also mentions her sister: 'Jane is these few days making a pair of stays and new cloaks for her & me. Thomas got the cloth in Dublin: it is napt [brushed].'[114]

Many young women used their skills to get apprenticeships. Anne Grubb was the daughter of a baker in Mountmellick. When his business failed, he returned to his native Clonmel and struggled to run a small bakery in Irishtown, a poor quarter beyond the West Gate. After his death his widow was told by the Committee of the Poor that the youngest son James, aged eight, needed a guarded education. However, with three children still at Mountmellick School, she could not afford it and they had to assist her. In 1822 the eldest daughter, Anne, left the school at the usual age of fifteen. The sewing skills she learnt

---

[108] Jane Austen made one for her niece, and this still exists.
[109] Marsh, 2006, p.16.
[110] Ahern, 2009, p.214.
[111] Crawford, 1969, p.1.
[112] Betsy Shackleton, in Corrigan, 2009, pp.288-289.
[113] Jackson, 2011, p.13.
[114] Jackson, 2011, p.21.

there enabled her to be apprenticed as a milliner to her uncle, Robert George Grubb, who had a shop on Main Street, Clonmel. Indentures (contracts of apprenticeship) usually lasted from five to seven years. The master supplied board, lodging and clothing, as well as teaching the trade, and the apprentice had to submit to a very strict code of behaviour. Indentures could be broken for immoral conduct such as walking out with a man. Anne, a very beautiful girl, fell in love with a young English officer stationed at the British Army Barracks, but, sadly, one February evening they drowned in the river Suir. Reports in the newspapers show they were both very popular and an immense crowd of both Protestants and Catholics as well as Quakers, followed her oak coffin. Her story has become part of the folk history of the town.[115]

As an apprenticeship required some financial outlay, Dublin Monthly Meeting administered a charity fund which, in case of hardship, could provide the apprentice fee. According to surviving information from the1870s and1880s, most of the indentures for girls could be for two, three or four years and were for apprenticeships to drapers, where a knowledge of fabrics and sewing was important. Two such girls came from Brookfield, the agricultural school for the children of disowned Friends. One was fifteen-year-old Mary Jane Hunter, who attended Monkstown Preparative Meeting, Dublin, and was apprenticed for three years to Mary Halliday, a widow who had a draper's shop in Kingstown (Dunlaoghaire). The other was Harriet Grubb who, although not a member, also attended meeting regularly. Her indenture was for two years with Switzer's, a large department store on Grafton St., Dublin, where she was specifically taken on for the 'Berlin & Art Needlework Trade' (i.e. embroidery).[116]

Higher education
Few women received serious schooling beyond the age of fourteen and little need for it was seen. Girls from better-off families tended to be given accomplishments such as drawing, music and sometimes French, often with an idea of preparing them for marriage. This was frowned on in Quaker families, and might even make grounds

for disownment. Anne Shannon's highly regarded private school which also took non-Quaker girls is most likely to have had music and drawing classes. Becoming a governess was a possible employment for a girl without much money. Finally, in1870, it became possible to learn the piano at Mountmellick Provincial School, when it was recognised that girls who might become governesses needed some musical competence.

There was little opportunity for women to gain any sort of more advanced education before the second half of the nineteenth century. It would be many years before either teacher-training or any college education for women happened. A few schools such as Suir Island or Anne Shannon's school in Mountmellick brought girls to a slightly higher level, sometimes taking them up to the age of eighteen. William Mullins, a Quaker, ran a very successful private school for boys in Mountmellick. His daughter Anne (1823-1880) became a significant figure in the development of education for girls. She may have been educated at home and then finished at Anne Shannon's. As a young Friend she initially helped women to earn money with their sewing skills. Her own ability to draw is evidenced from her designs for Mountmellick work which still exist.[117]

After her marriage to John Jellicoe who owned a flour mill, Anne moved to Clara, where she soon realised that the only work available was for men in the mills. So, in 1850 she set up a school for Ayrshire work, also known as 'sewed muslin' to distinguish it from tamboured muslin where the design is worked with a special hook. Examples of Ayrshire work can be found in Margaret Armstrong's Folio. This technique was based on a firm white muslin, developed in Scotland, and was suitable for embroidering delicate flowers, using satin, overcast and other stitches. It was ideal for collars especially the wide pelerines of the 1830s, children's clothes, handkerchiefs and caps. Up to 1860 Ayrshire work was exported to many countries, particularly North America, and Glasgow firms employed vast numbers of girls and women as outworkers, many thousands of them in Ireland, especially Ulster.[118]

[115] Ahern, 1998, p.69. Also, Grubb family papers including an undated article from *The Nationalist*.
[116] FHLD, Deed Box IX, folder 9.
[117] Houston-Almquist, 1985, p.12.
[118] Swain, 1982, p.15.

In 1853 Anne Jellicoe changed to lace crochet work, which offered better rates. Crochet lace-making was taught by the convents after the Famine and promoted by merchants at the Great Exhibition in London in 1851. By the 1860s it was providing employment to some 12,000 women especially in the Cork area, as well as a large number from Co. Monaghan.[119] Such work allowed many of these girls to earn enough to pay for their passage to emigrate, but in Clara this activity ceased in 1856 once women could get work spinning and weaving linen in Goodbody's new sack-making factory.[120]

When John Jellicoe acquired a flour mill in Dublin and they moved to that city, Anne was appalled at the poverty. The advent of factories using the newly invented sewing-machine meant that many skilled needlewomen, working at home, could hardly earn enough to survive. The factories were overcrowded, under-ventilated places where between 50 and 200 women worked ten hours a day, often without a proper break, for 2 shillings to 6 shillings per week. They prepared and finished the work for the women who were the machinists and who, depending on their dexterity, could earn from 7 shillings to 15 shillings per week.[121]

In 1861 Anne Jellicoe was invited to prepare a paper for the first Dublin Meeting of the National Association for the Promotion of Social Science. This Association had been founded in England four years before, with a membership of men and women on equal terms, and it became a forum where social problems affecting women were discussed. Anne Jellicoe's paper was entitled *On the conditions and prospects of young women employed in the manufactories in Dublin*. When asked for a follow-up paper the next year in London, she noted the need for an education which would benefit both the women and the factory. All the overseers were male and the reasons given for this were that a woman would not be capable of the job because of her ignorance of machinery, her deficiency in

arithmetic, and her inability to control women workers. Jellicoe pointed out that training could remedy such problems. In the field of design, she declared that a woman overseer with artistic ability could be trained to make patterns more suitable for the factory than the current male designers who were art-college educated but lacked the women's experience in production.[122]

Also in 1861, Anne Jellicoe was a co-founder of the Irish Society for Promoting the Training and Employment of Educated Women. The committee had twenty-eight Dublin professional and business men together with thirty-eight 'ladies', with four 'women' and four men forming the management committee. One of the first findings was that 'distressed gentlewomen' were so badly educated as to be virtually unemployable.[123] Beyond the accomplishments of a little French or German, drawing, music and dancing, knowledge was often felt to be unnecessary and even unbecoming for a lady. Being a governess was about the only occupation for a distressed gentlewoman, and the market was already oversupplied. All this led Jellicoe to become one of the founders of The Queen's Institute, in Dublin. The Queen's Institute (1861-1881) was the first technical college for women in the British Isles.[124] Of the various training classes, the most successful was the sewing-machine one, together with those for telegraph clerks and law-writing. The latter provided part-time work for twenty-nine women, most of whom were daily governesses whose income was more precarious than that of a live-in governess.[125]

Anne's idea of a training college for governesses proved abortive, but in1866, with the aid of Dr Trench, Protestant Archbishop of Dublin, she founded Alexandra College to offer a liberal, university-type education to women, modelled on Queen's College, London.[126] The enthusiasm of Trench and other clergy combined with that of a group of Trinity College Dublin professors led to the project receiving support from the highest

[119] Longfield, 1982, p.39.
[120] O'Connor, 1995, p.129.
[121] Ibid, p. 131.
[122] Ibid, p. 130-133.
[123] Ibid, p.134-135.
[124] Raftery and Parkes, 2007, p.73.
[125] Cullen & Luddy, 1995, p.135'
[126] Parallel developments to Alexandra College were Margaret Byers' Ladies Collegiate School (1859) and Isabella Todd's Ladies' Institute(1867) in Belfast. The development of higher education for Roman Catholic girls, despite the work of the Ursuline, Dominican and Loretto orders, was held back by the attitudes of the Church, especially Cardinal Cullen, even though he was a former a pupil of Ballitore school.

social circles. Girls of fifteen and over came to study, but almost immediately the deficiencies of their education became apparent and this necessitated remedial work. The next year the best students who were over eighteen were granted reduced fees in return for being assistant teachers to tutor the less advanced. By June 1872 Jellicoe had persuaded the Council to establish a feeder school to provide properly grounded students for the College. The comprehensive and well-taught curriculum included grammar, mathematics and Latin. A further related development was the establishment of a highly successful series of Saturday lectures given in Trinity College and open to all women. These lectures covered a wide range of topics starting with astronomy, Greek literature and English poetry.[127]

Alexandra College was able to spearhead higher education for Irish women. In 1884 the new Royal University of Ireland became the first university in Ireland that could grant degrees to women on a par with those granted to men. They could not study in the University, but were permitted to take the exams. The first group was known as the nine Graces, and of these six had been educated at Alexandra College where five were already on the staff, and three had studied privately.[128] Between 1882 and 1895, 269 women received degrees at the Royal University.[129] In 1904 women were admitted to study at Trinity College Dublin, and the first degrees there were awarded in 1908.

---

[127] Ibid., p.142.
[128] Raftery and Parkes, 2007, p.110.
[129] Raftery and Parkes, 2007, p.121.

CHAPTER THREE

CLOTHING AND COSTUME

Simplicity and plainness

The school curriculum as discussed in the last chapter makes clear the importance of plain sewing together with the ability to cut out garments economically. The emphasis placed by Friends on simplicity dates from the seventeenth century. In cut and fashion, the dress of the early Quaker was that of everyone, without extravagance or unnecessary ornamentation. It would have varied according to work, economic situation, age, position in society and where they lived. Clothing is not static but evolves continuously and is influenced by many factors, including availability of materials, fashion (or reaction against it) and social status.

In order to understand the attitude of Friends in this regard, and before examining the sewing done by Quaker women, it is necessary to look first at men's costume in the seventeenth century. Until the latter part of the eighteenth century, the dominant male, like the peacock, dressed as gorgeously and expensively as possible in the latest fashion. At the Field of the Cloth of Gold in 1520, Henry VIII of England and Francis I of France tried to outdo each other in the richness of their power-dressing. In the mid-seventeenth century Louis XIV insisted that all his noblemen should reside at Versailles where he could keep an eye on them. Deprived of much of their real power, they provided a glittering Court which was used to enhance royal prestige. Charles II, returning in 1660 from his exile to the court of Louis XIV, brought with him the most outrageous and expensive fashions ever worn by men and, as James Laver put it, 'The general effect of men's clothes at this period was of fantastic negligence, well suited to the moral climate of the Restoration Court.'[130]

Court costume included petticoat breeches which were immensely wide and worn over knee-breeches. This extraordinary garment, which lasted till the 1680's in France, was covered with ribbons and bows and lace ruffles, all of which cost a fortune. Further ribbons tied in bunches at the knee ornamented the garters. Equally ornamented was the extremely short doublet, with slashed sleeves to show off a superfine shirt, and to complete the ensemble the crown of the hat was

Court costume with petticoat breeches (1660s).

[130] Laver, 1969, p.112.

loaded with ostrich plumes. Fox acidly commented on the man dressed in the world's fashions as having 'a store of ribbons hanging about his waist, at his knees, and in his hat, of divers colours, red, white, black or yellow, and his hair powdered [...] three or four gold laces about (them) [...]a pair of double cuffs and a feather in his cap.'[131] He saw this as a waste of time and resources. At a more elevated social level William Penn, a courtier and a man of sophistication, had no use for such modes. His *Maxims relating to the Conduct of Human Life* include several on 'Apparel':

> Excess in apparel is another costly folly: the very trimming of the vain world would clothe all the naked one. Choose thy clothes by thine own eyes, not another's. The more plain and simple they are, the better. Neither unshapely nor fantastical; and for use and decency, and not for pride. If thou art clean and warm, it is sufficient; for more doth but rob the poor, and please the wanton.[132]

In his maxim on 'Respect' he writes: 'Never esteem any man, or thy self, the more for money; nor think the meaner of thy self, for want of it; virtue being the just reason of respecting, and the want of it, of slighting anyone.'[133] Thomas Ellwood, a young Quaker who was a friend of the Penns and also of the puritan poet John Milton, wrote in his *Journal*: 'I took off from my apparel those unnecessary Trimmings of Lace and Ribbands and useless Buttons.'[134]

In Ireland, Leinster Province Meeting was established 1670 and one of its first minutes was an order to Thomas Boale not to sell lace and ribbons. In 1676 the National Meeting testified against 'making and selling [...] things which truth will not allow of [...] gold and silver lace, gaudy ribbons, silks.' By their order fourteen Quaker tailors met in Dublin in 1687 and agreed not to cut and make garments for Friends according to the current fashions worn by those who were regarded as 'the people of the world'. Coats were neither to have full pleated skirts nor the huge cuffs with needless large buttons, a style also brought over from the court of Louis XIV.

The extravagance of dress among those connected with the Court was in complete contrast to that of the Puritans and the early Quakers. Contacts with Dutch Protestants, particularly in the east of England, also had an influence on dress. The sombre costume of the rich, powerful and pious burghers of Holland was an adaptation of Spanish modes, and this was copied in less costly, plainer and more practical materials by the English middle and lower classes

Portraits of the late sixteenth and early seventeenth century show fitted doublets fastened with a large number of functional small buttons set close together down the centre front. One doublet, reputed to have been worn at the Coronation of James I in 1603, had no fewer than forty-two buttons.[135] A doublet belonging to a middle-class Irishman whose clothes have been preserved because of his burial in a bog circa 1670 has eleven buttons in front and four to close the fitted sleeve, which is cut in two parts in a style that reflects the influence of English tailoring.[136]

Seventeenth-century middle-class Irishman with both doublet and coat.

[131] Gummere, 1901, p.180
[132] Penn, 1993, p.32, 'Some Fruits of Solitude in Reflections and Maxims relating to the Conduct of Human Life' nos.73-78.
[133] Ibid, no.253.
[134] Gummere, 1901, p.12.
[135] Arnold, 1985, p.74.
[136] Dunlevy, 1989, pp.81-83.

George Fox, by James Holmes,
after Gerrit van Honthorst. Stipple engraving,
published 1799. (FHLD)

Charles I in hunting costume
after Van Dyck portrait.

Gerrit van Honthorst's portrait of Fox (1654) when he was thirty shows a similar doublet fastened with small buttons, of which fourteen are visible, very like the one worn by the sleeper in the frontispiece of the 1679 edition of John Bunyan's *Pilgrim's Progress*.[137] The Honthorst portrait shows Fox wearing a large hat, doublet and cloak. These basic male garments can also be seen in Van Dyke's portrait of Charles I in hunting costume, but executed in very different fabrics. The King wears a white satin doublet, the breeches are in a rich red material, and his silken stockings are gartered with jewelled ribbons. Fox's stockings were plain homespun and in hot weather his doublet and breeches were of stuff (wool).[138] He is often referred to as 'the man in leather breeches', but in this he was in no way unique. Leather was a hard-wearing material widely used for breeches, jerkins and buff coats.[139] According to Sewell, Fox wore it for convenience in travel, and to avoid constant repairs to his clothes. We also know from an autographed letter in FHLD that William Penn,

as a present for a friend in Lewes, brought back an American skin to make a pair of breeches. Penn himself added 'I have wore one three or four years colourd, & much likt by some great ones, and 3 or 4 have been beging me for some of them.'[140] Will Hartas (1784-1864), a Yorkshire farming Quaker, said leather breeches could be passed down from father to son, and still have a vast amount of good wear in them.[141] At Clerkenwell school in 1780 the wardrobe for boys being sent out as apprentices included two pairs of leather breeches.

In the Honthorst portrait Fox wears a cloak. The well-cut Spanish-style cloak became fashionable in Elizabethan times and remained in universal use till supplanted by the coat. In his *Journal* Fox relates that both cloaks and coats were torn off the backs of about eighty Friends at a meeting just outside London in 1658.[142] The middle-class Irishman found in the bog has the longer French-style coat introduced after 1666, but otherwise he is dressed like Fox, including a felt hat almost

---

[137] The print made of the Honthorst portrait is probably a far more authentic picture of Fox than the nineteenth-century Chinn one which adorns many meeting houses today. The upturned eyes are a way in which baroque artists indicated spirituality.
[138] Fox, 1924, p.52.
[139] Gummere, 1901, pp. 44-45, Waterer, 1959, pp.18-21, Dunlevy, 1989, pp.121-122.
[140] Grubb, 1937, p.30.
[141] Kendall, 1985, p.59.
[142] Fox, 1924, p.174.

identical to that worn by the latter in 1654. Tall and wide brimmed, it too is of the same shape as that of Charles I.[143] However, the king's hat is adorned with ostrich plumes; Fox's is plain and somewhat battered, and the Irishman's has an ornate cord as a band. This style of hat was popular in the first half of the seventeenth century. Later on, crowns became lower, and in the 1670s a 'French hat, large enough in the head', was bought for Fox.[144] The frequently engraved Chinn portrait depicts him wearing this type of hat, which continued in use among many Quakers long after it went out of fashion. James Abell was still wearing such a hat in Cork into the nineteenth century.[145]

Fox's hat might have been weather-worn but his shirt was of fine linen. In 1652, he was seized by the constables because of the uproar his preaching occasioned in the town of Patrington. Upon his being searched for incriminating documents, it was discovered that, despite his unprepossessing clothing, he had fine linen which would not be worn by a vagrant.[146] As was the norm, his shirt was collarless. Separate stiff lace collars or ruffs had been fashionable in the early seventeenth century, but by now the unstarched falling collar of lace, as seen in the portrait of Charles I, or one of plain linen was worn. A simpler version was the rabat, a strip of white linen tied round the neck, such as can be seen in Dutch paintings of the time. In the portrait of Fox at thirty the rabat is tied loosely in a bow. In contrast, the cravat of the young William Penn in a portrait of 1666 is far more generous and of much finer quality, as could be expected of a rich young man, whose father, Admiral Penn was a courtier.

Apart from his linen, we know that Fox carried a comb-case in his pocket and this may have been of tortoise-shell.[147] George Fox's hair has the short, plain Puritan cut, whilst a portrait of the young William Penn shows the latter with curling locks of hair falling over his shoulders. Short hair could be a political statement and in itself was

not necessarily an indication of a pauper. The French king Louis XIV had a luxuriant head of hair, and his courtiers adopted wigs to emulate his extravagant coiffure, a style taken up by the Cavaliers and Royalists. The craze for wigs arrived in England with the Restoration of Charles II in 1660 and this was subject to negative comment by many sober Puritans. In the 1670s William Penn was accused by some scandalised Warwickshire Friends of being a 'Perriwigg man'.[148] To allow the periwig to sit more easily, coats at this period had no collars, a style that strict Quakers retained well into the nineteenth century, and seemed to think constituted a part of their identity, since it showed that they had no interest in fashion.

Horrified by the vanity and loose living of the fashionable, together with their waste of resources, early Friends emphasised plainness. Joseph Pike (1657-1729) of Cork perceived simplicity in dress and in household furniture as 'an outward expression of the principles of self-control and moderation'.[149] The superfluous, whether in the form of ribbons and lace, unnecessary buttons or more fabric than was needed, was to be avoided. Patterns, stripes and decorations were denounced. In 1688 thirty Dublin merchants, clothiers and tailors expressed the view that it was right 'according to truth for Friends to wear plain apparel' and decided not to make or sell flowered printed stuffs or striped fabric. Apart from arriving at conclusions of this nature, the tailors' meetings also kept a watchful eye on the standards and quality of their goods. Shoemakers were also subject to the concern for simplicity. In 1701 the National Meeting told the shoemakers to examine their trade and make sure that they made 'such shoes as suit the plainness of our profession', and were not 'guilty of making fashionable shoes' whether for men or women.[150]

The custom of wearing special clothes for mourning was strictly forbidden by Friends, as being both unnecessary and very expensive. In 1758 Mary Goff and Elizabeth Goff of Horetown,

---

[143] See Dunlevy, 1989, pp.64 and 81-83.

[144] Kendal, 1985, p.60.

[145] Water-colour portrait in FHLD. A late example of such a hat can be seen in the Quaker Museum in Ballitore.

[146] Penney, 1911, p.54.

[147] Fox, 1924, p.202. In the nineteenth century the Shackleton family still possessed a tortoiseshell comb reputed to have belonged to Fox.

[148] In 1677 George Fox wrote a letter explaining that Penn suffered from hair loss as a result of childhood smallpox and his later imprisonment in the Tower of London, and that he sensibly wore a partial hairpiece on which he did not spend enormous money (Hodgkin, 1947, p.214).

[149] Grubb, 1930, p.102.

[150] Ibid, pp. 95-101.

Co. Wexford, were severely reprimanded, 'for they put on apparel in imitation of mourning for the dead contrary to our rules'.[151]

Quakers and colour

There is a popular myth that Quakers disapproved of colour, and even today Friends often have the retrospective assumption that they always wore grey. John Punshon's excellent study of English Friends is entitled *Portrait in Grey*, but evidence from writings, portraits and extant clothes does not indicate that this was the norm. Unnecessary ornamentation or ostentation were disapproved of and plain fabric was recommended, but no particular colour was specified. 'Quaker grey' seems to be a late nineteenth-century fashion concept. In 1899 the Duchess of Abercorn attended the Dublin Horse Show 'dressed in a soft shade of Quaker grey' and in 1901 the Countess of Fingall attended the Viceregal garden party 'charmingly dressed in palest Quaker grey'.[152]

Joan Kendall, in her article 'The Development of a Distinctive Form of Quaker Dress', points out that there was no lack of colour and no uniform style of dress among early Friends.[153] In 1700 Margaret Fox (formerly Fell) wrote:

> In so much that poor Friends is mangled in their minds, that they know not what to Doe: for one Friend says one way, and another another, but Christ Jesus saith, that we must take no Thought what wee shall Eat, or what wee shall Drink, or what we shall put on: but bidds us consider, the Lilies how they grow in more Royalty than Solomon: But Contrary to this, wee must looke at no Collours, nor make any thing that is changeable Collours as the hilles are, nor Sell them, nor wear them: But wee must bee all in one Dress, and one Collour; This is Silly poor Gospell.[154]

Two years earlier she had warned about the danger of young Friends getting 'into an outward Garb, to be all alike outwardly; but this will not make them true Christians: It's the Spirit that gives Life'.[155]

Quaker men continued to wear colour up into the nineteenth century but this, like their choice of fabric, might well be influenced by their station in life. Joseph Gurney (1691-1750) was painted wearing an elegant coat of blue silk.[156] Dr. Fothergill (1712-1780) 'always wore a light suit of cloathes, a small cocked hat, and a white wig - mild, and courteous in the whole of his demeanor, he joined to the seriousness of the Friend, the manners of a gentleman'.[157] The coats of both Gurney and Fothergill were without extra ornamental buttons on the cuffs. George Braithwaite (1714-1753) is depicted in a green coat, which is double breasted and has a collar.[158]

James Jenkins, a natural son of Zephaniah Fry and a close relative of Elizabeth Fry's husband, attended the Meeting of Devonshire House (London) when a boy and later recalled:

> The colour of the cloathes of the young men were marone [maroon] light mixtures, bright snuff, pea-green, and peach bloom, the dark ones so much now in vogue they deemed only fit for their grandfathers.[159]

Other colours noted by Jenkins for men were liver colour, bark colour, a whitish colour, and claret. According to him both red and green waistcoats had appeared in Meeting.[160]

In 1770 Samuel Neale, regarded as a 'weighty' Irish Friend because of his respected spiritual authority, paid a visit to Philadelphia. He had a new pair of black velvet breeches made for the trip, but when he reached America he was informed that if he wore them his ministry would not be cordially received and so he brought them home unused.[161]

---

151 FHLD. Records MM VI F2, p.153.
152 Irish Times, 24 August, 1899 and 24 August 1901. Quoted in Smith, 2013, p.65.
153 Kendall, 1985, p.61.
154 Quoted in Kendall, 1985, p.62.
155 Ibid.
156 Photograph of a portrait, FHLD.
157 Jenkins, 1984, p.148.
158 Portrait owned by Peter Lamb, a direct descendant.
159 Jenkins,1984, p.15.
160 Ibid, p.217.
161 Ibid, p.76.

A year later, in 1771, Isaac Collins, at his marriage to Rachel Budd of Philadelphia, wore, 'a coat of peach blossom cloth, the great skirts of which had outside pockets; it was lined throughout with quilted white silk. The large waistcoat was of the same material.' His bride's fashionable dress of light blue brocade had a white satin stomacher, embroidered in colours and laced with a blue cord. It was worn over a large hoop. These clothes would seem to have been acceptable in Philadelphia which had many 'gay' Friends as well as 'plain' Friends.[162] The term 'gay' was defined by Samuel Johnson in his dictionary of 1755 as 'airy, cheerful, merry, frolicksome'. It did not carry any of its twentieth-century reference to sexual orientation, but did have a secondary meaning of 'fine' and 'showy', which was associated with 'the world's people' from whom more devout Quakers wished to distance themselves.

Around this time James Jenkins visited Waterford and noted that the Friends there 'differed from the plain Friends of England by some wearing a dark blue coat, and waistcoat, black breeches, speckled stockings, large silver buckles, great projection and display of wig above the shoulders; and all this with a plain triangular hat. [...] In winter, instead of the Great-coat long cloaks were generally worn by men.'[163] At London Yearly Meeting in 1792 he refers to Josh. Pike, the great Dublin banker, who with his fierce wig, large cocked hat, black waistcoat etc., looked so little like a friend, that the door-keepers stopped him, until it was ascertained that he was one of the Irish representatives.'[164] In 1786, at Tim Bevan's funeral, Jenkins' friend Henry Rutt said: 'About fifty years ago, most of your plain friends wore black stockings, cross (or outside) pockets, and large curled wigs, but, as I have since observed, that drab-coloured stockings, and the natural hair, is most common, so it seems, your ideas of plainness are not always the same.' He also added 'as it was the custom of each plain friend in those days to choose a colour, and stick to it, Bevan always appeared in light drab.'[165]

The term drab was in common use at the time. John Townsend (died 1801) 'uniformly wore a suit of drab-coloured cloathes, between a light and a dark shade.'[166] The word drab derives from the French word *drap*, which simply meant cloth. Originally the reference was to an undyed fabric and when used as an adjective in the eighteenth century tended to signify a dull light brown or yellowish-brown (1775). By 1880 the Oxford English Dictionary defined 'drab' as dull and wanting brightness, and from this the meaning seems to have shifted to a notion of dreary grey.

Despite this perception of the Quaker dressed in grey, the evidence does not point to this colour being favoured by male Friends. In the nineteenth century the fashion was generally dark colours for men's coats.[167] The emphasis was on cut rather than colour and this was adopted by the wealthier or more worldly Friends.

Appropriate attire
As clothing evolved over the years, strict Quakers often clung to outmoded garments, but the numerous reminders about plain clothing in the minutes of meetings indicate that younger Friends were constantly tempted to disregard this advice. After the 1820s trousers were normal wear. Breeches were worn at Court and by senior clerics, and also in the country where they were often made of leather or cord.[168] Strict Quakers clung to wearing breeches as the true garb of a plain Friend.

Despite recommendations, there has never been a specific Quaker dress code. Plain Friends stuck with what they regarded as simplicity, and it is often necessary to take into account both profession and socio-economic standing. An inventory taken in 1759 at the death of eighty-two-year-old Benjamin Lay, who had emigrated with his wife from England to Pennsylvania in 1731, mentions a variety of garments in different materials. Apart from a number of coats and jackets, most probably of woollen cloth, there are 4 leather jackets and a pair of leather 'britches', a skin coat, a 'buckrim' coat (probably cotton or coarse linen), and also a velvet coat.[169] Obviously these would have been worn according to the activity and the season. A nice example of appropriate clothing can be found

[162] Gummere, 1901, p.161.
[163] Jenkins, 1984, p.64.
[164] Ibid, p.243.
[165] Ibid, p.197.
[166] Ibid, p.393.
[167] Yarwood, 1978, p.102.
[168] Laver, 1969, p.169.
[169] Gummere, 1901, pp.44-46.

in the case of John Fry (1733-1803) who is known to have worn a dirty gabardine and an old hat early in the morning when he might have been making blacking (polish), treating a flea-ridden dog or cleaning filth out of a pigeon-house, and supplying its inhabitants with food. Then he would change his clothes prior to spending the hours of business at the Stock Exchange and the Bank of England.[170]

Quakers may not have been leaders of fashion, but most did follow it from afar. Our information mainly comes from writings and inventories. Relatively few portraits survive, since Friends' testimony against the 'vainglories of the world' included 'making a counterfeit presentment' (i.e. having one's portrait painted).[171] Commissioning a portrait was in itself an indication of gay rather than plain Friends. There are portraits and descriptions of some who mixed more widely, such as the Goffs, Gurneys and Dr Fothergill. We know that the banker and trustee of Ackworth David Barclay, who died in 1809, dressed very well in a full suit, a smart cocked hat and a wig with tiers of curls. He was both a very eminent Quaker and a personal friend of the royal family.[172]

At all levels of society men would have their main garments made by tailors.[173] Personal linen and shirts were always the women's province. Thomas Carleton of Ballitore listed extra clothing for a journey undertaken in 1678. This included 2 shirts, 10 handkerchiefs, 9 bands and 4 caps.[174] Men in the seventeenth century wore day- and night-caps of linen, silk and satin, which were often embroidered or cord-quilted.[175] The Mountmellick pupils' clothing cashbook has an entry for three eighths of a yard of linen to make Alex Wylie's nightcap, and this seems to have been a standard amount.

Stockings might be bought, or else made by the women of the house, and sometimes included a motif (clocking). A rare surviving pair of fine white stockings with clocks, possibly a stylised flower such as a tulip or rose, has a legend knitted around the tops: 'Joseph Pike his stockings knit by his wife in the year 1750.'[176]

The Mountmellick cash book carefully notes the quantity of worsted needed for stockings for different sized boys. 12oz. was allowed for 2 small pairs of stockings and 15oz. for 2 large pairs. These would have been produced by the girls in knitting class. Such work provided valuable training and was also a significant way of saving money.[177]

Women's clothing in the early years of Quakerism
The outrageous male styles originating at the court did not have a counterpart in women's dress. There was not much change in female dress during Charles II's reign. The long, pointed waists gradually became tighter, and, as large collars ceased to be worn, a neckerchief might cover the shoulders.[178] Already by the time of Charles I, portraits show that heavy fabrics, richly embroidered and supported by farthingales, had given way to the simple elegance of plain satins draped over petticoats. Deep rich blue and crimson were fashionable, and black was worn a lot. Decoration consisted mainly of ribbon, lace and pearls.[179] These great ladies were painted in their best clothes. Outside court circles what was worn would be influenced by status, age, money and where one lived, but few illustrations exist apart from those made by foreign visitors. Wenceslaus Hollar provides us with small but extremely precise pictures of English women of different classes.[180] His engraving entitled *Autumn* (c.1654), depicts a middle-class woman, and if this is combined with bills in Sarah Fell's Household Account Book and extant letters, we can get some idea of how Margaret Fell herself might have dressed. Puritans, especially in the East of England, had many contacts with Protestant Holland. The sombre costume of the rich, powerful and pious Dutch burghers was an adaption of Spanish modes, and this was copied in less costly, plainer and more practical materials by the English middle and lower classes. Painters such as Vermeer, Jan Steen, Frans Hals, and

170 Jenkins, 1984, p.409.
171 Kendall, 1985, p.58.
172 Jenkins, 1984, p.478.
173 Dunlevy, 1989, pp.137-138.
174 National Library of Ireland, MS 4715, in Dunlevy, 1989, p.85.
175 Colby, 1972, p.98.
176 Owned by Judith Badman. The length of the stockings is 56 cms.
177 FHLD has a case made of bamboo, holding very fine steel knitting needles. Donated by the Goodbody family.
178 Laver, 1969, p.112.
179 Stewart, 1986, pp.139-143.
180 Laver, 1969, pp.108-109.

Gabriel Metsu record contemporary costume, and in depicting people of all classes they provide valuable documentation which, used judiciously, can help our understanding.

Hollar's *Autumn* wears a boned bodice coming to a deep point in front and is laced with ribbons. The sleeves are three-quarter length, ending in wide turn-back cuffs. The foundation of the bodice would have been two layers of heavy linen with whalebone inserted between them and held in place by lines of stitching.[181]

Female dress after Wenceslaus Hollar's *Autumn*, c. 1650.

The Fell accounts for November 1673 show that whalebone costing 4d was got for Sarah Fell's sister Mary Lower. Many purchases of ribbons are recorded and these include yardage, colours and cost. Also mentioned are various other braids, including eighteen yards of 'fillit' (fillet), possibly used for trimming the bottom of a skirt. Ten years later Sarah writes from London that she has managed to get for her mother 'black cloth for a gown, which is good and fine,' and is sending it with the necessary haberdashery of sewing silk, laces and 'gallowne' (galloon) ribbon - a narrow

close-woven braid of gold, silver or cotton, used for binding dresses. At this period, when it was common for the bodice to be separate from the skirt, Sarah advises her mother that the gown should be made without the skirt being separate, that being the current fashion and 'usually so worn both by young and old'.[182]

The bodice was cut low and a white collar, similar to those in Dutch portraits, was made by diagonally folding a square linen neckerchief. Sarah and her sisters Rachel and Susannah bought 'alamode' neckerchiefs of light, glossy, black silk which was the latest thing. In April 1676 Rachel chose one with the corners rounded off to make a cone shape. Frans Hals illustrates both styles in his portrait of the Lady Governors of the Old Men's Almshouse (1664). These looked elegant and modest. Similar white neckerchiefs and a black

Lady Governors of the Old Men's Almshouse after Frans Hals, 1664.

round one can be found in Heemskerck's (Quaker) Meeting at London's Bull and Mouth in the 1680s.

Sarah Fell's choice of black cloth for her mother indicates a fabric which was very expensive because of the complex dyeing processes needed to achieve this colour.[183] George Fox purchased black Spanish cloth for a gown for Margaret: 'It cost a great deal of money, but I will save.'[184] He was happy to get good quality material for her, despite having no interest in his own garments. When Margaret sent money to George to buy himself clothes, he used it

[181] Waugh, 1987 p.37.
[182] Ross, 1949, p.348.
[183] Kay-Williams, 2013, p.89.
[184] Webb, 1865, p.294.

to purchase a piece of red cloth for a cloak for her. After this she gave up sending him money, as he always spent it on presents for her.[185]

A woman's basic undergarment was a long, linen shift or chemise whose visible neckline and sleeve ends might be frilled, embroidered or ornamented with lace. Its cut was like that of a man's shirt. A shift was also worn for sleeping. The Elizabethan farthingale had gone out of use by the 1620s and the skirt was now supported by up to three petticoats worn over the shift. Made of linen or wool these also kept the wearer warm, especially during winter in those days of scant heating. The gown itself was sometimes left open in front to display the uppermost petticoat. Petticoats were often quilted and consisted of two layers of fabric with teased wool sandwiched between them.[186] Some were flat quilted, but others had patterns raised with cord. It is likely that such garments were stitched by the Fells and their maids, as no payments for work of this nature are recorded. These could have been made of their own homespun linen and there are payments for dyeing petticoats various colours, red, ash, black and dove.

In the evening a garment known as a 'nightrail' was sometimes worn informally at home. This was a loose wrapping gown also called a bed gown or nightgown. That of Margaret's daughter Isabel was made of expensive imported Indian muslin.

Hoods were worn throughout the seventeenth century and continued in use in the eighteenth when outdoors. The Fells bought black hoods, like the one shown in Hollar's *Autumn*. Expensive items, these were most probably of velvet or silk. In 1670 Margaret Fox's son-in-law sent her from London a white sarsanet (soft silk) hood together with a white mantle.[187] Two fustian hoods for everyday use were also acquired around this time.[188] In Heemskerck's picture of a Quaker meeting, the women have both black and light coloured hoods, and two are still wearing the old fashioned tall hat of the 1640s over them. When the Fell sisters and their mother bought new felt hats in the 1670s

they would almost certainly have acquired ones with the new lower crown.[189]

Autumn's white linen apron has a narrow, worked border, probably of cut and drawn threadwork with needlepoint lace stitches. Given the prohibitive cost of imported lace, a capable young woman would make her own collars, cuffs, and edgings for caps. Whitework band samplers were made by girls who were already highly skilled in stitching, and such work occurs on several seventeenth-century English Quaker samplers in the Fitzwilliam Museum.[190] Cut work and needle lace were also used to ornament shifts. FHLD has an early nineteenth-century wooden doll dressed as a plain Friend. She wears a shift, the sleeves and neck of which are ornamented with integral needle lace, an indication that the skill had not been entirely forgotten.

Hollar's picture of *Autumn* does not let us see the shoes, but his personification of *Winter* is shown wearing leather shoes with well-shaped high heels. In March 1675, Sarah Fell paid five shillings for two pairs of shoes from Anthony Shaw, a Kendal shoe-maker. As shoes were relatively expensive items, wooden pattens or overshoes were worn in wet weather to raise the feet above the mud.

At Swarthmoor, stockings were made of yarn or worsted spun by Margaret and her daughters using home-grown flax or their own sheep's wool.[191] Payments were also made to women on the estate for spinning yarn and worsted, and to others for knitting stockings. Worn stockings would be re-footed. Sometimes the Fell's got their stockings dyed sky-blue, sea-green or red, and the accounts also refer to gloves being dyed.

Individual entries for each sister and their mother for haberdashery indicate that the Fells did a lot of their own sewing. They bought threads, pins, and on one occasion 100 needles. Linens, both 'Scotch' (coarse) and 'Holland' (fine), blue calico (an Indian cotton fabric) and dress materials

[185] Ibid, p.293.
[186] Discussed in more detail in Colby, 1972, chs. 4 and 5.
[187] Gummere, 1901, p.125.
[188] Kendall, 1985, p.60.
[189] The account book notes that Sarah sold lambswool to the hatter for felting.
[190] In the sixteenth century Barnaby Riche's tale Of Phylotus and Emilia (1581) describes a rich man's wife, after she has dined, choosing from her exampler which ideas and patterns would be best in a ruff, in a sleeve, in a coif, or in a handkerchief; what lace would do best to edge it, what stitch, what cut.
[191] Ross, 1949, p.260.

were usually bought in Lancaster or London. Plush and wool cloth of various types such as flannel, broadcloth, serge, fustian, drugget and frieze could also look very elegant if well cut, besides being very suitable in a cool climate. The account book records payments to the tailor for making up garments, particularly outer ones, and these were often in a local Cumberland tweed.[192]

Hollar's *Winter* wears a hood and, because of the season, has also a mantle and a vizard mask. In October 1674 Sarah bought such a mask to protect her face outdoors. She had to ride on horseback a great deal, whether managing the estate, overseeing the welfare of local Friends or travelling to other Meetings or even to London. She would have worn a cloak and a 'safeguard' (overskirt) to protect her from dirt and the weather and the accounts also mention a riding coat made up for her at a cost of five shillings and sixpence.[193] A riding coat was defined by Randle Holmes in 1688 as 'a long Coat buttoned before like a Man's Jacket with Pocket-holes; and the Sleeves turned, and buttons'.[194] Such a coat can be seen in a portrait of Lady Martha Rodes where it is accompanied by a skirt or petticoat. Further detail for a riding habit of this sort is provided by a letter written by Lady Rodes to her son John staying in London in June 1690. She asks him to obtain some material, and if necessary, to ask the advice in the matter of a Betty Ash:

> a silk dust Coat to ride in, for I find Camlet is so thick for this hot weather, I cannot well endure it. I would A Grave Colour; it is a slight kind of silk, and will not cost much. I would have as much as to make me A riding coat and petticoat; if it be a yard broad, 3 breadths will be enough for the petticoat.[195]

Lady Rodes and her son lived in Barlborough Hall, Derbyshire, and were both serious Quakers. The outfit depicted in the portrait is vastly different from stock images of Quaker female attire but is fairly typical of what a woman of her class would have worn for riding.

In December 1683 Sarah sent a 'manteau' of coloured stuff to Swarthmoor for her sister Mary

Martha Rodes in her riding suit, late seventeenth-century portrait. (Photo in Lampson, 1910).

Irish woman with short jacket green apron and white hood, c.w 1700; short fur-lined jacket (manteau), after Gabriel Metsu, second half of seventeenth century; middle-class English woman with jacket after Hollar.

[192] Ibid, p.261.
[193] Ibid.
[194] See Rothstein, 1984, p.18 and Arnold, 1972, pp.3-4.
[195] Lampson, 1910, p.17. Some boxes of their letters, including one from William Penn, were kept at Barlborough Hall.

Hannah Middleton, old photo of portrait by Richard Houston. (FHLD)

Lower.[196] Such an upper garment was loose-fitting and flared out from the shoulders with wide three-quarter length sleeves.[197] The loose fit made it suitable for lining with fur, which requires air-space and room for movement. It is very likely that Mary sent hers to the furrier in Kendal for a rabbit skin lining.[198] In the work of Metsu and other Dutch painters of the seventeenth century well-to-do women are often portrayed wearing jackets of this type, but none are known to have survived.

Another Hollar engraving shows a middle-class English woman wearing a fitted jacket. Called a 'waistcoat' at this period, this was unboned. Randle Holme in 1688 describes it as 'a garment generally worn by the middle and lower sort of Women', but it was also used as undress (informal dress) by the upper classes. Elizabeth Wright, a Quaker, of Sidwick, in her will dated 1718, bequeathed to her cousin, Agnes Harrison, her 'best searge under waistcoat', and to Agnes Fisher her 'best wastcoat with long sleeves'.[199] Worn informally in the seventeenth and eighteenth centuries, waistcoats could be plain, embroidered or quilted.[200] Plain Quakers would have avoided embroidery but warm quilting would have been appreciated. A Yorkshire woman Friend's will of 1755 lists two black quilt coats, one lined with blue.[201] These may have been similar to a quilted satin hooded jacket of this period in the Snowshill collection. Now in a very fragile condition, it, together with its matching petticoat, is a very rare example of such a garment.[202]

Women's dress in the eighteenth century
From the relatively small number of extant portraits we gain some knowledge of what better-off Friends might have worn in the late seventeenth and eighteenth centuries. William Penn's first wife Gulielma Springett (1644-1694) was the young and beautiful heiress to the wealthy Puritan Sir William Springett. In her portrait the dress is fashionable but, as befitting a Friend, without any unnecessary adornment. Interestingly, Hannah Middleton, who married Joseph Gurney in 1713 in Norwich and was an ancestor of Elizabeth Fry,

is depicted in an identical costume for her portrait by Richard Houston. It is possible that Houston painted the head from life, then told an apprentice to copy Gulielma's dress. Later this portrait was made into a very popular print as typifying a beautiful Quakeress.

The dress in the Hannah Middleton portrait is an elegant gown of silk, long waisted and very low-cut with a fine handkerchief which is tucked under the front lacing. However, there are no ruffles or lace and under the cuffs can be seen the simple finish of the sleeve ends of the chemise. A black hood, typical of the period, is worn over the white cap, and a pair of long gloves completes the ensemble.

William Penn's second wife Hannah Callowhill (1664-1726) came from a rather austere community of wealthy Quaker merchants in Bristol and her portrait shows an older woman in a dark dress fastened right up to the chin, with her straight hair centre-parted. However, the black hood covering her head is of silk and has the additional detail of a fine pleated edge to its cape.

Hannah Callowhill after a portrait
in Gummere, 1901.

---

[196] Ross, 1949, p.349.
[197] Arnold, 1972, p.3.
[198] The furrier 'makes and lines coats, cloaks, hoods and other garments' (Jost Amman 1568). See Arnold, 1985, p.3. According to the account book the Fells sold rabbit skins.
[199] Kendall, 1985, p.62.
[200] Colby, 1972, p.97.
[201] Kendall, 1985, p.63.
[202] Bradfield, 1981, p.21.

Mary Goff, old photo of her portrait. (FHLD)

Elizabeth Goff, old photo of her portrait. (FHLD)

The three main types of gown in the eighteenth century were the closed robe, the open robe which was split up the front to reveal the petticoat, and the informal wrapping gown which had fullness in the back, was crossed over or wrapped in the front and was secured with a brooch or girdle at the waist. All of these can be found in Quaker dress. The alternative to a full gown was a jacket worn with a skirt, which at this period was usually referred to as a petticoat. The materials used could range from silk or linen through to basic woollen stuff, depending on who the wearer was. The following examples of gowns are from portraits of well-to-do Irish Friends and are of silk.

In 1721 Mary Fade (1700-1753) of Dublin, married Jacob Goff who had large estates in Wexford. Her gown of satin is fastened with three clasps in the centre front with the ends of the fine handkerchief tucked inside. Her deep cuffs are typical of the1730's and 40's and the cap which frames her face is tied under the chin.

Elizabeth Goff, née Wilson, of Edenderry (1739-1817), was painted wearing an informal wrapping gown of about 1775. Such a gown

was often loose at the back and crossed-over or wrapped in front where it was fastened with a brooch or sash. The gleaming silk sleeves would appear to have fashionable ruched pieces at the elbows rather than the large cuffs of an earlier period. Elizabeth has no neck-handkerchief and so her elegant chemise is visible. Her hair falls gracefully onto her shoulder. The photos of both of these Goff portraits were very faded making it impossible to ascertain exactly what might have been the original colours of the gowns.

Colours varied from the very sombre shades of plain Friends like Hannah Callowhill to the much brighter ones of gay Quakers. When writing about eighteenth-century Pennsylvania, Amelia Gummere notes that 'white satin petticoats, worked in flowers, pearl satin gowns or peach-coloured satin cloaks' were worn. She then mentions Sarah Logan Norris in a deep blue gown, and Mary the wife of Isaac Norris in crimson and blue. Mary's granddaughter, Mary Dickenson wore deep red, but the dress of her daughter, Maria Logan, indicates the increasing tendency amongst Friends towards plainness and uniformity.[203]

[203] Gummere, 1901, p.158.

Top: Sarah Dennis and her daughter Elizabeth Penrose
after their portraits, c.1760.
Below: Elizabeth Penrose after later portraits.

It is very interesting to compare Elizabeth's clothes here with what she wears in an informal family portrait executed around 1772. Now the wife of Cooper Penrose, a very wealthy Cork Quaker merchant and patron of the arts, she is depicted wearing a simple closed robe of red silk over her chemise, but has neither a white cap nor a handkerchief.[205]

A 1775 portrait of Elizabeth in charcoal and sepia wash on paper shows her in the gardens of Woodhill House (the Penrose residence) in an open robe of the palest grey satin over a matching petticoat, with a folded white lawn handkerchief, secured with a large ribbon bow. A fine black silk shawl, long white gloves and an elegant straw hat decorated with pale ribbons, complete her outfit.[206]

Plaited straw hats were very fashionable and so were chip hats made of thin strips of shaved pine, willow or poplar which were plaited, stitched together and shaped into a headpiece on a block. A popular straw hat known as a *bergère* or shepherdess hat had a low crown and wideish brim. In 1720 York Quarterly Meeting warned Friends to keep out of the fashion of wearing hats with crowns too little or too large, whether of straw, chip, black felt or beaver.[207] In New Jersey, Ann Whithall, again bewailing the worldliness of the young, saw no contradiction in going to Meeting in a straw bonnet lined with pink silk.[208]

In 1779 Lydia Mellor wore a chip hat with pink ribbons for her marriage to Abraham Shackleton in Ballitore. She had an impeccable Quaker lineage being a direct descendant of Judge Fell and Margaret Fell, and according to her sister-in-law was carefully educated by her mother.[209] Elegant and always neat, Lydia chose a pinkish-fawn corded poplin for her wedding dress, as this fabric

Sarah Dennis, née Newenham, was a member of a wealthy mercantile family in Cork. Her portrait and that of her daughter Elizabeth are attributed to Thomas Pope-Stevens and were painted circa 1760. Both wear gowns made of plain silk, one brown and the other yellow; the sleeves, now narrower, still have cuffs, and the stomachers are white. Sarah's muslin cap, similar to Mary Goff's, is tied under the chin. Her transparent handkerchief is tucked in, while Elizabeth's is outside, conforming to Quaker 'advices', but elegantly tied with a ribbon. No jewellery is visible but a black ribbon sets off the neck, a fashion disapproved of as 'a sorrowful sight indeed' by Ann Whithall, an American Friend.[204]

[204] Both portraits are reproduced in Murray, 2008, pp.24-5.
[205] Ibid, p.26.
[206] Ibid, back cover.
[207] Gummere, 1901, p.142.
[208] Ibid, pp.160-161.
[209] Corrigan, 2009, p.59-60.

Dark brown silk dress c. 1785 with neckerchief.
(FHLD)

Cinnamon silk dress, c. 1785.
Green poplin apron c.1770 on chair (FHLD)

would also wear well afterwards as Sunday best.[210] Irish poplin, a mixture of silk and wool, had been developed in Dublin by Huguenot immigrant weavers, and by 1700 had become famous. Heavy poplin was widely used for coats and one is mentioned by Mary Shackleton in a letter of December 1774.[211]

The pattern of Lydia's dress may have been similar to two contemporary silk dresses in FHLD. One is cinnamon coloured and the other dark brown, and, unusually, neither has been altered. Very few dresses of that period have survived intact in their original form. Both are closed robes with neat waists emphasised by full skirts that are slightly longer behind. The bodice consists of a number of carefully shaped pieces, each lined with

white cotton and top stitched together. The seams are then made with very even running stitches. The centre front overlaps and is closed with pins (a standard fastening at the time). The skirt opening is a front fall, pleated into a band, with ties going round the back like an apron. All this indicates a date of 1780-1795. Fashionable in cut, but being of plain fabric without lace ruffles, these dresses would have conformed to Quaker simplicity. They may have been made for an older woman as the style of the cuffs is earlier. The low neckline would have had a fine white handkerchief of muslin or cambric tucked into it, and a white cap would have completed the ensemble.

Not all Quakers regarded total simplicity as fundamental to their beliefs. In July 1784 Rebecca

[210] Together with the note about the hat the family gave two small pieces of poplin from her wedding dress to FHLD. Also remaining with family members are a sampler stitched by her and an embroidered seat cover.
[211] Dunlevy, 2011, p.245. FHLD has a piece of the green poplin apron that was worn by Elizabeth Shackleton (1726-1804).

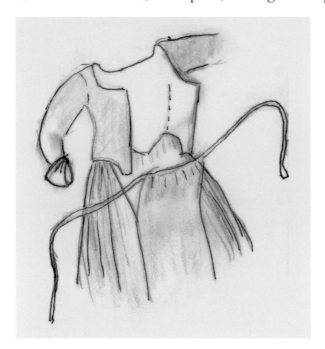

Front fall-opening of dress c.1785.

6. When Girls go out as apprentices or servants, the stewardess is to send with them

A hat and cloak
Two gowns
Two petticoats
Two under ditto
One pair of stays
Six shifts, four of them new
Two Hessian aprons
Four coloured ditto
Two white ditto

> All in good condition.

Four coloured neck-handkerchiefs
Two white ditto
Four pocket ditto
Four pair of stockings
Two pair of shoes
Six caps
Two night caps
Three pair of sleeves
One pair of pattens

> All in good condition.

A deal box, with lock and key, of three shillings price.

Also, A Bible, and the books before-mentioned.

Clerkenwell School, 1780, clothes list
for female apprentices (FHLD)

Jones stayed in Norwich with the Gurneys, a very rich family who, at the time, would have been described as 'gay' Friends and who, unlike 'plain' Friends, enjoyed worldly things. The seven Gurney daughters partook in music, dancing, theatre and singing, but later one of the youngest would become Elizabeth Fry, a major figure in the introduction of schooling and sewing into women's prisons. Rebecca may have been surprised by the Gurney lifestyle, but commented perceptively that:

> Many of the youth here and in London are wide in their appearance from the ancient standard of plainness; but there is a tender part in them, so very susceptible, that 'tis beautiful to behold, and what I have wished was the case with the gay and thoughtless amongst that class in my native city generally.[212]

At Ackworth School pupils were required to have robust and simple clothing, but there was no mention of uniformity of colour, and neither was this a requirement on any of the clothes lists of the Irish Friends Schools.

An idea of what a poorer Friend might have worn can be got from the list of clothes which the Committee of Friends School and Workhouse at Clerkenwell specified should be sent with each girl

when they left as apprentices or servants. From this we can surmise what Sarah Lynes, aged fourteen, might have had when she went as a governess to Clonmel in 1787. The list specifies that everything should be in good condition but not necessarily new. Luckily a notebook of her employer, Sarah Pim Grubb, survives and it is possible find what had to be replaced over the next few years.[213] Nothing was purchased to make another gown, so she most likely got one handed down from someone else:

1788:--2 prs. shoes, 1pr. pattens, worsted, stuff for petticoat, gloves, linen to mend clothes, stuff to mend petticoat, and 1 pr. of shoes.

1789:--a pair of stays & case, a lace for ditto, yarn to make linen for shifts, bobbins, cambric for caps, muslin for caps, 1yd. lawn which made 2 handkerchiefs, weaving 18 yds. linen @ 4d. yd. [for shifts or petticoats?], lawn for 4 handkerchiefs, a bonnet, 3prs.stockings, 7yds. [illegible, but possibly coat fabric] with body lining & making same, 2 pocket handkerchiefs, 2 yds. linen for [?]

1790:--2 prs. shoes, & 1 pr. pattens, Cloth for a cloak & making cloak, check [checked fabric] & tape for 4 aprons

1791:--2 prs. stockings

---

[212] Jones, 1849, p72.
[213] Sarah Pim Grubb notebook, FHLD.

Eighteenth-century corset, front and rear view. (FHLD)

Worsted (thread) was got in 1788, possibly for knitting stockings, but after this, stockings were bought. Otherwise she seems to have made up and mended her own clothes apart from the coat and cloak. The 1yd of lawn for 2 handkerchiefs would have been cut diagonally to produce 2 triangular ones to use as neckerchiefs. The four, coloured neck-handkerchiefs on the Clerkenwell list correspond to normal everyday wear for servants, with the two white ones appearing on First Day.

Underwear

Knickers were not normally an item of women's underwear before the nineteenth century, and the earliest ones often consisted of two separate legs attached to a waistband. Apart from the shift, which was long, and the petticoats supporting the gown, a woman's shape would be determined by her corset (the French term) which in English was called a 'pair of bodies' or 'stays'. An eighteenth-century pair of stays given by the Bewley family to FHLD, is fully boned and reaches high up under the arms where chamois leather binds the edges

to prevent chafing. Half-boned stays were put on children as young as three, and one pair is indicated on various Quaker school clothing lists around 1800.[214] These were not worn next to the skin but over the shift. To protect the gown from rubbing, an extra undergarment or slip was made to cover the stays. Such slips, made of 'chequer' (checked fabric) were required for Lisburn in 1812, and the Pupils Clothing Cash book of Mountmellick records the 'makings' (i.e. fabric) for such garments. As an alternative, in the nineteenth century, the shift was sometimes cut so that the top flapped over the stays. Corsets were supposed to contribute to health and straight backs, and according to the Regulations of 1785 for Mountmellick, the girls' deportment was to be supervised while walking in the garden.[215]

The padded roll, used since Elizabethan times to support full skirts and give the required silhouette was not disdained by Friends. A modest 'bum roll', as they were elegantly called in the later eighteenth century, is also held in FHLD.

[214] Waugh, 1987, p.45.
[215] Anon, 1886, p.20.

Bum roll: Dublin print, 1819.

Mary Shackleton: sketch of a lady wearing an apron, 1769. (KLS)

Garters were essential for both men and women to keep their stockings up, and might be tied above or below the knee. Dublin Men's Meeting of July 1687 complained that the 'heathenish customs' at weddings of 'giving off the bride's garters and throwing her stocking' were still practised. The direction in which the stocking fell was supposed to show the person who was to be married next.[216] We do not know what happened at the wedding of Sarah Handy and John Pemberton on 15 February 1744, but her silk garters are still being handed down in the family and were given to the latest bride in 2018. These garters, made by Sarah's father, Thomas, who was a weaver, each measure 132cms long and 3cms wide and one end is finished with a 4cm fringe. Woven into them are the name and date, as well as various motifs including a vase of flowers, five hearts, and the crowned harp, which was used as a silver mark in Dublin in the seventeenth century and later as a quality mark by the weavers. Ribbon-weaving and the making of fringes was a highly specialised trade, and this industry was strong in Dublin. Another Quaker ribbon-weaver, John North, worked with Margaret his wife, their daughter and their eldest son Abel

in their home in the Coombe and was obviously comfortably off, as his will of 1724 left £500 to be shared equally amongst his family.[217]

Stockings for men and women came to just above the knee and could be of silk, worsted or woollen yarn. In Leadbeater's *Cottage Dialogues*, Rose has worsted stockings for winter, and dark cotton ones for summer, as white would get ruined and stained by her leather shoes. Worsted stockings were specified on the Irish Quaker school lists, but Mountmellick also allowed cotton in summer. In previous times, as can be seen from the Fell accounts, all colours were possible under the long skirts. Apart from plain worsted, Quaker women using very fine needles also knitted stockings in cotton or silk; this work could be done when neighbours came to chat. Debby Fuller and her mother, both of whom had left Ballitore as a result of the 1798 uprising, had died by 1799, leaving 'a great many silk gowns and quilted petticoats, and fine cotton stockings with clocks in them of Debby's knitting'.[218]

216 Grubb, 2018, p.23.
217 Dunlevy, 2011, p.55.
218 Corrigan, 2009, p.268.

Machine-knit green silk stockings with clocks are on a doll of the 1730s, said to have been bought for Anne Petticrew (1724-1814), of a Dublin Quaker family.[219] In the first half of the nineteenth century either white or flesh-colour was the fashionable choice.[220] However by 1878 Anna Pim's trousseau had only one pair of white stockings (for the wedding), but six pairs of woollen stockings and a dozen pairs of Balbriggan machine-made ones.[221]

Aprons, hoods and bonnets

Aprons were worn by women at all social levels and had the added practical function of protecting the dress which would generally be valeted, but seldom washed. They could be decorative or even indicate status. Dunlevy in 1989 published an illustration of a middle-class Irish woman of around 1700 wearing a full-length green apron. In 1711 Jonathan Swift, Dean of St. Patrick's Cathedral Dublin, bought a fashionable green silk one for his friend Stella. Green was the popular colour at the time. Quaker Minutes from Dublin, Aberdeen and London frequently advise young women as to the style and colour of their aprons. Aberdeen Meeting in 1698 approved, 'either green or blue, or any other grave colours, and not white upon the street or in public at all, nor any spangled or speckled silk or cloth or any silk aprons at all'. In 1735 Queen Caroline and her daughters received May Drummond, who, in addition to being young and attractive, was a very able minister, known to have preached to audiences numbering 3,000. As well as enjoying the discussion, the Queen was pleased with her plain dress and green apron, thinking it, 'exceedingly neat and becoming'. A letter of Richard Shackleton's dated 'Ballitore, 14th Third month, 1776', indicates that the green apron had now become special for wearing 'on the solemn occasion of assembling for Divine worship or other religious performances'.[222]

Two bonnets (one more cutaway); hood worn by Mary Ridgeway over a white cap; over-hood to protect bonnet from the rain. (FHLD)

[219] This doll is now in NMI.
[220] Yarwood, 1986, p.396.
[221] Dunlevy, 1989, p.158.
[222] Gummere, 1901, p.134-137.

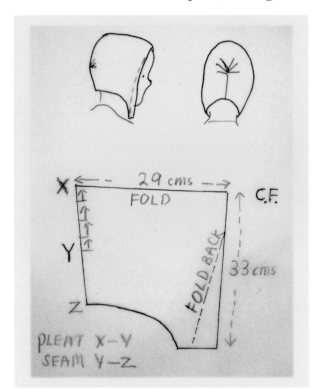

Pattern for Mary Ridgeway hood.

When the American Sarah Dillwyn came to London Yearly Meeting in 1784, she observed, 'the women here dress extremely neat and exact, a few of the plainest with black hoods and green aprons. Some go to meeting without aprons, but generally carry fine muslin or cambric ones in their pockets, to put on when they get in the house; if we don't bring one, they always offer.'[223] These latter would be dressy aprons. Many women then adorned theirs with fancy needlework, but Friends would have kept theirs plain. Ballitore Quaker Museum has on exhibit a mid to late eighteenth-century apron of fine dark brown silk voile.

A full-length green poplin apron of very fine quality was worn by Mary Ridgeway of Mountmellick, a notable minister, and is now in the FHLD collection with a note indicating a date of around 1770. After over two hundred and fifty years, its richness and vivid colour remain striking. In Ballitore, according to Betsy Shackleton, her grandmother still continued with 'a green tabinet apron, another symbol as characteristic as the black hood. Both of these were only worn in meetings and only by Friends who were most strict or in the highest estimation.'[224]

Together with her green apron, a black silk hood that belonged to Mary Ridgeway also survives. Absolutely minimalist, it is tied by narrow ribbons, and the back is designed with folds radiating from a central point to provide the necessary fullness.

Another type of black silk hood had long ends or lappets and was also still being worn for going to meeting in the 1770s. The hood was soon to be superseded by the Quaker bonnet. In itself the bonnet developed out of the new simplicity of the fashionable 'world's people' who, tired of the monstrous creations balanced over the enormous hair-dos of the 1780s, superseded these with simple straw hats and attractive small bonnets. With Friends, plain versions of the latter replaced the out-of-date black hood and in turn became the orthodox headgear for many years. A few older people still retained the black hood, one of the symbols of a plain Friend, but most opted for the Quaker bonnet, which was worn over the usual indoor cap of white lawn, cambric, muslin or gauze. Caps might be pleated or ruffled, but embroidery and lace trimmings were taboo.

Bonnet brims were stiffened with pasteboard or straw. In wet weather Friends often protected these with an oilskin cover. By 1800 the Quaker bonnet was the new conformity. The 'world's people' might alter bonnet shapes and decorate madly, but not Friends. Woe betide anyone who used gathers on the crown instead of pleats. However, looking at dateable silhouettes, it is obvious that the form of the bonnet or cap did not show a total lack of awareness of what was more generally worn.

Bonnets and caps. Bonnet boxes. (FHLD)

223 Ibid, p.137.
224 Corrigan, 2009, pp.40 and 264. Monsieur Tabinet was a French Protestant refugee, who was famous for weaving a particularly high-quality poplin.

Abraham Shackleton, sketch, 1768, 'A Lady pinning her cap.' (KLS)

Changing fashions and Quakers

Betsy Shackleton obviously fascinated by what the better-off Quakers were wearing, describes a variety of clothes at meeting in Ballitore in the 1790s. She speaks of the wealthy Ducketts 'so genteel, all dressed in silks', Debby Fuller with her 'high-coloured silk gowns that made a rustling sound as she walked into meeting and Anna Taverner wearing a 'harebine [thin woollen] gown of the most delicate shade'. She also expresses her pleasure in viewing the summer gloves and light gowns. Her young aunt Mellor, a sister of Lydia Shackleton, was very fashionable with her high-cauled bonnet, kept up by a wire, with a broadish ribbon round it, which she wore over a 'dressy' style of hair. Many of the less affluent would have worn their best gowns of stuff or calico. Betsy refers to the less well-off Molly Haughton, who sat on the side seat and wore a large black satin cloak, a hand-me-down that had belonged to the late Susan Bailey.[225] She was also conscious of social status: 'On the seat behind me sat Hannah Haughton, Jenny Boake, and other grown-up young Friends of our rank'.

Fashionable hat, Ireland 1786; straw gipsy hat; simple bonnet c.1800; three variants of Quaker bonnets.

[225] Corrigan, 2009. These details are scattered over pp.262-267.

Betsy Shackleton, silhouette. (FHLD)

Portrait of Edward Carroll, c.1794, showing frilled collar. (FHLD)

Portrait of Rebecca Goff (1785-1832). (Private collection)

Mrs Fayle's clothes, after Nancy Bradfield,1981.

In the wider world outside Ballitore, during the years following the French Revolution, fashion for both men and women was undergoing significant change. The heavily structured dresses of the eighteenth century made way for a more natural line. Even before the Revolution in France, queen Marie-Antoinette, in a reaction against the formal and structured court costumes of heavy and rich fabrics, wore a one-piece chemise dress of fine muslin when expecting her first child. This garment tallied with the new ideas of simplicity advocated by Jean-Jacques Rousseau and others. Aided by the ready availability of fine cottons and muslins resulting from new manufacturing techniques, the simple white chemise dress became the rage. Such a dress is depicted in the portrait of Rebecca, Elizabeth Goff's granddaughter, who married Francis Davis in 1809.

Large petticoats and stays were abandoned. The emphasis was now on a slender line, achieved with soft fine fabrics, and sometimes a small bum pad attached to the back of the dress, as in the case of two dresses of 1806-1810 that belonged to the Quaker,

Mrs Fayle. One was a fine white muslin dress and the other a 'charmingly simple grey silk dress'.[226]

Mrs Fayle's long linen mittens of a style often seen in the mid-eighteenth century, but without embroidery, have also survived. We also know that she wore a black silk Quaker bonnet. In a picture from around 1820 she is shown wearing a mob cap and a neckerchief, both of transparent muslin, and a shawl round her shoulders for warmth.

By the 1820s the mob cap was popular. Susannah Greeves (b. 1800) who worked in the small family shop in Dungannon, wrote in 1823 to her sister in America that most of the young people were wearing mob caps.[227] Mrs Fayle's mob cap had lappets whose frills would be pressed with a very small crimping iron, and not pleated. A crimping-iron would have been needed to maintain these frills and those on boys' shirts. In Lisburn, Dorothy Lamb, a strict plain Friend, showed rather excessive zeal when she objected to the crimped frill on a cap and seizing it proceeded to flatten it with her fingers.[228]

In 1809, arriving in Cork for a family wedding in June, Margaret Boyle Harvey of Philadelphia, expecting the worst, commented, 'In general Americans despise Ireland.'[229] She was astonished to find the sophistication of furnishings, food and clothes. She had smuggled through the customs a piece of lightweight silk, which her sister-in-law, Anne Church, arranged to have made-up into a

Crimping iron. (FHLD)

[226] See Bradfield, 1981, pp.371-374. These two dresses were given to Nancy Bradfield by Lady Corfield, a great-great-granddaughter of Mrs Fayle. Both are illustrated in Bradfield.

[227] Jackson, 2011, p.86.

[228] Creeth, 1921, p.49.

[229] Harvey, ms., p.36.

fashionable dress by the mantua maker. Anne would not allow her to wear a cap, but got her an expensive straw gypsy hat, white gloves, a gauze neckerchief and a white silk cord for her waist. Kid shoes and flesh-coloured stockings completed Margaret's ensemble. Anne wore a gown of blue sarsanet, with a white silk cord around the waist, flesh-coloured stockings and white kid shoes. In addition, she had a handkerchief with a lace frill to it and a lace shawl thrown over her shoulders. Their fashionable gowns would have been similar in line to those worn by Mrs Fayle.

Simple gowns of muslin were very popular and had become cheap enough to be affordable by young women. The wearing of such garments scandalized many older people, especially those Friends, who saw this as following the immodest ways of the world. In Lisburn, Samuel Douglas's sister Mary, as a young woman, was reprimanded by Dorothy Lamb: 'One would think thee hadn't on any petticoat.' Mary then pulled up her skirt to display not one but three petticoats, the last being knitted.[230]

Further indication of the wearing of multiple petticoats comes from two dolls in FHLD. One is a luxury German Sonneberg doll of wood and kid with a papier-mâché head that belonged to the Pim family. The doll wears an elegant chemise dress, the hem of which is finished with a suggestion of needle-lace. On her head is a very smart black velvet bonnet worn over her transparent frilled cap, and her green silk caped-cloak is lined with pink. Like Mary Douglas, she too, under the muslin dress, is equipped with three petticoats, including one of flannel.

The other doll, also early nineteenth-century, is a simpler, large, wooden peg or Dutch doll (from Austria), and this too has three petticoats, one of grey stuff, one of white flannel and one of cotton. Dressed as a plain Friend, she is attired in a dark brown serge skirt and tailored collarless jacket. She has a large white shawl and her Quaker bonnet is worn over a fine white cap. A slightly surprising detail is the finishing of the sleeve ends and the neckline of her shift with needlepoint lace (detached buttonhole stitch) where it can't be seen.

An indication that Quaker women were not completely insensitive to fashion is the fact that a new dress was often acquired for attendance at Yearly Meeting. Mrs Greer records that 'Going to Quarterly Meeting in Youghal one needs a new bonnet, shawl and gown.'[231] In their book, *The age of dolls*, the Colemans have a diverting mention of a Quaker doll in the 1820s that was provided with a new outfit for Yearly Meeting each year.[232]

The making of dolls' clothes was an enjoyable occupation in which girls could use their sewing skills. Mary Shackleton (later Leadbeater) as a child in the 1760s, wrote to her sister, Sarah:

> a disaster befell me, last night as I was making a Bonnet for thy little Baby [doll], I mean as I was trying it on, it bounced from me I do not know whither, I search'd narrowly for it, but cou'd not find it; So I fear it is 'Gone never to be heard of more', but I intend to make another, I have made the Cloke [cloak], if the head [hood] be not big enough I hope thou wilt excuse me, for the Silk would not allow it any bigger & I suppose she will not wear the head much.[233]

These dolls are another reminder that there was no such thing as a single Quaker style of dress. Elizabeth Fry, who had been a gay young Friend wearing purple boots and a red cloak, chose later to dress as a plain Friend in browns. In her case her sober dress made her more acceptable when visiting prisons.

A sober dress did not necessarily mean avoiding what was in fashion. Elizabeth Jacob who had been approved of by Robert Grubb as mistress of Suir Island School, was described by a pupil, Sarah Strangman (later Mrs Greer), towards 1818:

> Her dress was neat, and costly too. Her gown, of very dark brown tabinet, was made as the gowns of our aristocratic Friends always are, so very long, as to require holding up when walking even across a room; and her petticoat, of the same material, was just short enough, to shew the white cotton stocking, and the highly polished short quartered shoe, with its broad ribbon tie. The muslin of which her caps and

[230] Creeth, 1921, p.49.
[231] Greer, 1852, p.49.
[232] Coleman, 1965, p.3.
[233] FHLD, Pamphlet Box 10, no. 79.

neck-kerchiefs were made, was of a fabric fine enough for Majesty to wear. The time bestowed on washing, ironing, clear-starching, and tacking, was amazing; but they were perfect structures of delicate folds, when completed.[234]

Rather younger than Elizabeth Jacob were the five sisters aged between seventeen and twenty-five that Mrs Greer remembered from a Munster Quarterly Meeting, probably in 1821. They were all good-looking, but dressed exactly alike, in 'dark greenish tabinets, muslin kerchief plated [pleated] over the dress and muslin mob caps.'[235] It may have been Quaker economy to have all the dresses cut from the same bolt of cloth, but there is also the possibility that it was the thing for girls to dress alike. In a letter of 21 March 1824 to a cousin in America, Mary Sinton from Dungannon, describes the preparations for her sister's marriage to John Walpole, where five of the girls were to have the same gowns:

Grödnertal doll, c.1830. (FHLD)

Items of clothing worn by Grödnertal doll. (FHLD)

[234] Greer, 1852, p.37-38. Sarah Strangman (1806-1891) married John Greer in 1829. She indulged in ribbons and blonds (silk lace net) from the moment she left school until her father requested her to lay them aside, and resume a Quaker style of dress, though not in its extreme plainness. She wrote a rather jaundiced account of Quakers and Quakerism. The Suir island records were lost in a fire, so we do not know exactly when she attended the school.

[235] Greer, 1852, p.55.

E. (the bride) Mgt & Martha & Thirza & I are all to have gowns of the same - light dove coloured Levantine – a kind of thick twilled silk - which comes as cheap now almost as tabinets and is much worn. We will all have pillareens [pelerines], the same & silk hfs [handkerchiefs] tied round our necks & frills &c., white gloves & shoes as near the colour of the gowns as possible - E. to have to have white sattin shoes & bonnet to please John - Thirza & Anna are to have light silk shawls - Anna has a beautiful new Lutestring gown which will do her. We are all but E. to have sattin bonnets near the colour of our gowns so I think we will look very nice – what does thee think? … John's friends are all quite gay, but we are determined they shall not be the means of making any change in our dress. But his aunt is a plain steady Friend, though Lady Mayoress [of Dublin].[236]

The Sintons were not affluent enough to give a stylish wedding dinner. Straight after the marriage the young couple went about acquiring goods for their linen drapery and flannel blanket trade and opened their shop in High St. Dublin. Mary Sinton wrote that John Walpole seemed 'not a bit like a Friend but I do believe as good and better than many who make a plain appearance.'[237]

At the time of the Sinton wedding, waistlines were becoming lower and corsets again became essential. For the fashionable, huge full sleeves helped emphasise the narrow waist. A portrait of Jane Goodbody, shows her dressed in this style in blue muslin, with a transparent neckerchief and frilled cap, white shawl and a watch pinned to her belt.[238]

About 1830 'a simple blue muslin dress' was the garb of Sarah Greer, when, as a young wife, she received a morning visit from an elderly female overseer. Following a long silence, Sarah was informed, 'a real Friend ought not to wear blue; but it is not that alone; look at the vain fashion - look at thy sleeve and at thy skirt - what waste

of material.' Sarah replied, 'Thy dress is just what a real Friend's ought to be […] dark green, Irish tabinet with narrow sleeves and skirt of a moderate width'.[239] Sarah argued that her muslin cost not one-tenth the money spent on the tabinet. Earlier, when dresses were narrow and straight, the back might trail a little on the ground, even for day wear. The back of the gown of the elder who visited Sarah Greer was slightly longer and had to be held up for walking. This may imply a dress in a style current in 1810, which would already have had a few years' wear, and Sarah was slyly hinting at the 'extravagance' of the cost of the fabric. However, Sarah's flimsy, fashionable, muslin gown would have been wearable for two seasons at most. A fashion plate of 1832 shows a coloured muslin dress like Sarah's with very full sleeves and wide skirt revealing the ankles.[240]

In Thomas Fowler's very large painting of the Garratt family of Granite Hall, Dunleary (Dunlaoghaire) in 1832, the three daughters stand out in their dresses of muslin in light colours with very full sleeves. Their mother's red dress is of rich silk, fashionably cut with very wide sleeves and her frilled cap is trimmed with coloured ribbons, which match her blue mantle. Her husband, a very prosperous Dublin businessman, does not wear the out-of-date breeches and collarless coat of the plain Quaker. The family's clothes proclaim them gay Friends and a feature of the picture is a grand piano, which may have led to their disownment in 1843 for having their children instructed in music (as well as becoming insolvent).[241]

It is clear that many Quakers, especially younger ones, were constantly torn between dictates of plainness and dressing with a certain degree of style. A good example of the latter is the matter of the bonnet, a subject discussed by Susanna Greeves of Dungannon in a series of family letters between Ireland and America in 1819. In a letter to her sister Anne O'Brien, she wrote: 'Jane and I are getting Black Mode Bonnets as I tell you they

---

[236] Jackson, 2011, p.89, Letter 47.
[237] Ibid.
[238] Jane was the daughter of Mark Goodbody and Elizabeth Pim. Both Pim and Goodbody families were very successful entrepreneurs in the 19th century. In 1824 Jane married Dr. John Eustace who had trained as a doctor in Edinburgh and Dublin and was now Medical Superintendent of Bloomfield, Friends Mental Asylum in Dublin. In the portrait, reproduced in Goodbody, 2011, plate 4, her face doesn't show any signs of the smallpox she had as a tiny baby and which carried off two of her brothers.
[239] Greer, 1852, pp.230-233.
[240] Reproduced in Holland, 1955, Pl.48.
[241] Testimony of disownment, FHLD, MM II F4, p.43.

Thomas Fowler, portrait of the Garratt family, c.2m50 x 1m 50, 1832.. (Private collection)

are all the tone. The Hoggs have them and Jane Nicholson. We sent for the mode to Dublin.'[242] Five years later, Anne received another letter on the subject of bonnets and caps:

> I am sure thy bonnet must be past mending as thee mentions in a letter to sister Mary that thee never got one since thee left Ireland - my sister Jane and I now send thee one which I hope thee will like […] I send two caps which is the same shape of the kind Jane and I wares; it is also the same kind the Sintons wares, also sister Mary, only hers is not quite so deep in the middle piece. I made them of coarse linen and if thee likes the shape, we send some finer so that thee can make them. I tacked up one and measured up the size of my head so that, should it either be too deep or too wide, thee will be a better judge how to make the rest. I would have made thee more of them but not knowing but thee would reckon them too gay. I also send one of my own night caps that if thee would like them, thee could make some of the muslin up the same kind. It is just the shape of my day caps, only wanting the jaws. I send the pattern on paper so thee can make any alteration thee likes on them.[243]

Anne also received a letter from her sister Jane written on the same day, and still talking about bonnets:

> silk for a bonnet which I hope thee may like: from the description thee gives of the American ones, I think they must be very ugly; and if they were, I think it would be a pity to spoil good silks. With it I send thee a pattern such as is worn here, which thee can think off: the crown is pleated and sewn to the front, the way the old women's used to be, with this difference that they cock up in front a little instead of lying straight back, which gives them a very smart look. The friend's fashions change like everything else.[244]

Further comments on the Quaker bonnet are found in a paper by E.C., a former governess, written in 1901, which seems also to indicate a consciousness of social status:

> Looking back to the 'Thirties' and 'Forties' my remembrances of Friends are intimately connected with the peculiar garb. The Friend's bonnet, the grey or fawn shawl, the muslin handkerchief, the crimped cap, the quiet grey,

[242] Jackson, 2011, p.42, letter of 1 December, 1819.
[243] Ibid, p.92, letter of December 20, 1824.
[244] Ibid, p.98.

Portrait of Deborah Davis Grubb, c.1840. (Private collection)

brown, and drab colours. Almost all women Friends; some plainer than others. A flat Friends' bonnet was thought the plainest kind. It was gayer to have one with the crown sticking up, and the same rule held with the cap, the flatter the crown the more orthodox. No pretty bright ribbons were allowed, or jewellery, or curls, and as for flowers and feathers and plaited hair, they were regarded with horror. I perfectly remember, when going to my first situation as a governess in 1843, it was thought best for me to have no other bonnet than the orthodox one. I pleaded for a straw bonnet, which I sometimes wore, but no, it was averred the straw might give employers an unfavourable impression. We thought far too much about dress in those days. The very anxiety to be plain made it of too much importance, and we were apt to criticise each other. To many young minds the plain dress was a constant grievance.[245]

Even more affluent Quakers might wear basic simple garments in calico or stuff for housework in the earlier part of the day, but change into something more elegant later on. In the Greeves-O'Brien correspondence already referred to, Anne O'Brien received a letter from her daughter Mary O'Brien, describing Abraham Bell's well-appointed household in New York:

Up before 7 - found breakfast nearly ready. After it the men went to the office leaving the girls alone. I believe they keep just one girl yet. Rachel says it is sweeping day so she has been busy sweeping. Mary is getting some apples (of which they have plenty on their farm ready to stew and Anne is darning stockings......The girls wear calico in the morning. Yesterday (evening) when I came in, they were dressed very tidy. Rebecca had a black crepe, Mary brown silk, and Anne Moutier Derbur [Provencal cotton?]..... the house is very large with carved mahogany furniture, gilt mirrors, marble display tables ...[246]

With the 1840s many middle-class Quaker women, while avoiding excessive ornamentation, followed changes in the line and style of fashionable

garments. In a letter of 1845 to her brother Joseph Sinton O'Brien, Margareta Jane O'Brien writes: 'Tell Lydia the fasion for making dresses is tight sleeves and full wasts, eather pleated or gayed [gored?].'[247] Although written in the USA, this is very similar to what was being worn in Ireland in the 1840s.

About 1840 Deborah Davis and her husband Samuel Grubb, a successful Tipperary miller, had their portraits painted. Her hair is in neat ringlets and framed by the frilled edging of the fine cap. A transparent white tucker with delicately embroidered flowers on its collar, also frill edged, acts as a fill-in to her fashionable off-the-shoulder black silk dress. This has diagonal pleats across the bodice which descend to a point in the front over a full pleated skirt. Half way down the long narrow sleeve is a short flounce. Such details together with the cut, are very much in the contemporary vogue while the sober colour suggests a serious Friend. Despite her obviously fashionable clothing, Deborah had the strongest of Quaker principles. A few years later, on behalf of a Quaker soup kitchen, she wrote a firm letter to the Under-Secretary in Dublin Castle about the Potato Famine stating that unless the government intervened the people would die.[248]

Two very elegant wedding dresses from 1841, held in FHLD, also show how some Irish Friends were completely up to the minute in the latest styles. The fashion plates in ladies' magazines would be anxiously pored over, fabric bought and a picture shown to their dressmaker. Elizabeth Todhunter, of a well-to-do Dublin family, married Joshua Harvey in 1841. Her dress follows virtually the same design as a day dress in a deep beige silk and cashmere mixture, dated between 1839 and 1845, which is in the Gallery of English Costume, Platt Hall.[249] The Todhunter bodice is overlaid with flat pleated folds of the same silk as the dress, and these descend from the shoulder to the centre-front. The new fitted sleeves, tailored in two pieces, are decorated above the elbow with double pagoda flounces trimmed with piping. Elizabeth's outfit also includes a large satin wrap for warmth

---

[245] Quoted in Jackson, 2005, p.119.
[246] Jackson, 2011, p.190, letter of 2 September, 1840.
[247] Ibid, p.307, letter of 19 May, 1845 from Buffalo, USA.
[248] Ahern, 2009, p.130. Deborah Davis Grubb was an excellent businesswoman, but was also capable of embroidering a large hexagonal seat (still in good repair) and writing a long poem about the Fitzgeralds.
[249] This dress has been closely examined in Arnold, 1972, pp.64-66 which includes sketches and a pattern.

Elizabeth Todhunter wedding dress, 1841.
(FHLD)

Godsey-Shaw-Dowd wedding dress, 1841.
(FHLD)

and a Quaker bonnet. It is not clear whether the accompanying veil was worn in conjunction with the bonnet.

A superb white silk wedding dress from the Godsey Shaw Dowd family dates from the same year. By this date a white dress symbolising purity for a bride was becoming a tradition. Over a short-sleeved bodice there is a fitted long-sleeved jacket, again with the fashionable diagonal pleats. Such a jacket would have made it suitable for wear on other occasions. While no Elders could complain of colours and patterns, the lace that adorns all sleeve ends might have seemed somewhat extravagant, as would the magnificent Limerick lace veil that she also wore.

Like everybody else, Friends would have worn their best clothes for Meeting. The dark brown silk taffeta dress of Anne Best, née Dobson, of Richhill, Co. Armagh, would have been a suitable garment for Sunday. Dated about 1850, the skirt, with woven woollen braid on the hem, is lined with brown calico, which gives it body, without the excessive fullness popular in this period of large crinolines.[250] The bodice has a simplified version of the diagonal pleating seen on the earlier wedding dresses, but the overall effect suggests that she was a plain Quaker.

In 1853 when Jane Marion Wakefield was married at Ballitore she chose a dress in a simple style which, though very elegant, could also be worn afterwards as a day dress. Her wedding ensemble is

---

[250] NMI, DT 1962.5. Described in Smith, 2013, pp.56 and 91.

Princess-line dress 1875-8 in beige Irish poplin (part of the skirt missing). (FHLD)

now held in the Ballitore Quaker Museum where it is described as being of a 'slate grey/purple silk tabby weave with small 'v' motif; machine sewn, 3 pleats on each side of the bodice, glass buttons; cream silk hooded shoulder scarf; cream silk deep brimmed poke bonnet with pasteboard brim.' After the wedding Jane returned north with her husband, John Grubb Richardson.

The heiress, Hannah Woodcock Perry, on her marriage to Marcus Goodbody at Monkstown Meeting, Dublin, in December 1848, wore a gown specially designed for that occasion. Of cream silk trimmed with machine lace it is lined throughout with heavy glazed cotton and the large stole is edged all around with swansdown. This now occupies pride of place in NMI.[251]

A late example of Quaker restraint combined with fashion is a dress dated 1875-1878 from the Jacob family, also in FHLD. Made of beige Irish poplin, it is in a completely new style, the 'princess-line', which was introduced in 1866 by Worth, the leading couturier in Paris. Gone are the huge crinoline skirts pleated at the waist. The front of the gown is cut in one piece without a waist seam and gored side panels give a smooth line to the skirt. The back would have had extra material gathered up into a bustle, but in this case that is missing, having possibly been recycled to make a child's frock. Underwear would have included a bustle petticoat with flounces at the back and a long corset. The Snowshill Manor collection has a very similar day dress which includes the small, neat high collar with piped edges, fitted sleeves with cuffs, a special watch pocket and 18 small, grey silk-covered buttons closing the front opening.[252] The English example also has a multitude of trimmings in various colours and fabrics, which would have been eschewed by the Quakers, and it is precisely this absence of decoration that gives the Irish dress a superior elegance.

Photographs show many older Friends continuing to wear the plain clothes of their youth. Less well-off friends could not afford much change unless they were very adroit with the needle. What is noticeable, however, is a tendency to use good quality materials which meant that garments lasted a long time and would be handed on.

In his prize-winning essay of 1858, the young John Stephenson Rountree had already ascribed the decline of Quakerism in Great Britain and Ireland to 'deadening traditionalism' and the weakness of individual members. He pointed to the official insistence on antiquated forms of dress, speech and manners. What might be regarded as unsuitable clothing became a major subject of debate. A piece written in 1859 and entitled *An honest confession of the cause of decadence in the Society of Friends with a glance at a few peculiarities of the Society* by a member declared: 'Dress [...] as fashionable as you like [...] but straight collar - lined with velvet and half compromised by being dog's-eared - and you are all right [...] But let him dress all in greys with a turn-down collar [...] I am sorry to see thee following the fashions of the world.'[253] Apparel

251 NMI also holds the embroidered waistcoat that Marcus had for the wedding.
252 Sketch and pattern, Arnold, 1977, pp.34 and 93.
253 Quoted by Kendall, 1985, p.25.

could be an impediment to serving on committees, attending business meetings and even be a reason for disownment until 1860 when, after three years of serious discussion and controversy, London Yearly Meeting finally agreed that clothing could be left to the discretion of Friends.[254] The testimony to plainness was replaced with the advice, 'Be careful to maintain in your conduct and encourage in your family that simplicity in deportment and attire [...] which become the disciples of the Lord Jesus.'[255]

[254] Brayshaw, 1921, p.88.
[255] Kendall,1985, p.71. Quoted from Minutes of London Yearly Meeting 1860.

Chapter Four

Household Linen and Soft Furnishings

Robert Burton, in his *Anatomy of Melancholy* (1628), dealing with the treatment of depression and mental illness, sees occupation as the best cure for melancholia:

> Now for women [...] they have curious needle-works, cut works, spinning, bone-lace, and many pretty devices of their own making, to adorn their houses, cushions, carpets, chaires, stools, (for she eats not of the bread of idleness Prov. 31, 27).[130]

Most of the needle-work mentioned here would have been undertaken by women to improve their homes. In the sixteenth and seventeenth centuries even the wealthy had comparatively little furniture. Some tables, stools, chairs and simple food cupboards, usually made of oak and sometimes carved, would be set in panelled rooms. A study of furniture involves both wood and soft fabrics, the latter in the form of such things as upholstery, hangings, cushions and carpets. In poorer homes furniture would be minimal or barely existent. In all cases it could disintegrate with age and wear, whilst household textiles would be mended and patched till they were only fit for cleaning rags. Inventories and wills do record some of the furnishings, but the wording may require a degree of interpretation. Together with letters and journals, which sometimes have passing references or descriptions, they help us form an idea of the furnishing that Friends had, and very occasionally some actual material object has survived.

In the absence of artefacts, reference may made to both English practice and to what was probably general in Ireland. Many of the early Irish Quakers were of Cromwellian Puritan stock, and their emphasis on simplicity and truthfulness in life and behaviour led to plainness of speech, apparel and furniture.

William Edmundson, had been trained as a carpenter. 'Valiant for truth on earth'[131], he saw simplicity in life and dress as an essential form of self-discipline. Influenced by him, the National Meeting of 1694 called together Quaker joiners and ship's carpenters who reported back later that all furniture should be plain: tables and chairs without carving, chests of drawers not bow-fronted or with inlay, and no unnecessary mouldings on beds or clock-cases. Even the carving of figureheads for ships was condemned.[132] That same year Tipperary Monthly Meeting appointed overseers to visit homes and advise them to ensure that they kept nothing that was contrary to the simplicity of the truth.[133]

English Friends never went to such lengths. Swarthmoor Meeting house was happy to have 'two large arm-chairs very heavily made, altogether of wood, and carved on the back; one for George Fox and the other for his wife'[134] while there were two large elbow oak-chairs, embellished with carved work and the date of 1694 in Highflatts Meeting house, Yorkshire.[135]

In Ireland, Friends such as William Penn and General Goff's descendants, were people of considerable substance and as the years went by many other Friends, being successful, could afford fine furniture. One such Friend was Joseph

[130] Sixteenth edition, 1838, printed from the authorised copy of 1651, pp.358-359
[131] Harrison, 2008, p 81.
[132] Grubb, 1930, p.100.
[133] Ahern, 2009, p.187.
[134] Savery, 1844, p.238.
[135] Jenkins, 1984, p. 321.

Pike (1657-1729) who moved from poverty to considerable wealth. In 1668, Joseph was eleven when his father Richard Pike died as a result of imprisonment in Cork for his beliefs. At the age of eighteen, following the sale of the small family business, Joseph set up in the wool trade with an initial capital of £3 and went on to become one of the most prosperous merchants of the city. Later he received from William Penn a grant of 10,000 acres of land in Pennsylvania. Like William Edmundson, who had been instrumental in his spiritual development, Pike came from a lower socio-economic group than Goff or Penn. At the Half-Yearly Meeting in 1692 he produced a diatribe against the unnecessary, but in so doing gave a few hints as to what the wealthy friend might have had:

> fine veneered cases of drawers, tables, stands, cabinets, escritoires of walnut and olive wood varnished and nicely set forth. Some had carved chairs, large mouldings and cornices, some had hangings of diverse colours. Some very large looking glasses with toppings. Some pretty fine curtains with fringes.[136]

Fringes, like ribbons, were a specialist branch of silk weaving, and very expensive indeed.[137] Used just for decoration on furnishings and fashionable dress for both sexes they were showy and unnecessary. The 'hangings of diverse colours' could have been printed chintz, imported from India, or they may have been embroidered.

Quakers of a more ordinary sort were very unlikely to have had more furniture than what was essential. An inventory of 1705, attached to the will of William Willin (Willan), a farmer and weaver of Co. Wexford, lists only two old feather beds and 'furniture', two old flock beds and 'furniture', two chests and one box, two old tables, five old chairs and four joint stools.[138] Clothes were either kept in chests or hung on wooden pegs in the wall.

Beds and bed furnishings
The word 'bed' was applied to what today might be called the mattress, whilst the 'furniture' of the bed refers to the bed frame and the accompanying soft furnishings. Willin also possessed seventy-three sheep which supplied wool for spinning and weaving. Flock is waste wool and this would have been rather cheaper than feathers as stuffing. Willin's wife Mary's poultry would have provided feathers. A very large quantity needed to be collected for the bed. These then had to be sterilised, one way of doing this being to put them in the oven after bread baking. A cheaper type of mattress filling was straw or chaff which Willin would have obtained after the corn was threshed, and chaff was also probably used for the pillows.

The textiles for the beds were produced at home. After combing or carding the wool, Mary and her daughters would have done the spinning. William would then have woven the fabric for the bed curtains, bedlinen and woollen blanketing, after which the women did the making-up and the stitching. A new rug is also noted and was probably a coarse woollen coverlet, also woven by William.

The bed was one of the most important items of furniture, but could range from a straw-filled palliasse on the floor to a substantial piece of furniture with fine hangings. The poorest Irish slept on a shakedown of loose straw thrown on the ground. Anne Willan Grubb (daughter of William Willin), following a series of disasters, was found by the visiting Elder, Elizabeth Fennell, with 'her children in a very poor cabin with great marks of poverty about her.'[139] Since Quakers would sell their furniture and other belongings rather than be in debt, this was most probably a one-room thatched mud cabin with no beds but just straw under the bedding.

William Willin's beds may well have been what today we call four-poster beds. Such beds were widely used by the middle classes and simpler ones were constructed in poorer homes. At this period windows were usually left naked but the curtains which surrounded the bedstead had the double function of providing warmth in draughty cold houses and also privacy. Houses did not necessarily have specially designated bedrooms. Such a bed

---

[136] Quoted in Harrison, 1991, p.63.

[137] Dunlevy, 2011, p. 34.

[138] County Wexford Records No.6 Wills 1680-1720, p.284. Copy in FHLD, Grubb coll. SGA 3. Willin was what in Ireland is termed a strong farmer, roughly the equivalent of a yeoman farmer in England. He owned a cart, a plough, corn (rick) in the haggard and spring corn growing, 22 cows and heifers, a bull and 15 other cattle, 6 garrens (horses) & mares & foals, 2 small pigs. His 73 sheep had a higher valuation than anything else.

[139] Ahern, 2009, p.275.

might be found in the principal living-room which was known as the parlour.[140] In 1687 James Taylor, a Quaker clothier in the city of Dublin, had 'in the great chamber, 1 large featherbed and bedstead with green fine bayse [baize] for hangings and vallins [valance], with 1 rug, 2 blankets, a green counterpane, 1 bolster and 2 pillows.'[141] Robert Fayle, a farmer in Offaly, had 'in parlour 1 bed, bolster and pillows, quilt, bedstead and hangings'.[142] A bed stood in the corner of the cottage living-room where Molly Webster, kept her Dame school, as well as brewing herbal medicines.[143]

At an earlier period in grand houses richly worked hangings on the four-poster beds, together with wall tapestries, supplied both colour and comfort. From paintings of the early 1600s it has been deduced that curtains of plain coloured cloth or velvet decorated with bands of embroidery also existed.[144] In some cases the hangings were not embroidered directly, but instead the motif was worked on smaller pieces of linen or silk and then cut out and the resultant 'slip' was appliquéd onto the ground fabric. The Duke of Hamilton's home, Lennoxlove, has yellow damask curtains which probably originated as bed hangings and are decorated with a number of slips representing birds, flowers and figures of the kind found on early samplers.

In 1687 George Fox bought a small-holding from the Swarthmoor estate and paid for the setting up of a meeting house with a guest room. This was furnished with a four-poster ebony bedstead hung with *pintado* curtains.[145] Imported from India, these chinz fabrics with their exotic and colourful designs were expensive and very desirable for both furnishing and dress. About twenty years later at Levens Hall near Kendal a set of patchwork bed hangings complete with quilt was made from Indian chinz pieces.[146]

Bed hangings were important, but the type of fabric could vary enormously. Less expensive than chinz or silk was the fustian (linen union) bought for curtains by Sarah Fell in 1674. Probably for bed hangings, these could have then been embroidered in crewel wool with exotic foliage and flowers. Inspired by Indian chinz, such designs were popular in the seventeenth century, and sometimes birds and animals were added. Crewel thread was two-ply, spun from worsted wool and slightly twisted. Very fine, strong and lustrous, it took dye well.[147] Such hangings, besides being comparatively quick to work, draped well.

The Swarthmoor Hall household accounts record the costs of making a bed, complete with the bedding and the fabrics involved:

Mar. 11th 1675 pd. Tho. Wilson wright [carpenter] & his men for makeinge a trundle bedstead, & other worke 5 dayes   2s. 6d. using estate timber. [In November 1673 they had spent 15 days sawing a tree into bedsteads & boards for the Fells.]

Mar. 14th 1675 pd. At Kendall for a bed coard   1s 1d.

June 25th 1676. Pieces of cloth for bed coverings & yarn for fether bed ticks were sent to Kendall for dyeing

Jan. 26th 1677 pd. Geo. ffell for weaving 18 ells of fether bed Tikin(ticking) 7s. 4d.

Apr. 22nd 1678 pd. Geo ffell " "   26 ells of feather bed tickin(g). 11s.

At 5d. per ell the ticking seems expensive, but this was a type of hard, strong linen that had to be exceptionally close-woven to contain the feathers. Feather beds were valuable heirlooms and regularly appear in wills and inventories.

[140] Grubb, 2019, p.29.

[141] Goodbody, 1971, pp.54-55.

[142] Ibid, p.61.

[143] Corrigan, 2009, pp.272-273.

[144] Toller, 1980, p.13. Mary Stuart, Queen of Scotland had her own embroiderer whose job it was to design and draw out the patterns which she could then work directly on the fabric. Hangings and cushions still exist in Hardwick Hall worked while Mary was a prisoner there.

[145] Ross, 1949, p.331. 'Pintado' (Portuguese) and 'chitta' (Indian), both meaning 'spotted/speckled cloth', were textile trade terms for mordant-worked and dyed cotton textiles. Colours were brilliant and fast when washed. See Gittinger, 1982, pp.197-198.

[146] Colby, 1972, p.121.

[147] Marsh, 2006, p.147.

A number of other entries refer to the textiles used for beds and bedding:

> Apr. 1st 1675 pd. For 3yds. of course cloth for 2 chaff(e) bolsters 1s. 9d.
>
> Oct.16th 1673 pd.Issabell Atkinson [a widow, she also weeded and dressed peat] for spininge 18½ lbs. of woole for blankets & mixt cloth 2s. 5d.
>
> Dec.11th 1673 pd. Geo. Fell for weaveinge 18 ells of blankettin 2s. 1d.
>
> Jan. 15th 1673 pd. Ja. Walker for milling & dressing 19 ells of blankettin 2s. 2d.
>
> Feb. 15th 1676 pd. Ja. Walker for milling & dressinge19 yds. for blanket 1s. 10d.
>
> Apr. 13th 1676 pd. "   "   fuller "   " 42 yds. for blankets, & bedcoverings 3s
>
> June 25th pd. Rich Stable for whiteninge 60 yds of teare or hempeclothe 2s. 6d.
>
> June 28th 1677 pd. "   "   40yds. of linen cloth 1s 8d.

Bed hangings of plain blue, red or green serge were listed in the Inventory of J. Eves of Edenderry in 1729.[148] William Penn's old home in England had been an example of a luxuriously equipped Puritan house where many expensive fabrics were used. The furniture for a bedroom known as the 'blew chamber' included:

> 6 pieces of Tapestry 10 foot deep, one bedsteed, silk Quilt, Suit of Curtains vallens of sky colour tabby and lin'd with yellow sarsnet, a mat, cord, rods, 1 pillo, 4 blankets, A little old Carpet, Trunk, looking glas, a stand, 5 blew old and 1other some old blew hangings of bays, one picture and nurses chair, one green satten Quilt and one pallet, 8 yards of crimson sarsnet in 2 chariot Curtains.'[149]

The bedstead, either a four-poster or surmounted by a tester, with its valance and set of sky-blue silk curtains lined with yellow soft silk and hung on rods, would have had a basic frame laced with about 20 yards of hempen cord which supported the bed mat made out of woven or plaited rushes or straw. A feather bed (mattress) would have been put on top of this, and, in addition, the pillow, four blankets and the silk quilt. The sheets were taken from the linen closet next door, where there were twenty pairs of flaxen ones and two pairs of fine Dutch linen, along with a large number of napkins, tablecloths and towels. The pallet bed with its green satin quilt would have been pushed under the bed by day. Useful space savers, pallet beds were also called trundle or truckle beds and these provided an extra sleeping place in a bedroom. In cottages it was not uncommon to find sleeping alcoves screened off by a curtain.

According to an inventory of 1694, the prosperous Dublin Quaker weaver John Johnston had beds in three rooms. In the 'back chamber' was a feather bed with 'blew curtains & blew rug'; in the 'fore Street chamber' he had 'one bedstead sarge [serge] curtains feather bed and bedding', and in the 'little fore Street Roome' there was 'one bedstead a flock bed & bedding & green painted hangings'.[150] The green-painted hangings may well have been pintado.

When the girls' boarding school in Edenderry opened in 1764 Samuel Neale provided ticking, feathers and blankets for twelve beds and bolsters. The linen for twenty-four pairs of sheets was, unsurprisingly, supplied by the northern Quakers Thomas Greer and John Christy, and the four-poster beds, hung with linsey woolsey curtains, were provided by William Greenhow, Joseph Inman and Thomas Bewley.[151] Each bed may well have accommodated two if not three children as was customary at the time, and this would have been the case for Mountmellick Boarding School which opened in 1786 with wooden beds. It is not clear whether the latter had curtains or not. In England bed hangings were not used at Ackworth in 1779.[152] However, in 1835 the boys' beds in the Friends' school at Bootham had 'nice little curtains round the bed-heads.'[153]

Bed curtains might hang on the frame, or from a tester suspended from the ceiling. Towards the end of the eighteenth century the four-poster bed was giving way to a simpler type of bed with the

---

[148] Grubb, 2018, p.29.

[149] Hodgkin, 1947, p.135.

[150] Inventory of 1694, referring to Johnston's will of 15 November 1691. Goodbody, 1978, pp.41-43.

[151] Bell, 1919, p.20.

[152] Grubb, 1792, p.260.

[153] Sturge, 1931, p. 44. Quoted from a letter from Anne White, a pupil at the Mount School, to her parents, then running Ballitore School.

Susanna Pim's doll's bed, 1837. (FHLD)

curtains draped from a small round frame or ring suspended over it. As an alternative to this, the hangings were placed over a curved frame which formed a canopy. A fine contemporary copy of a canopy bed of this type was made for Jonathan Pim's eldest daughter Susanna who sadly died in 1837, aged 8. This miniature bed complete with its doll, and now in FHLD, is in perfect condition so it must have been carefully put away and not played with after her death.

The little Pim bed has a tightly stuffed feather bed as a mattress and this rests on a slatted wood base. A plain bottom sheet and a top sheet with a finely frilled flounce are covered by two cream wool blankets with red blanket-stitched edges. Both the pillow and the bolster have their own separate cases, beautifully worked, with tiny tape ties to fasten them.

The wood frame is stained brown, to represent mahogany, and the head and foot boards are of the same height. At the back the bedhead is lined with fine cotton, as is the canopy. The curved frame of the canopy means that the curtains cannot draw with rings on rods. Instead there is a kind of tailored loose-cover made of fine white cotton which can be pulled back and held with ties. Unlike the embroidered or rich fabrics of earlier four posters, this can be taken off for washing in the annual spring-clean. Not long after this, doctors pronounced closed curtaining to be unhealthy, and a consequence of this was its removal, whilst bed posts were cut shorter.

The mattresses in Mountmellick were straw palliasses which were not in good condition when the school moved in the 1790s. The Committee suggested that 'a suitable amendment' would be to lay light feather beds on them. Then, in 1797, they replaced them with 'mattresses filled with curled hair'.[154] The new mattresses were of horse hair and made by a harness maker. [155] At Friends School Lisburn the marriage of the master Samuel Douglas with the mistress Sarah Dickenson, celebrated in 1803, provided a holiday for the pupils, but the

[154] Anon, 1886, p.18.
[155] O'Neill, 1977, p.23.

Four poster bed; settle bed; press bed.

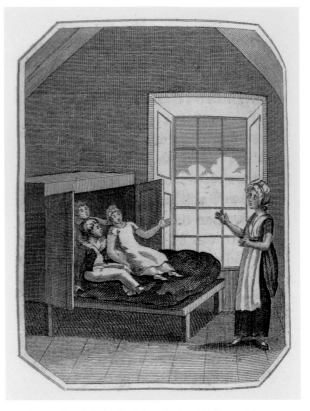

Press bed (labelled 'settle bed') from Mary Leadbeater story 'The Settle-bed'. (FHLD)

time was used profitably for the senior girls who were put on to refilling the palliasses with straw.[156]

Four-poster or tester beds with their hangings were often simply defined by their mattress as either a feather bed or a flock bed. In 1689 an inventory with the will of James Hutchinson who had come to Tipperary about 1660, shows him to have been wealthy, with no less than twelve winged chairs, three feather beds and bedding, three flock beds with bedding, and a settle bed.[157] This last item is interesting being a particularly Irish design.

In the kitchen, the Irish settle bed was a seat by day, with the bedding stored inside, whilst by night it could be unfolded into a bed for two. Sleeping in what effectively was a box also allowed for some degree of shelter in a draughty house. The Irish settle differed from the English one which was a seat that could serve for storage, but did not become sleeping accommodation. The early Quakers took note of this, as they adapted to living in a new

country. We know from the inventory of 1694 that John Johnston had 'a settle bed for servants & beding' in his 'kitching'. Likewise, in 1697, Joseph Deane of Meath street, a Dublin shearman, had in his kitchen 'A settle Bedstead [and] flock bed'. Another Quaker, Thomas Weston, a miller of the town of Athy, Co. Kildare, in an inventory of 1709, mentions in addition to '1 oak settell bed' a 'Press Bed, one fether bed, one boulster and two pillows'.[158]

The press bed was another space-saving item of furniture. Folding out of what appeared to be a small press or a chest of drawers, this was much used in small rooms such as parlours and kitchens in eighteenth and nineteenth-century Ireland and Britain, and later sometimes became known as a Murphy bed in America.

Goldsmith's poem, *The Deserted Village* (1770), recalls the hospitality of an Irish inn:

---

[156] Creeth, 1921, p.50. Replenishing the mattresses whether with straw or feathers was a necessary but tedious task. At Baltyboys, Co.Wicklow, in July 1849 Elizabeth Smith (not a Quaker), was sorting two years' collection of feathers and 'filling up the bedding' for the large house which she was struggling to maintain. (Grant, 1991, p.457.)

[157] Ahern, 2009, p.213. Capt. James Hutchinson was the son of Sir Thomas Hutchinson and a brother of John Hutchinson, one of the judges who assented to the execution of Charles I.

[158] Goodbody, 1971, p.57.

The white-washed wall, the nicely sanded floor,

The varnished clock that clicked behind the door;

The chest contrived a double debt to pay,

A bed by night, a chest of drawers by day.[159]

Seventeenth-century chair from Sycamore Street Meeting house, Dublin. (FHLD)

Upholstery

In the Elizabethan age chairs had no padding. By the late sixteenth century embroidered cushions were introduced to relieve the hard seating and, by the seventeenth century, padding the seats and backs added comfort to wooden chairs. Leather made a hard-wearing covering, which was done by a professional. On Mar. 22, 1675 Sarah Fell notes: 'pd. Tom. Lucocke Sadler for brasse nailes, & for mending & fitting some chaires & Stooles 2 days 2s.' and 'pd. him for Lether & for mending a portmantle (bag) 1s. 6d.'

FHLD possesses a leather-seated corner chair which is said to have been part of the furnishings of Dublin's Sycamore Street Meeting house when William Penn visited. This design continued in use for a long time, and a century later Richard Shackleton, wearing his velvet cap, used to relax of an evening on a similar chair.[160]

Upholstered wing chair 1700; caned couch with squab.

The John Johnston inventory of 1694 mentions amongst other items a parlour furnished with 'one foulden oaken table and six oaken chairs', other rooms with six chairs and stools and a 'fore Street chamber with twelve cane chairs.

Caning, introduced shortly before 1660, came from the rattan palm and was imported from the Malay Peninsular by the East India Company. Cheap, light and comfortable, it became especially fashionable for seats, initially in London where so much was destroyed in the great Fire of 1666.[161] Squabs were loose cushions that added to comfort and lengthened the life of the caning by spreading the weight on the seat. These might well have been covered with velvet or needlework. Around this period more fully upholstered furniture also came into use. In1755 Sarah Sleigh of Cork, a widow, left her daughter, Sarah Sleigh, all her effects including six oak cane chairs, cane couch with its 'squab', and a 'beaufet' [buffet or sideboard], as well as household linen.[162]

---

[159] There were also bureau beds, based on the same principle, and on HMS Victory Nelson had a chair that folded out to become a bed.
[160] Corrigan, 2009, p.282.
[161] Gloag, 1969, p.177.
[162] Goodbody, 1967, No.201, p.154. The term 'beaufet' and the use of oak would suggest a seventeenth-century piece of furniture. In Cork in 1755, Joseph Pike's son William owned a dining table of walnut, which, with mahogany, had become a more fashionable wood. He also had cane bottomed chairs (p.149, no.190). An interesting detail in this will is the inclusion of a rack and dog-wheel, a mechanism whereby a dog inside the wheel would turn the spit to roast the meat.

Elizabeth Pim sampler, 1729-1750, 30.5cms x 35.5cms. (FHLD)

Oak chair c. 1620 in V&A.

Examples of stylised flower head in diamond: E. Pim; German, sixteenth century; Grace Caitlin (1719); two flowers (E.Pim); detail of German sampler 1688.

Upholstery on chairs needed a durable form of embroidery and this led to the use of crewel thread in cross, tent, or Florentine stitch, all of which were quick to work. Needlework very likely covered the twelve winged chairs listed in James Hutchinson's will. Plants, animals, birds on sprigs and even some figures are amongst the traditional motifs on two armchairs of 1635 in Hardwick Hall. A continuation of the naturalistic Elizabethan-style flower motifs, now arranged using two alternating plants in repeating rows, is a feature of an armchair of about 1620 in the Victoria and Albert Museum, London (V&A). The more formally treated flowering plant as a repeat arranged regularly over a plain surface was a feature of Mughal textiles, which were imported by the East India Company and widely used and imitated in England.[163]

Seventeenth century spot or random samplers often have flowers or fruit in an all-over pattern on a plain ground. Sometimes stylised flower-heads were placed within a diamond. This motif could be repeated to form a diamond trellis pattern as can be seen on an early sixteenth-century German sampler in the V&A and a Danish one of 1756 in the Fitzwilliam museum.

Grace Caitlin, a London Quaker girl, used the diamond trellis on her band sampler of 1719. Elizabeth Marsh a Quaker originally from Worcester, England brought this design along with other band patterns to Philadelphia. There she and her daughter, Ann Marsh, both superb embroiderers, worked as teachers, and their influence lasted from the 1720s to the 1790s. In Philadelphia nine pieces of work with this geometric band pattern are known. The earliest of these was worked in 1725 by Sarah Logan, daughter of James Logan, administrator of Pennsylvania for William Penn.[164]

In early eighteenth-century Ireland, Elizabeth Pim made a spot sampler which included a blue carnation within a diamond shape. This sampler, worked intermittently over a period of twenty-one years, was begun in 1729 when she was eleven years old. It comprises a number of motifs that could be used for upholstery or, equally, on the embroidered purses and bags carried by men and women. The use of crewel wool, not silk, and the working of all the motifs in cross-stitch is a further indication that Elizabeth was thinking in terms of upholstery.

[163] Robert Skelton, referred to in Gittinger, 1982, p.74. These were probably inspired by the European herbals thought to have been presented as gifts to the court about 1619.
[164] Ring, 1993, pp.328-336.

The earliest motif (bottom right), dated 1729, and the one next to it, each have as central elements a pair of identical flowers with encircling ornamentation such as can be found on Dutch Marken samplers of the seventeenth century. Unlike earlier ones based on herbals, the flowers in this case are stylised, and if extracted from their surroundings can be seen to be suitable for a repeat pattern of a type that occurs on seventeenth-century samplers for upholstery.

A repeat design for flower sprigs and another with strawberries appears in 1788 on a sampler by seven-year-old Sybil Tatum, a little Quaker girl in New Jersey, and a late example with alternating tulips and carnations was worked by Elizabeth Mee in 1812. Lydia Mellor Shackleton, in addition to making a sampler in 1761, embroidered a set of chairs (one of which is still in the possession of a descendant) with a central rose motif and bunches of flowers in the corners.

The shell-shaped petals of one of Elizabeth Pim's flowers were often executed in Florentine work. This technique, with its shading and blending of colours, may have been brought to Florence with the Hungarian bride of a Medici in the fifteenth century, but its distinctive patterns remain popular today for embroidery, woven fabrics and brocades. Traditionally used for bed hangings, the eighteenth century found Florentine work good not only for chair covers and stool seats but also effective on small items.[165] The Florentine stitch was also known as Barghello or Irish stitch. The Women's Meeting in Dublin in 1721, 'desired [...] that Friends [...] do not suffer their children to learn Irish stitch, or work chair covers in different colours, it being a grief to some'.[166] The purists disapproved, thinking the use of this stitch led to unnecessary decoration, but others saw no problem with it, and Irish stitch was still being taught in Molly Webster's little school in the late 1790s.[167] Jane Richardson's sampler of 1797, which may have been made in the North of Ireland, has various upholstery patterns, including two bands worked in Florentine stitch. Fine Quaker examples of the use of this stitch can be seen on two embroidered

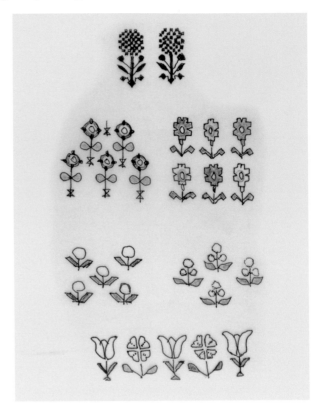

Two flowers (1729) from Elizabeth Pim sampler;
Two overall repeat stylised flower patterns
on mid-seventeenth-century English sampler.
(V&A);
Overall flower and strawberry designs from
Sarah Tatum sampler (1788);
Alternating tulip and rose pattern from
Elizabeth Mee sampler (1812).

letter-purses made for Samuel Sandwith in 1749 and for Joseph Sandwith some years later.[168]

Turkey work

Admiral Penn owned Macroom Castle, Co. Cork, where the family lived in William Penn's youth, and later Shanagarry Castle. We do not know how these were furnished, but it is possible to obtain a good picture of how fabric was used for furnishing from the inventory of the 'Dining Roome' of his house in Wanstead, England, in the 1660s. This lists:

6 forrest Hangings 9 foot deep [tapestries],
11 needlework chayres and a cloath Couch,
one dozen of truky [Turkey] work chayres and

---

[165] Humphrey, 1986, p.100. See also p.116 for illustration of a wing chair worked in Florentine stitch c.1725.
[166] Grubb, 2018, p.38.
[167] Corrigan, 2009, p.272.
[168] Samuel Sandwith's purse is in a private collection. That of Joseph Sandwith (1757-1841), together with a silver snuff-box, is in the FHLD collection.

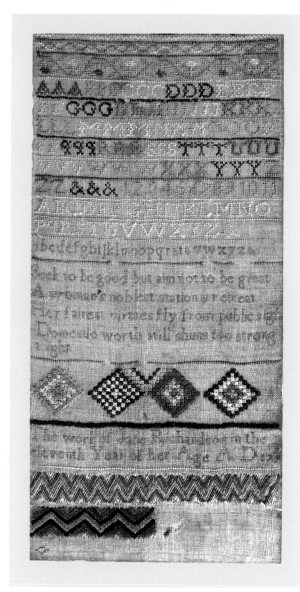

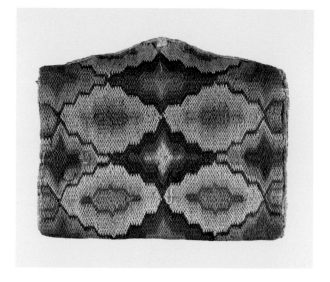

Joseph Sandwith letter purse. (FHLD)

Jane Richardson sampler, 1797,
52cms x 24cms. (Private collection)

couch of the same, 2 tables, 2 carpets, 4 window curtains, rods and stuff, one great glas and one picture over the chimney of 3 frigotts [frigates].[169]

References to Turkey work occur quite frequently in the mid-seventeenth century. Admiral Penn's friend Richard Boyle, Earl of Cork, ordered elaborately upholstered chairs and stools with fringes of crimson silk and silver together with 12 high stools of turkey work for Lismore Castle, Co. Waterford.[170]

The Cromwellian General Waller, in a claim for compensation when his castle in Co. Limerick was sacked in 1641, listed turkey work chairs, turkey cushions, richly embroidered satin cushions, etc., amongst his furnishings lost.[171] A wealthy Cork alderman's inventory has '6 stools covered with turkey cushions, one Turkey & other carpets.'[172] The John Johnston inventory of 1694, as well as the chairs already mentioned, has seven turkey-work chairs, one of them 'great' (possibly a large armchair).

A Turkish carpet was the ultimate in expensive sixteenth-century luxury and was placed carefully on the table where it is often depicted in paintings, especially by Holbein and Lotto. When placed on the floor it had something of the status of the modern red carpet and on festive occasions might be hung from balconies for the passage of a king or potentate.

The turkey work referred to in Irish inventories may have been actual Turkish carpeting, or an imitation by English weavers who often made panels of it for seats.[173] In Turkey the distinctive patterns of the carpets were also executed in embroidery, and the same practice was common in England. There is a very clear link between Elizabeth Pim's sampler and some of the traditional

[169] Hodgkin, 1947, p.135. Admiral Penn's wife was from Rotterdam and their inventory lists several pictures including one of frigates, a genre pioneered by the Dutch which then became popular in England.
[170] See Somerville-Large, 1979, p.66.
[171] de Breffny & ffolliot 1975, p.51.
[172] Ibid., p.47.
[173] Gloag, 1969, p.684.

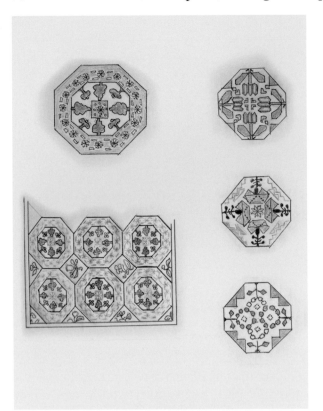

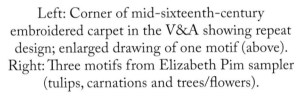

Left: Corner of mid-sixteenth-century embroidered carpet in the V&A showing repeat design; enlarged drawing of one motif (above). Right: Three motifs from Elizabeth Pim sampler (tulips, carnations and trees/flowers).

Geometric stars and octagons: Left, Elizabeth Pim; Memling gul carpet C.15; Selcuk carpet C.13; right, Lady and the unicorn tapestry; Judyth Hayle school samplers, 1693; carpet motif on sampler, German C.16.

designs found on Turkish carpets.[174] Coming from an affluent Quaker family, in all probability she would have seen turkey-work and then imitated the designs. In Ireland no specific references to the teaching of turkey-work have been found, but it was sometimes included in the curriculum for girls in America. When Mary Ann March advertised her school in Maryland in1751 she indicated that teaching would include 'all sorts of Embroidery, Turkey Work, and all sorts of rich Stitches learnt in Sampler work, at ten shillings a quarter.'[175]

Embroiderers, both professional and amateur, copied the oriental designs in cross stitch to make their own table carpets. A mid-sixteenth-century embroidered carpet in the V&A contains octagon medallions, the design of which can be found on

a large-pattern Holbein carpet in an unknown painter's *Rites of St. Giles* (c.1500), now in the National Gallery, London.[176] The outer border of each octagon on the V&A carpet supports a circle of stylised trees whose crowns almost touch a centre square containing a geometric star. Between the octagons there are English flower inserts.[177] Elizabeth Pim's sampler includes four different octagons with trees and plants growing towards the centre from within a modified geometric border. These include tulips and carnations, both popular in Turkey.

The octagon is a recurrent shape in early Turkish carpets, often with a star or a cross, or with the form of a diamond superimposed on a square in the centre, the whole surrounded by smaller units

---

174 The term Turkish here is used here to refer to carpets originally produced by the various Turkish tribes without a specific geographical identity.
175 Ring, 1993, p.500.
176 Illustrated in Aslanapa, 1988, p.88.
177 Clabburn, 1981, p.56. According to Clabburn the overall design draws on Caucasian patterns, and the border of interlaced strapwork is based on Kufic script.

of stars, octagons and stylised motifs.[178] Known as a *gul* motif, this is particularly associated with the paintings of Holbein or Memling. Triangles facing inwards might decorate the edge of the medallion. A table carpet with a border of octagons, stars and flowers is depicted in the late medieval tapestry, *The Lady with the Unicorn*, now in the Musée de Cluny, Paris. An octagon medallion containing a square set diagonally, within which is a star and in the very centre, a flower, can be found in the Elizabeth Pim sampler.[179]

Samplers worked in Holland and Germany in the seventeenth century also have motifs taken from oriental carpets.[180] Dated 1640, a sampler from Marken, Holland has an octagon identical to that of Elizabeth Pim.[181] Pim's range of colours is very similar to that used at Marken and they have retained amazing intensity. Maria van Hemert observed of the Marken samplers that the colours had not faded and seemed to be more permanent than those used later.[182] She also noted that those most commonly found on the seventeenth-century Marken samplers are greenish yellow, light blue, golden yellow, natural, a warm dark red and a lighter, bright red closer to crimson. This is very like what can be seen in Pim's work, suggesting that the thread used by her was imported from the Netherlands. We know that Sarah Fell bought Dutch thread. Dutch dyers had a reputation for fine quality dyeing and much cloth was sent from England and Ireland to be dyed there. Up until 1699 Joseph Pike had an extensive trade in serge from Cork to Holland and Flanders. Two other Cork Quaker merchants were Daniel Cullimore and Isaac Mee. Cullimore's trade ranged across Europe, and he sold French and Spanish indigoes and dyestuffs, Dutch linseed oil and painting colours. More specifically, Mee was a colour merchant and salesman of dye-stuffs.[183]

List carpets and rag mats

Concern with the home meant that the housewife, by working hard in the evenings, might attempt to make the furnishings more attractive, and in so doing find an outlet for artistic skills. Running a house was far more onerous than today, and all but the poorest had maids to help them, thus providing much-needed employment and training in skills. When Margaret Boyle Harvey came from Pennsylvania as a bride to Clonmel, it was pointed out to her that she should not make her own carpet but give the work to others. It is not known whether the carpet or mat in question was a rag mat or a stitched one, but the making of a carpet out of rags is yet another example of thrift. The good housewife used up old clothes and fabric to make list carpets or rag mats.[184] In the second half of the eighteenth century the original earthen floors of most of the houses of Ballitore were replaced by boards or stone flags, so it was now feasible to put down a mat. It took Mary Leadbeater and six friends two weeks to weave a list carpet. The warp was nailed to the floor and the weft was worked with wooden needles threaded with long strips (lists) of old textiles. This was then taken out of the frame with the help of Richard Shackleton, and to finish it an M. Dickenson assisted with the sewing. The second part of the carpet was then put in the frame and when it was completed it was laid down in the parlour and the furniture was rearranged. Mary Leadbeater obviously enjoyed the whole business:

> While a carpet was making the parlour was all in confusion; it was a time of delightful variety and idleness, and everyone was pleasant.[185]

Bed covers and quilts

In the days before the sewing machine, sheets, towels, napkins and other household linen all involved a great deal of time-consuming work, as every item had to be hemmed by hand. When these

---

[178] Bennett, 1989, p.22. The geometrically-constructed star occurs on a thirteenth-century Selcuk carpet described in Aslanapa, 1988, p.13-14.

[179] Small versions of this motif as a band were sometimes worked on samplers by pupils of Judyth Hayle's school in Norfolk around 1700. Three are in the V&A collection, and others can be seen in the Fitzwilliam collection.

[180] A motif on the early sixteenth-century German sampler in the V&A can be found on small-pattern Holbein carpets. See Ganzhorn, 1991, p.250-251.

[181] Reproduced in Van Hemert, 1978, as a frontispiece and on p.8.

[182] Van Hemert, 1978, p.9.

[183] Harrison, 1991, p.17.

[184] Very comfortable list slippers were also made. Newtown school specified these for both boys and girls in 1798.

[185] Corrigan, 2009, p.297.

became worn, other skills came into play including almost invisible darning. For poorer people flour bags were a cheap alternative to linen or cotton. Flour used to be sold in large unbleached calico bags and when well washed these were made into sheets and nightdresses and could be used for lining quilts. On the backing of a Carlow quilt dated 1869 'S. and A. G. Davis' is just legible, this being the name of a Quaker mill in Enniscorthy.[186]

In a letter of April 1790 Mary Leadbeater wrote: 'Settled down to quilting - I love the social work.' After a busy day she obviously enjoyed sewing in the company of friends. We do not know what quilting technique was being used, whether it was patchwork or had a single colour top, sometimes known as a 'wholecloth'. In her book *The Cottage Fireside* (1826) Abigail Roberts recommends having a green drugget quilt for everyday and making a patchwork quilt out of old gowns for best.

The green satin quilt of the Penn Inventory in the 1660s would have been a wholecloth one. The two layers, top and lining, could have been flat quilted but were more likely to have been filled with sheep's wool and then quilted. Sometimes embroidery in coloured silks was added. When Princess Elizabeth, daughter of James I, married the Elector Palatine in 1609 her trousseau included, '3 quilts of fustian, lined with taffeta, filled with wool, and sewed with silk'.[187] Bed covers like those in the Penn inventory could either have been quilted in the same colour or else in a contrasting one, and this type of quilt continued in Wales and Northumbria into the twentieth century.

The technique of cord-quilting was fashionable in Europe during the sixteenth, seventeenth and early eighteenth centuries. It usually consisted of two layers of white linen but without any wool wadding between them. The pattern was drawn in two parallel lines and worked in fine backstitch forming a channel through which the cord was threaded. More than any other type of quilting, patterns raised with cord rely for their perfection on great skill and accuracy. The cord technique gives body to the fabric, helping it to drape well

Jane Wilson cord-quilt, detail showing stitching. (FHLD)

and the resulting sculptured appearance could look magnificent on a bed by day. Cord-quilting was principally made in larger houses, while poorer people were more likely to use the faster running stitch for their warmer wadded quilting. In 1772, Jane Wilson, the daughter of a well-to-do Quaker land-owner in Edenderry, married Joseph Sandwith. A year later she finished a superb cord-quilt some 270cms x 270cms with delightful scrolling floral designs reminiscent of earlier Jacobean textiles. Sadly, Jane had no children but her sister Elizabeth, who married Jacob Goff of Horetown, had twenty-two.[188]

Textiles were often passed down the female side of families. This quilt went to Elizabeth's daughter Charlotte, who married Joshua Edmundson, and then passed it down to Jane Edmundson, who married Joseph Fisher Shackleton. Their daughter, Chrissie Shackleton, gave it in the 1960s to her

---

[186] Jones, 1979, plate 10. The author remembers sleeping under an eiderdown of flour sacks dyed orange and stuffed with sheep's wool, made by her mother in the 1940's, whilst the scratchy feel of a flour bag nightdress was recalled by a seventy-year-old Irish librarian in August 2017.
[187] Colby, 1972, p. 99.
[188] FHLD has a photograph of an oil painting of Elizabeth Goff.

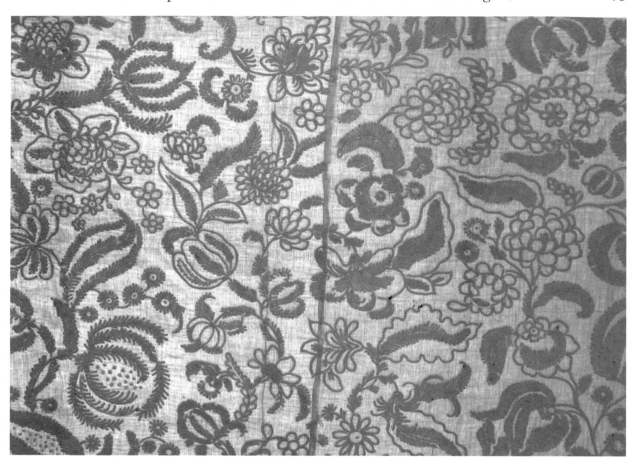

Jane Wilson cord-quilt, detail, backlit to show pattern. (FHLD)

cousin Doreen Foley née Edmundson, and the latter's daughter, Judith Badman née Foley, brought it to FHLD.

Patchwork quilting was another technique in the Irish Quaker repertoire and would have appealed to thrifty women who could then legitimately enjoy the creative aspect. Skill in design and sewing could make a very attractive bedspread out of a lot of small scraps of fabric. Life in a war–torn country was not easy for the first Irish Quakers, many of them former Baptist soldiers, but it is reasonable to assume that their wives continued to use their home-making skills. Not surprisingly, no early bed covers have survived in Ireland. However, a good idea of patchwork quilting of the period can be

Mount Wilson, a fairly typical example of a prosperous Quaker farmhouse. (FHLD)

Horetown House in the eighteenth century. (FHLD)

seen in an English one worked by Priscilla Redding, whose father, a soldier and Baptist preacher, had been the Governor of Deale castle. Her cot cover of the 1690s is carefully designed with a centre block inside an octagon, and concentric borders using a variety of silk velvets, satins, silver and silver-gilt tissues in geometric shapes. The reverse is an English or Dutch block printed cotton and a thick layer of wool is sandwiched between this and the top. In 1713 Priscilla Redding worked a wholecloth white silk quilt for a grandchild.[189] The complete set of patchwork bed furnishings made around 1708, which still survives at Levens Hall near Swarthmoor, includes a bed cover, the top of which is pieced from scraps of expensive imported Indian prints, and the whole is quilted in a simple diamond pattern with red thread in running stitch.[190]

In 1724 the Quaker Parke family emigrated from Carlow to Pennsylvania and were followed by Mary Parke and her husband Thomas Valentine in 1725. Shortly before her departure, Mary received a letter from Robert Parke of Chester County requesting her to buy material and to bring it over for her sister Rachel, most probably to make a quilt: 'Raichell Desires thee wod bring hir some bits of Silk for trashbags [ragbags] thee may buy them in Johns Lane - also [-] yards of white Mode or Silk for 2 hoods.'[191]

In the early nineteenth century the Goff sisters of Horetown used 2,648 diamonds of glazed printed cottons to make a magnificent 'Sunburst' quilt of concentric octagons. The stitching and accuracy of the piecing are exceptionally fine.[192]

At a far more modest level, the three women of the Hudson family of Ballitore, which included a mentally disabled son, earned their living largely by sewing, and this included both quilting and the making of patchwork quilts.[193]

Mountmellick work

Another form of coverlet was a cotton one embroidered in what is known as Mountmellick work. Because Mountmellick had been a significant Quaker town, this type of needlework is often thought of as Quaker, and indeed was a technique that was taken up by many Quakers. With the decline of the weaving and spinning industries in the early 1800s many women in the once prosperous town found themselves without employment. One response to the desperate economic situation of such women was the creation of a new style of embroidered household linen. This was the brainchild of a local Protestant, Johanna Carter, who ran a school of 7 Catholics and 8 Protestants in a small thatched cottage where, in 1824, she lived on an income of £9 a year. She had the idea of white work embroidery for household linen, using easily available materials of robust white cotton fabric and thick thread like crochet cotton. This type of work was also taken up by the girls in the Quaker school.

Much quicker to execute than most whitework, it sold well, and being very washable was good for household linens, especially tray cloths, dressing-table cloths, pillow shams (made to be thrown over the pillow by day) and bedspreads. Well-drawn designs, based on plants from Irish hedgerows and garden flowers, worked boldly with intelligently

---

[189] Like many Quakers Priscilla kept a spiritual diary. See Prichard, 2010, pp.52-55.

[190] Colby, 1972, p.121.

[191] Miller, 2003, p.80.

[192] Reproduced in Jones, 1979, No.15. A similar quilt of 3,803 diamonds was completed in 1837 by Rebecca Scattergood Savery, a Pennsylvania Quaker, for her grand-daughter, Sarah, and is now in the Philadelphia Museum of Art.

[193] In London, when visiting Newgate Prison, Elizabeth Fry discovered from the women their need to learn to read and sew. Encouraged by her, they organised themselves in the Lancastrian system of groups of twelve with a monitor, and learnt to make and mend their own clothes. This was followed by making patchwork bedcovers, using scraps and surplus materials readily supplied by Quaker drapers. Consisting of hundreds of tiny hexagons pieced together, a quilt, made in Newgate under Elizabeth Fry's auspices is in the collections of the Strangers' Hall, Norwich. Elizabeth Fry was aware that there was a demand for quilts in New South Wales and made a business deal with Dixon & Co. of Fenchurch St. who were exporters. The quilts were sold in the colony, and most of the money earned was saved for the prisoners pending their release or transportation. It was also arranged for each woman embarking on the convict ships to be given: A large bag or hold-all with a Bible, 2 aprons, 1 cotton cap; and a smaller bag with 2 stay-laces, 2 combs, a knife and fork, 1 ball of string, 1 pair of spectacles if necessary, 1 thimble, 8 darning, 1 bodkin, 1 piece of tape, 1ounce of pins, 100 needles, 7 balls of sewing cotton, 2 balls of black worsted, 24 hanks of coloured thread, and 2 pounds of patchwork pieces. On the long voyage, an industrious convict could make a patchwork coverlet to sell or to use on arrival in Australia. The well-known 'Rajah Quilt' (1841), made on the ship of that name, is slightly different in that during the three-month voyage it was worked collectively by the 180 women to express their gratitude to the 'Ladies of the Convict Ship Committee'. This is mainly of triangles and squares in plain and printed cotton, with appliqué and embroidery in the centre and on the borders. Now in the National Gallery of Australia it is the only quilt known to have survived from the 12,000 women on the 106 ships said to have been visited by Elizabeth Fry.

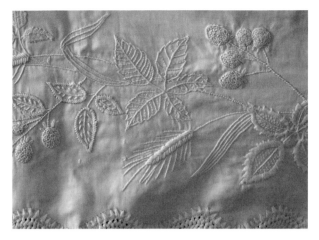

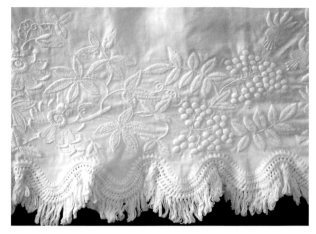

Mountmellick work. Detail of pillow sham.
(FHLD)

Mountmellick work. Detail of pillow sham.
(FHLD)

chosen stitches so as to be almost in relief, were framed by a border of buttonholing with a deep knitted fringe. Arranged informally the plants might be naturalistic in outline, but for the fillings the individual embroiderer chose from a large range of traditional stitches and this, together with a considerable variation in density, made for work of individuality and charm. Mountmellick work became very popular with the middle classes, especially after1890, when Weldon's published 8 booklets of instruction.

Three fine Mountmellick bedspreads worked by Quakers are in the collection of FHLD. In 1879, at the age of seventy-five, Jane Newsome of Cork completed a bedspread measuring 270cms x 270cms for the marriage of her son John to Sophia Alexander of Limerick. For an elderly person the technique would have been easier to handle than fine cross-stitching but still needed considerable skill to choose the most effective stitches. In her analysis of the stitches used on this bedspread, Jane Almqvist Houston notes the use of padded satin, overcasting, bullion, French knot, seeding, Indian filling, cable plait, buttonhole, diamond trellis, Cretan, double feather, and snail trail.[194]

Though using the technique of Mountmellick work, the designs of the three bedspreads are rather more formal. The Newsome one has the centrally placed basket of flowers, which was often the basis of the design on bed furnishings in the early eighteenth century.[195] Here it is enclosed in

a formal ribbon frame intertwined with flowers which itself is surrounded by a scrolling vine with bunches of grapes. The scrolling vine, often growing from an urn or vase, is a very ancient motif of which examples can be found in Roman and Byzantine mosaics.[196]

The second bedspread also has the scrolling design, but with oak leaves not vines enclosing the basket of flowers. Besides such frequently-used motifs as odd shells or butterflies, both of these have the heavy fringe typical of Mountmellick work. The third has the basket with its surrounds, but a simple embroidered edge takes the place of the fringing.

Along with the bedspreads FHLD has several pillow shams in the classic Mountmellick style. These are embroidered on three sides with freely drawn hedgerow ferns, leaves, flowers and berries.

Motifs and pattern books
The arrival of the printing press in the fifteenth century made available a number of new sources of design with herbals and books on botany, bestiaries, and prints. In the sixteenth century general pattern books for the trades were also utilised by the needlewoman. Coming from Germany, Venice and France, they were rapidly adapted into English and might be purchased by the newly affluent mercantile middle classes. To transfer a pattern, holes were pricked in the paper. This was then laid on the fabric and pouncing powder was applied

---

[194] Houston-Almqvist, 1985, p.19.
[195] On eighteenth-century bed furnishings see Clabburn, 1981, no.54.
[196] In Tunisia, the Sousse Museum contains a third-century Roman mosaic of Bacchus with this motif (Djelloul, 2006, p.27) and a sixth-century Christian Byzantine mosaic with birds, a palm tree and scrolling vines in a vase. (Ibid, p.34.)

Seventeenth-century stumpwork, 34cms x 45.7cms. (FHLD)

and pressed through the holes leaving dots on the material. The paper being removed, the design was carefully inked in. Few complete early pattern books have survived this operation.[197]

Johann Sibmacher's *Neues Modelbuch*, published in Nuremberg in 1597, contained patterns that were copied in John Taylor's *The Needle's Excellency* (1631), in which an introductory rhyme promised designs for:

> Flowers, Plants and Fishes
> Beasts, Birds, Flyes, and Bees
> Hills, Dales, Plains and Pastures
> Skies, Seas, Rivers, Trees.[198]

In Britain what are known as spot samplers would have a random selection of small patterns and motifs of such things as birds, flowers and insects. Motifs like these were worked on the petticoats which can be seen in portraits of Queen Elizabeth I in 1599 and Lady Dorothy Cary in 1614.[199] Examples of such motifs can also be found in blackwork on the collars of two small boys' shirts of the late sixteenth century.[200] Embroidery on costume went out of fashion in the time of Charles I, but many of the popular motifs continued to be used on textiles for household furnishings, whilst samplers remained in use for the collecting and trying out of ideas.[201]

Stumpwork
In England during the second half of the seventeenth century there was a short-lived craze for small pictures worked in tent stitch or stumpwork by amateur embroiderers. Generally worked by girls of well-to-do families, these took the form of small panels or pictures, mirror frames and decoration for little caskets.[202] Stumpwork was partially three dimensional with much raised and padded work, appliqué, detached button hole stitch, needlepoint lace, darned silk pile and beads, spangles, mica etc. The ground fabric was usually a creamy-white to contrast with the colours and textures of the embroidery and to enhance the effect of light and shadow.

The term 'stumpwork' derives from the word 'stamp' in the sense of something that has been printed (cf. French *estampe*). The designs might be derived from popular prints, particularly of Old Testament stories (New Testament images were felt to be too Catholic). These could be adapted and set in an imaginary seventeenth-century landscape which allowed the addition of motifs such as those advertised by Taylor. Professionally drawn pictures on fabric ready to embroider could be obtained from dealers who also sold novelties, threads and materials.

Rubens' painting of *The Judgement of Solomon* was widely known from a popular print by Boetius A. Bolswert (c. 1620). The subject allowed for a symbolic reading, and God's choice of a wise king as ruler could by extension be interpreted as a reference to the Stuarts. One working of this print was in canvas work, using wool and silk thread. The palace interior was replaced by a pastoral scene which allowed for the adding of a number of animals, birds, insects and flowers.[203] In another version the action is also re-set in the country, but with a cottage instead of a church.[204] In this case the animals include a lion, a rabbit, a fox and a stag, all of which were common motifs on spot samplers. The seated stag from earlier pattern books occurs on the oldest dated English sampler, by Jane Bostocke (1596), and can also be seen on a late seventeenth-century stumpwork panel in FHLD.

Family lore associates the FHLD panel with Margaret Pim's marriage to Caleb Beale in 1755 and it may have been a gift from a wealthy Friend. Considering the fragility of this type of work, it must have been carefully cherished to have survived. This panel would seem to have been composed at home using motifs from pattern books. Under three clouds is the popular stumpwork motif of a Renaissance palace meant to look like Henry VIII's Nonesuch, which he built to rival Francis I's Château of Chambord.[205] The rather grand building overlooks a landscape filled

[197] Ginsburg, 1991, p.217.
[198] Colby, 1964, p.157.
[199] Ginsburg, 1991, pp.132-133.
[200] Synge, 1986, p.132.
[201] Ibid, pp.40-44.
[202] Girls would already have achieved various samplers including a band one of patterns, an alphabet one and whitework which might include cutwork and needlelace; a collection of Martha Edlin's work culminating in a stumpwork casket can be seen in the V&A.
[203] Synge, 1986, p.98.
[204] Feller, 2011, vol. II, p.30.
[205] Colby, 1964, p.83.

with a variety of flowers, birds and flying insects scattered around. As was common practice, some of these motifs are outlined in black stitching. Two moths look different at first sight, but are in fact the same model repeated in other colours, whilst a snail and a caterpillar appear to be upside down. Across the bottom are a leopard, a pool with two fish swimming, a bird on an oak sprig and a seated stag. Each one is separate with its own mound. Birds on sprigs are another very old popular motif. A number can be found on the fourth-century mosaic floor of the basilica church of Aquileia in Northern Italy. *One Book of Birds sitting on sprigs* is amongst the titles listed by Peter Stent, in his catalogue of pattern books (c.1660).[206] The leopard and the stag were heraldic in origin, while the fish was an ancient Christian symbol.

The embroiderer of this piece of stumpwork chose the motifs simply to create an attractive parkland, but was most probably unaware of their significance. Some seem to have been worked separately as slips, and then appliquéd to the silk satin ground which is backed with linen. Other motifs are worked through both layers of fabric in a variety of embroidery stitches using polychrome twisted and floss silk. Plushwork and tubular coiled wire give the vegetation a three-dimensional quality, and the centre eagle is padded and seems to be about to fly on wings made of needle-lace supported by wire. As was usual in the seventeenth century, an attempt has been made to portray the individual flowers and animals using their natural colouring, including shading.

Although there is no overall sense of scale, the positioning of the different motifs indicates a degree of visual sensitivity resulting in a satisfying sense of balance and harmony. The various elements subtly direct our eyes to a central inner picture contained within an oval frame. This frame is a metal coil covered with rolled silk, and is decorated with three-dimensional foliage of needlepoint lace with a wire support. Inside the frame is a large country house of the period with several chimneys, a sign

of wealth in 1665 when chimneys were subject to a substantial hearth tax. The stepped gable, large windows and lack of fortifications, suggests it is in England, which, since the Wars of Roses, apart from the brief Civil War, had been fairly peaceful, unlike Ireland where few large mansions were built.[207] Different stitches are used to achieve an effect of stonework and brick or plastered walls. The luxury of glass windows is indicated by small pieces of light-reflecting mica with silk laid diagonally to represent the diamond-shaped panes which were used before larger sheets of glass could be made.[208] The open door of the palace gate-house is of tight needlelace, also on a wire frame.

Needle painting

The execution of a complete picture in needlework is known to have been enjoyed by some Friends. By the late eighteenth century, a fashionable form of embroidery was the copying of famous artists' pictures using long, irregular stitches to represent brush-strokes on the canvas. In some cases ladies could command high professional fees for this sort of work, and might even be exhibited at the Royal Society of Artists.

In the early 1770s Queen Charlotte, herself a keen needlewoman, commissioned from Mary Knowles (1733-1807) an embroidered portrait of George III after Zoffany.[209] Sophisticated, witty and good-looking, Mary Knowles was the wife of an eminent physician and had been received at court in Versailles and The Hague. She was a friend of Samuel Johnson, who referred to her as his 'Quaker lady', and also of Benjamin West (1738-1820), historiographical painter to George III. On one occasion she dined with West where she met the American Quakers William Savery and George Dillwyn, who were on a religious visit to Europe. After dinner they paid a private visit to The Queen's House (Buckingham Palace) to chat with the Royal family.[210]

In the later eighteenth century, the techniques of needle-painting were also employed in the

---

[206] Ibid, p.25.

[207] In Ireland the unsettled state of the country meant that the semi-fortified tower-house with bawn (enclosure) was safer. Where mansions were built they were usually in proximity to a walled town, such as Sir Walter Raleigh's house in Youghal, and the Butler house in Carrick-on-Suir, where Anne Boleyn was born.

[208] From the thirteenth century glass was blown in a round shape which was then trimmed to create a diamond-shaped pane. Such glass can still be seen in the 1682 Almshouse in Kinsale.

[209] Now in the V.&A. King, 1956, p.110, pl.56, mentions that Horace Walpole, in Strawberry Hill, had a landscape after Uden embroidered by Mary Knowles.

[210] Savery, 1844, p.281. West, born in America of a Quaker family, showed early evidence of artistic talent and Friends paid for his training.

Needle painting of ruined church on an island, 25cms x 31cms. (FHLD)

Court the sheen of the lilac and primrose satin sets off the embroidery of the hangings, while white satin is employed as the basis for the coverlet and curtains of the cradle of one of her children.[211]

A surround of free-flowing flowers, sometimes loosely entwined and usually executed in long and short satin stitch was occasionally worked as a framing device for a poem and a splendid example of this is a sampler worked by Deborah Newenham at Edenderry School in 1769. Map samplers were sometimes framed in a similar way. In 1813 Ann Rhode at Mountmellick surrounded an oval map of England and Wales with an elegant border of flowers in coloured silks.

Goldfinch on a rose (probably a commercial design), 29.5cms x 22cms,. (FHLD)

working of naturalistic flower groups in flat stitches in silk on a pale ground and used to adorn the plain-woven fabrics that were fashionable at the time. On Queen Charlotte's bed at Hampton

Embroidered romantic landscapes were popular and there are some Quaker examples. To create these scenes the usual technique was to draw the outlines of the picture on a panel of white silk. The Thompsons, a Dublin Quaker family, had an ancestor who, using grey crewel wool, embroidered a ruined stone church on a wooded island. The carefully textured trees were worked in silk chenille with random long and short stitches and stand out against the white silk which was left plain for the sky.

Two nearly identical needle paintings of a 'Goldfinch on a Rose' were embroidered respectively by a member of the Clibborn family of Anner Mills of Clonmel, and by a member of the Myers family of Cork. Though Quakers had many fine botanical artists it is most likely that both of these were made from nineteenth century commercial designs.

It was said of Elizabeth Carleton (born 1726) that 'She excelled in skill and ingenuity with her needle and was preparing to work a picture for an exhibition, when the ministry of a Friend on a religious visit to Ireland, was made instrumental to discover to her the vanity of the things in which she delighted.' [212] This sad story may partially explain the comparative lack of Quaker pictorial samplers in Ireland.

[211] King, 1956, p.109.
[212] Shackleton, 1822, p.15.

CHAPTER FIVE

THE SAMPLER

Stitches

Medieval embroiderers drew on a wide variety of different stitches, many of which would later appear on samplers. These include stem stitch, back stitch, chain stitch, split stitch, satin stitch, buttonhole stitch, cross stitch and couching stitch. Popular in sixteenth- and seventeenth-century Spain and England was the double running, or Holbein, stitch, which dates back to a much earlier period and can be found in Coptic work, including samplers. In fifteenth-century Italy, the Florentine stitch was much used and can be found on a small number of Quaker samplers. In the early eighteenth century, alphabets were still subordinate to patterns, whereas later they often tended to dominate. By this time the sampler was becoming a way of displaying skills acquired, and generally, until the modern period, it was more associated with schoolgirls than adult women. Most of the motifs and patterns found on Quaker samplers, like the stitches and alphabets, have their origins in the more distant past and have been adapted over the centuries. It is the choice and arrangement that may make the work identifiable as Quaker.

Cut work sheet border with seventeenth-century design, late nineteenth-century. (Private collection)

Band samplers

In the seventeenth century long, narrow, linen samplers were made with bands of border designs of the sort used for clothing and household textiles. Some would be white cutwork, drawn thread work or needle lace, which was made with buttonhole stitches (reticella).[213] Stitched with linen thread, these designs could be used on underwear or bed linen. Others, worked in bright silks, could also adorn curtains. Both types are found on ten band

samplers known to have been made by Quaker girls in London and were typical of the time.[214] Two other Quaker samplers of 1727 and 1729, also from London, were executed in hollie point, a technically demanding and time-consuming stitch related to needle lace, which was used to decorate baby clothes.[215] A small number of English Quaker band samplers dating from the early eighteenth century were worked entirely in polychrome silks in a shorter and wider format.[216] Most of these

---

[213] Longfield, 1978, p.2.
[214] Discussed in Humphrey, 2017, ch.8.
[215] Tarrant, 2014, pp.185-186. 'Hollie point' derives from the word 'holy' as this work was often used on ecclesiastical vestments. Given the young age of the Gerrey sisters, who belonged to a Quaker family in Southwark, these two samplers were possibly made as a prelude to working professionally.
[216] See Humphrey, 2017, ch.8.

Blessing Fenn sampler, 1710, 62cms x 24cms.
(NMI)

Ann Fenn sampler, 1713, 82cms x 24cms.
(NMI)

are from the London area and have variants of the usual reversed arcades of stylised flowers, sometimes some text, and maybe an alphabet. Ann Marsh's academy in Philadelphia was noted for its needlework, and the band sampler developed there to become an attractive square where pattern and text were carefully integrated.[217] Rebecca Jones, who completed her education there, produced a beautifully worked, coloured band sampler with a border, and this, together with two cut-work samplers, still exists.[218]

It would seem quite probable that band samplers which included needle lace and cut-work were made in better-off Quaker households in Ireland from the start. However, to date no seventeenth-century Quaker work of this sort has survived.

The earliest known Irish Quaker samplers were made by two little Fenn sisters sewing industriously in Cork. Their father was a prosperous merchant and their mother, Patience, was the daughter of Captain Morris of Castle Salem, Co, Cork.[219] The delightful but rather old-fashioned work suggests that they may have had an elderly governess or relative who taught them, copying from samplers made in her own childhood. In 1710 Blessing, aged ten, worked a band sampler 62cms long while her sister Ann, at eight years old, did one of 82cms. The long narrow shape, together with the colourfulness and lightness of the designs, looks back to samplers of the seventeenth century. Two of the band patterns in double running stitch worked by the Fenn girls occur on an English sampler dated 1649 and also on another mid- seventeenth-century one in the V&A.[220]

Further examples of these designs can be found on a number of samplers of this period. The earlier ones are in monochrome and may originally have served to decorate cuffs, collars and edgings of shirts and chemises. In Elizabethan times Holbein's

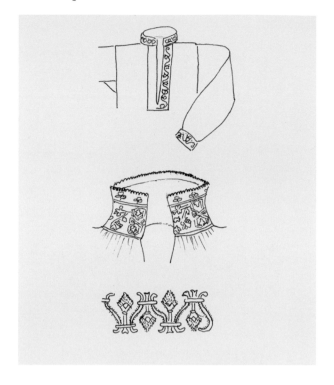

Use of embroidery on shirt collar, neck and cuffs; collar of Elizabethan boy's shirt (after shirt in V&A); Band design worked by Blessing Fenn.

portraits show that the collar and cuffs of a man's white linen shirt might have a monochrome design using black silk thread (or sometimes blue, red or even gold) in double running stitch.[221] As well as being very decorative, it made the collar firmer and is also reversible, unlike the back stitch which is only neat on one side. This stitch, sometimes called Holbein stitch, was most probably used for the decoration of the shirts which Katherine of Aragon was still making for Henry VIII after their divorce.

The double running, or possibly back stitch, that occurs on the Fenn samplers was also excellent practice for sewing seams neatly and quickly. To make the design more interesting, a mix of green, red and blue thread could be employed instead

---

[217] Ann Marsh and her mother Elizabeth, who had taught in Worcestershire before emigrating to America in 1723, ran this highly estimated school in Philadelphia for many years.

[218] Rebecca Jones was well equipped to be a teacher and on the death of her mother in 1761 she took over the school which she had run. Her mother had become reconciled to her becoming a convinced and plain Quaker and when Rebecca was in charge of her own school only plain sewing was allowed and 'the lighter and merely ornamental branches' of learning were avoided. Rebecca Jones's samplers are reproduced in Ring, 1993, pp.335 fig.353 and 346 figs.364-365.

[219] William Morris, a governor of three garrisons and a Baptist Elder of great repute, was granted a fortified tower-house which he renamed Castle Salem ('salem' means peaceful). He became a Quaker and his son was a friend of William Penn. Both samplers are in NMI, ref, DT: L.875.1 and DT: L.875.2.

[220] The 1649 sampler is in Nottingham Castle Museum (ref. 07.78). The V&A sampler ref. is 739-1899.

[221] See Arnold, 2008, pp.17-26, pp.61-62, pp.65-74.

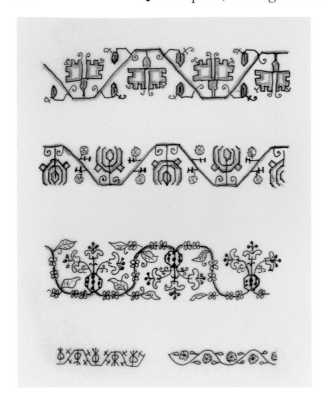

Blessing Fenn band designs. Carnation; honeysuckle, 'Lily pot', two simplified designs used for framing other bands.

Carved borders on sixth-century Ravenna ivory throne and marble panel, two Jane Bostocke bands, fourteenth-century Swiss embroidered cloth border.(After cloth in Basel Historisches Museum)

of monochrome, and this can be seen on these samplers where bands of repeating designs of highly stylised flowers are arranged within scrolls or arcades, the blooms alternately facing up or down. This is a classic border design which can be found more than a thousand years earlier in the scrolling plants on the ivory throne of Bishop Maximianus in Ravenna. In England Jane Bostocke's sampler of 1598 has at least six different small examples of such a border. On the Fenn samplers a number of bands have a narrow border on either side, often in the form of a line of repeating stylised plants, sometimes so schematic as to be barely more than a few stitches.

In the later seventeenth century bright silks were used, and stitches such as satin and tent made for more colourful and solid work. Gradually cross stitch and satin stitch would supplant the double running outline patterns. In contrast to her outline

designs in double running, Ann Fenn has a row of fleurs-de-lis worked in cross stitch, and a band of unidentified stylised flowers in satin stitch, both of which appear very solid. The fleur-de-lis was a stylised form of the lily of the Virgin Mary, but its original religious significance had been largely forgotten. For her carnation bands Ann employed cross stitch as did Blessing, who also used this stitch for the popular sixteenth-century honeysuckle band which she ornamented with flourishes in Holbein stitch.[222]

Matching stitches were commonly employed for alphabets and the divisions that separated them from other bands. [223] In one case Ann Fenn used eyelet stitch for an alphabet and the division. She then employed cross stitch for a second alphabet with its divisions, and for a religious text:

---

[222] Cross stitch, herring bone, satin, Florentine, rococo and trellis stitch were all used in 1720 by ten-year-old Dorcas Haynes. She did not employ double running, but her repeat bands of stylised flower and leaf patterns, reminiscent of the previous century, are robust and in vivid colours. See Humphrey, 1997, p.54.
[223] Crawford, 1989, p.26.

AVOID ALL VAIN AND IDLE TALK THAT DOTH CORRUPT THE MINDE. HARK TO THE   SOLID WEIGHTY TRUTH IN WHICH THOU SHALT COMFORT FIND.

Most of the children in the Fenn family died in infancy, but Ann lived on to be married to Joseph Sleigh of Cork and to have children. Blessing was delicate but struggled with ill health until her death at the age of thirteen. A serious and very good child, a testimony to her was published in a volume of *Piety Promoted.*[224] On her sampler Blessing Fenn stitched:

THIS WORK OF MINE MY FRIENDS MAY HAVE WHEN I AM DEAD AND LAIN IN GRAVE.[225]

The spot or random sampler

In its origins, Quakerism was firmly based on a literal reading of the Bible, and this led to a mistrust of any images or symbols and an excessive emphasis on the word. However, pictorial elements can be found on Quaker samplers. Their function was purely decorative and it is unlikely that anyone thought of the potential meaning of the images themselves.

Most of the motifs on the Elizabeth Pim spot sampler are of an abstract nature and have already been looked at in the context of designs for upholstery. However, two motifs stand out as rather different. Both have a pair of birds framing a central vertical element with a formalised flower or flowers. Elizabeth Pim was certainly unaware that this common embroidery design is also a version of an extremely ancient motif in which a stylised pillar with two birds relates to the Tree of Life, one of the most universal symbols representing the link between man and the heavens.

In Babylon the Tree of Life carried both the idea of renewal and of immortality. The biblical Tree of Knowledge in the garden of Eden is a version of this, and together with Adam and Eve, was depicted in numerous samplers in Protestant northern Europe. In contrast to the often dry and barren lands around them, both Jews and Arabs pictured the Garden of Eden with flowers, animals, trees and water, and *Djanna*, the Arabic word for paradise, also means garden. The name of the Alhambra gardens in Granada is *Djannat al-arifin*, meaning 'gardens of those who know the truth'.[226]

Already in Sumerian art the Tree of Life figured as a plant growing from a vase, often flanked by two or more guardians, and this would become a favourite motif of European folk art.[227] Around the Mediterranean, an early variant of the pool of water, appears as a two handled vase from which develops a scrolling vine. In Gaza a Jewish synagogue floor mosaic of 530 A.D. shows a vase out of which emerges a scrolling vine, enclosing animals, fruit and various offerings. In this case the vine itself has been interpreted as

Top: fourth-century Coptic tapestry ;
sixth-century Ravenna marble panel.
Below: sixth-century mosaic of Theodoulos
(Sousse museum); fifteenth-century doorway,
Devenish Island, Ireland.

[224] John Field, *Piety Promoted,* Vol. II of 'new edition', London, 1812, pp.15-17.
[225] An almost identical expression of this sentiment was also stitched on Sarah Logan's sampler of 1725 (Philadelphia). Reproduced by Ring, 1993, p.331.
[226] Piotrovsky and Vrieze, 1999, p.63.
[227] Further afield, the Indonesian Wayang puppet plays start with a tall, leaf-shaped representation of the Tree rising from a stylised pool or pot of water, which may be guarded by animals or birds.

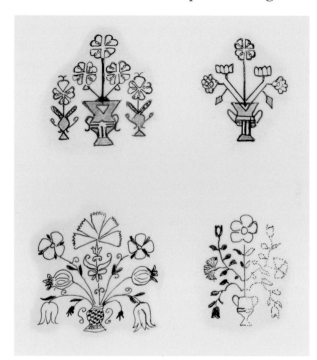

Vase of flowers motif: Elizabeth Pim, Sarah Tatum. Eighteenth-century Moravian embroidery, Esther Priestman 1804

representing paradise and the peacocks as symbols of immortality.[228]

On a sixth-century marble panel in the Byzantine church of St. Apollinare in Ravenna, two peacocks guard the cross which emerges from a small pot, whilst the whole is surrounded by vines. Much later, on Devenish Island, near Enniskillen, Ireland, a fifteenth-century monastery doorway rises up into a rod which forms a simplified cross with a bird on each side eating grapes from the vines.

By the seventeenth century these originally religious motifs were appearing in secular embroidery, with the vine often being replaced by flowers, particularly carnations, tulips and roses, all of which are associated with fertility, although their symbolic value had been forgotten. The vase of flowers continued as a popular decorative motif on samplers, bed spreads and tablecloths.

A small sampler of 1663 from Marken, Netherlands, has a number of miniscule versions of trees and blooms including a tiny tree with

Stylised tree with two birds: Marken, Marken, Austrian or Swiss sampler, 1675; Priestman (York School), Elizabeth Pim, Lisburn M.W. 1761.

228 Avi-Yonah, 1975, pp.54-56. Further examples of the theme can be found on a fifth-century bishop's tomb in Tunisia where doves drink the Water of Life from a vase surrounded by roses, and on another Christian tomb which depicts a peacock and other birds wandering among the roses growing out of the vase. The very elegant sixth-century Christian mosaic of Theodoulos, also in Sousse, has birds, including two peacocks, perching on the vines (now a Christian symbol), with a palm tree in the centre.

Vase with carnations and two birds.
Elizabeth Pim sampler, detail. (FHLD)

Tree of life with peacocks.
Elizabeth Pim sampler, detail. (FHLD)

very schematic branches and two flanking birds. Peacocks, or doves signifying love can often be found in embroideries of central and eastern Europe where a heart might take the place of the vase. On another Marken sampler two peacocks face a completely stylised brown plant with three small 'roots' at the base and three branches, above all of which floats a heart, and above that again a crown.

Elizabeth Pim has a motif dated 1730 where two peacocks flank the tree which has become a green vertical element with leaves and topped by a stylised blue carnation, above which is a crown. Lisburn Linen Museum holds a sampler dated 1761 which has obvious affinities with the Elizabeth Pim one, including a motif of two peacocks guarding a stylised plant, in this case surrounded by extra little diamonds, but without the carnation. However, a blue carnation almost identical to a Pim motif surmounts a double heart in a central octagonal motif.

Elizabeth Pim also worked a two-handled central vase, filled with red carnations. Perched on top are two tiny striped birds reminiscent of the striped birds, animals and angels that occur in late

seventeenth-century English embroideries and samplers such as those made in Iudyth Hayle's school in Norfolk.

A particularly interesting bird design, 'the pelican in her piety', appears on the Lisburn sampler. Its function here is purely decorative without any understanding of its symbolic value.[229] The religious interpretation is that the bird's blood flows to feed her young and is thus a symbol of Christ's sacrifice. This subject can be found embroidered on the medieval Pienza cope and two sixteenth-century samplers, one German and an English one by Jane Bostocke.[230]

A sampler worked by a Sarah Harris, now in the Smithsonian, also presents strong visual affinities with both Pim and Lisburn.[231] Like these it is a sampler in the older sense of a number of motifs being tried out on a piece of linen. Such a piece was not designed to be framed and the different elements are crammed into the available space without any specific reference to a top or bottom line. A feature that points to an earlier style of sampler is the single alphabet across the top, which can also be found on the Lisburn one. The format is that of the long sampler, measuring

[229] Much later, in 1804, Sophia Doggett of London stitched the same version as the Lisburn one, along with other medallions and half medallions (Feller 2012, p 41.).
[230] V&A references: T.114-1956 and T.190-1960.
[231] This was probably Sarah Harris who married Thomas Roberts in 1789. She lived in Cork and may well have known Elizabeth Pim, who moved there after her marriage to George Newenham in 1747. Sarah died in England in 1793.

M W sampler, 1761, 51cms x 43cms. (Lisburn)

70.5cms x 33.7cms, and it carries the dates of 1786 and 1788, indicating that, like Elizabeth Pim's one, it was worked over several years.

Some of the motifs are in complete octagons, others are in half octagons, where it is obvious that the other half would be a mirror image, and the maker found it unnecessary to work the full design. Pim's octagons appear as complete designs, but the half octagon is common to Lisburn, Sarah Harris and many Ackworth and York school pieces. In addition to these motifs relating to carpets, Harris has other designs, some of them almost identical to ones used by Pim. Amongst these is a double heart with the initials SH and the date of 1786. One of the octagons has a pair of flowers similar to the ones worked by Pim in 1729 as part of a potential repeat pattern for upholstery. Harris's

Pelican motif: Jane Bostocke; Lisburn sampler.

freer use of the octagon allows for the insertion of a small scene. One has a lady in a large yellow dress in a bower whilst a 'token of love' octagon features two little dogs framed by two flowers and a third contains the lion and the unicorn of the Royal coat of arms. A single crowned lion appears on both Sarah Harris and Lisburn. Hearts and crowns were popular in the eighteenth century and these also occur as part of a formalised design with the Pim and Lisburn samplers. As purely decorative items they found their way into many later Quaker girls' samplers, often as space-fillers.

The maker of the Lisburn sampler and Sarah Harris both treated some elements in monochrome, and by the 1780s the monochrome half-octagon motif can also be found in America. Monochrome used in the stitching of a number of half octagons similar in design to the Lisburn sampler can be found in 1788 in the work of Sybil Tatum in New Jersey. She stitched a number of octagons, two of which contain all-over repeat patterns of stylised

Esther Priestman sampler, 1804, 26cms x 31cms. (Private collection)

Prices for making LINEN continued.

	s.	d.
Shift Sleeves, fine, per Pair —	1	0
Ditto coarfer, per ditto — —	0	9
An Apron with a Seam, fine Holland,		
Irifh, or Long Lawn — —	0	8
Ditto without ditto, Muflin, or Callico	0	6
Ditto coarfe and fmall — —	0	4
Pocket Handkerchiefs, fine, hemmed		
four Sides, per Doz. — —	3	0
Ditto hemmed two Sides, per ditto	1	6
Ditto coarfe, per ditto — —	0	8

Houfe Linen.

	s.	d.
Sheets, fine, per Pair — —	1	6
Ditto coarfe, per ditto — —	1	0
Pillow Cafes, fine, per Pair —	0	6
Ditto coarfe, per ditto — —	0	4
Table Cloths, per Yard — —	0	1
Napkins, per Dozen — —	1	6
Towels coarfe 9d per Doz.—fine —	1	6

Additional for Marking *.

A Halfpenny per Letter, and a Farthing per Figure.

* This Addition to be given, at the Difcretion of the School-Miftrefs, for the Encouragement of thofe Girls who beft obferve her Inftructions.

Prices for marking and making linen from Rules and Orders for the government of Friends School Workhouse at Clerkenwell, 1780. (FHLD)

flowers, while the others have vases of flowers all in bright colours, including one vase identical to Elizabeth Pim's.

In England by 1789, pupils at Ackworth and York Schools used both the full octagon medallion, and also the half octagon, in both cases showing a preference for monochrome or a reduced colour palette. Placed within an octagon frame, a very simplified version of the tree of life turns up in their work, but by now the tree trunk has been reduced to a vertical element or pole supporting a very schematic carnation. It neither touches the ground nor connects to the branches, and in a final manifestation it is omitted altogether and we are left with two dicky-birds amid leaves. The vase of flowers also appears, but often worked only as a half motif.[232]

The Alphabet
In French the term for a sampler is *abécédaire*, and today samplers tend to be thought of as involving letters of the alphabet in needlework. Earlier samplers, however, did not necessarily involve letters at all or only used them rather sparingly. Pim has the letters of a single alphabet in various

colours but they are scattered about randomly, a feature that appears later on some of the Ackworth medallion samplers and which was worked as late as 1805 by a Mary Thompson.[233] In the seventeenth century, according to Colby, it was quite usual for a signed sampler to have initials placed within a tablet. Pim's tablet containing her initials is to be found in an octagon of 1731, with a saw-toothed border. In 1750 she added the initials EN at the bottom of the sampler, indicating her married name of Newenham. In the case of the Lisburn sampler, apart from the initials MW, there is, unfortunately, no clear indication as to who may have worked it.

With a shift from the recording of decorative motifs a sampler became increasingly a way in which simple lettering skills might be practised with a view to the neat marking of laundry. In a large household or institution, it was important for each person's clothes to be marked with their name so that the laundry could be returned to the right people. In Ackworth, which had 300 children, the clothes for washing were marked both with the initials of their names, and the number of their bill of admittance.[234] Small girls learnt to stitch the

[232] At both Ackworth and York, octagons and garlands are used to frame initials.
[233] Another example is Frances Rae's of 1797 (National Design Museum, Smithsonian Institute).
[234] Grubb, 1792, p.260.

alphabet at a very early age. In Mary Leadbeater's *Anecdotes taken from Real Life* (1809) Susanna, at the age of seven, was proficient enough to earn some money by marking her uncle's stockings, a more difficult task with knitting than with a woven fabric. According to the1780 Rules, the girls at the Friends School and Workhouse, Clerkenwell (London), besides making shirts and shifts and hemming bed and table linen on commission, earned additional money for 'Marking at the discretion of the School-Mistress'.

Later, girls in the Irish National schools, along with their plain sewing, continued to make lettering samplers as part of their training for the marking of linen. In the case of clothing, the Quaker ribbon-making firm of John and Joseph Cash, which had been established in Coventry in 1846, started using the Jacquard loom and by the 1870s was producing name tapes. These were specially valuable for institutional use, such as boarding schools, and would gradually supersede hand-stitched marking.

A Pennington sampler of 1738 has two alphabets, both in capital letters, of which many are doubled - e.g. AA. Each pair is worked alternately in green or yellow and these are variants of Roman capitals. The Roman M and N appear once but elsewhere the Gothic version of these letters is used. J and U are omitted as I and V often replaced them in spelling at the time. This must have been a laundry-marking sampler, as the names of Peter Pennington and Sarah Pennington are worked twice, followed by a series of paired initials. Regardless of punctuation, the lines are filled up, with arbitrary divisions of words which sometimes run on from one line to the next, as on the Ann Fenn sampler where the word 'weighty' becomes 'we ighty', a practice that is also found on some seventeenth-century tombstones.

The date of the Pennington sampler is given as 'May the 19 1700 and 38'. The Penningtons were a very well-known Quaker family and the reference to the month as 'May' is atypical. The names of many of the months and days have associations with Norse or Roman gods, and Friends preferred to replace this heathen practice with numbers. A typical example of this is a sampler in NMI

Ann Wright sampler, 1765, 40.5cms x 20.5cms.
(FHLD)

marked 'Sarah Lovell's work, '1ˢᵗ Month 9ᵗʰ 1782' (9 January, 1782), which immediately identifies it as a piece of Quaker work.[235] However, Sarah Pierson's northern Irish sampler of 1800 is dated 'September' and not the '9ᵗʰ month' according to the preference of strict plain Friends. Like the Pennington sampler, her work includes the paired initials of some of her siblings: JP (either Jacob or Joseph) AP (Alice or Anne), SP (Sarah or Susanna), and her brother Thomas, spelt in full.[236] Other initials are probably those of friends. Pairs of initials, a feature of much work made in Scotland,

---

235 NMI, ref, DT: 1994.22.

236 Sarah Pierson's dating of the piece as September and not the 9ᵗʰ month would also have been disapproved of by strict plain Friends.

Sarah Pennington sampler, 1738, 21.5cms x 17cms. (FHLD)

can be found on the 1761 Lisburn sampler and on various Ackworth ones, but also occur on non-Quaker ones in the north of Ireland and Scotland. The alphabets on thirteen-year-old Ann Wright's sampler of 1765 are like Sarah Pennington's, and are laid out in an arbitrary way but on an old-style, long, narrow sampler. Sarah Pennington has worked her lettering and its plain lines of division in cross stitch. However, across the top are simple, stylised borders in double-running stitch which hark back to seventeenth-century work.

Lettering and literature

The first alphabets on samplers in Great Britain and Ireland seem to be early seventeenth century and were probably school exercises. Marking was not the only use for lettering. In the will of Robert Jackson, a bookseller in Meath Street, Dublin (1778), there is special mention of a folio Bible with a needlework cover and it would be interesting to know whether this involved lettering or simply an embroidered design.[237] Plain Quakers eschewed religious images and focussed on alphabets and text. Literacy was very important for Protestants, and religious pieces of a suitably uplifting nature were often worked, as in the case of the following five text samplers from the second half of the eighteenth century. These are much shorter than the long band samplers of earlier times and all have a border completely surrounding the words, a practice which suggests a more consciously pictorial approach. Work of this nature was not usually a school exercise, but was done in the evening in the girls' free time as a pleasurable activity and an outlet for more creative skills.

In 1761 Lydia Mellor stitched *Remember thy Creator*, a religious poem by the popular hymn-writer Isaac Watts loosely based on Ecclesiastes XII. The text is in two columns, a format popular from the 1720s, which reflects the shape of the wooden tablets upon which the Lord's Prayer and the Ten Commandments were displayed in Protestant churches.[238] English samplers using this format often had a pair of flying angels blowing trumpets at the top, but in this instance there are two butterflies with a colourful satin-stitched flower in the centre. At first glance, Lydia's stylised floral arcaded border framing the whole appears simple and symmetrical. On looking more closely

one can find at least five or six different flowers including the rose, carnation and tulip. She omits Watts' last depressing verse, using the space for her name, date and a floral sprig, and introduces a tiny scrolling stem with buds to divide all this from the text. The net result has considerable charm. She probably brought it with her from England when her family came to take charge of the first official Friends School in Ireland at Edenderry, and today it remains in the care of her descendants in Ireland.

At Edenderry in 1769 Deborah Newenham (b.1755), the daughter of George Newenham, a very rich Cork merchant, and Elizabeth Pim, used black silk to stitch Elizabeth Carter's poem *On a Watch*. In contrast to Lydia Mellor's stylised floral arcade she has a glorious surrounding border of freely drawn flowers worked in polychrome silks on white satin. Naturalistic flowers were becoming fashionable in the second half of the eighteenth century and were worked in long and short satin and stem stitch.

The majority of surviving Quaker samplers have more stylised floral borders, usually in cross stitch. In 1795 at the age of eighteen Sarah Fisher,

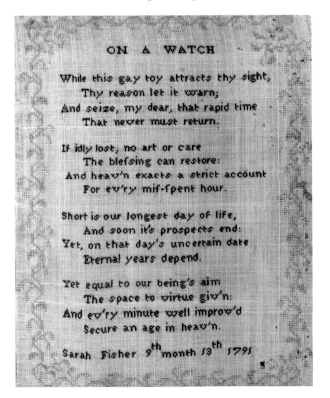

Sarah Fisher sampler, 1795, 21.5cms x 17.5cms.
(Private collection)

[237] Goodbody, 1967, p.145.
[238] Humphrey, 1997 p.64.

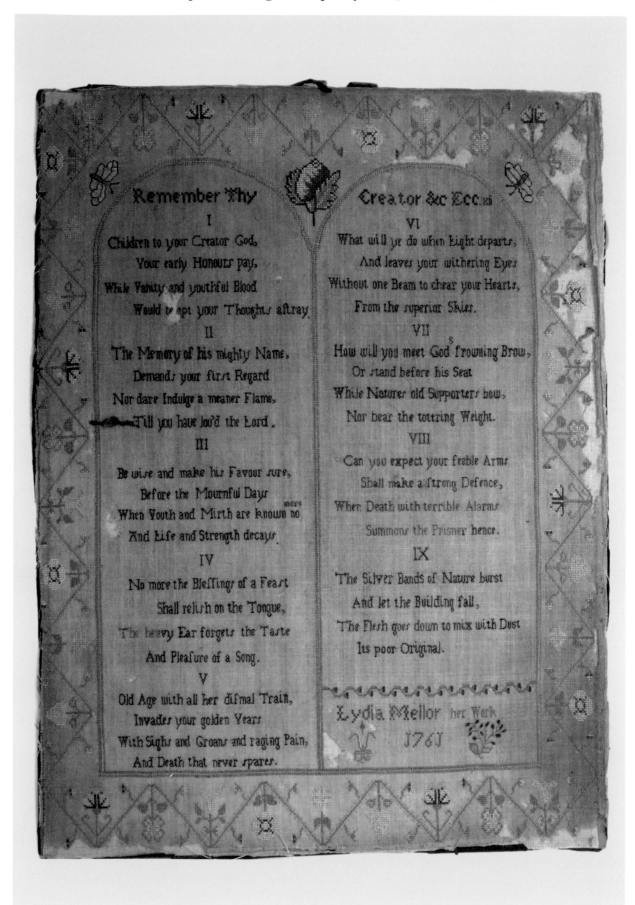

Lydia Mellor Sampler, 1761, 41.5cms x 31cms.(Private collection)

Deborah Newenham sampler, 1769. (Private collection)

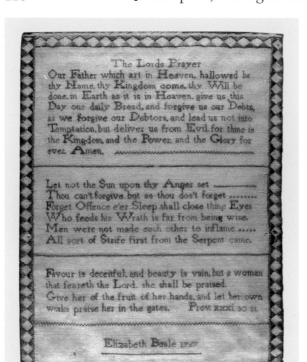

Elizabeth Beale sampler, 1767, 25cms x 18cms. (FHLD)

a great-granddaughter of William Edmondson, stitched *On a Watch* in black with a monochrome surround of a simple leaf-and-bud design executed in pale green silk. This precedes the earliest known example of this poem on an English sampler which, according to Colby, dates from 1796.[239]

A geometric border in satin stitch frames Elizabeth Beale's visually very satisfying monochrome sampler of 1767 worked in blue silk.[240] Two of her texts are from the King James Bible: The Lord's Prayer and Proverbs, ch.31 v. 30-31. In the text from Proverbs, King Lemuel's mother says princes must abstain from drunkenness, judge fairly, and plead the cause of the poor and needy. Then follows a beautiful description of the ideal wife. A wise woman, she is equally competent at buying a field to plant a vineyard or at managing the household, and she is superb at spinning and weaving. The third text is a paraphrase of 'Let not the Sun go down upon thy Wrath' and is in rhyme. Metrical versions of psalms and other biblical texts were a device

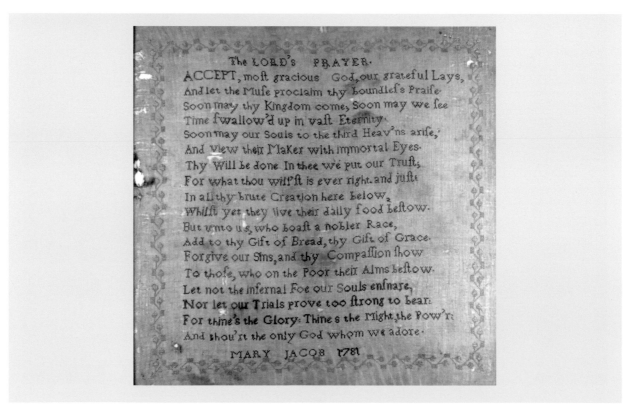

Mary Jacob sampler, 1781, 35cms x 35cms. (FHLD)

239 Colby, 1964, p.248. Carter's poems were often included in anthologies. Friends generally appreciated poetry, even if they did not approve of novels, and FHLD holds several such volumes inscribed with the names of their eighteenth-century Quaker owners (and sometimes succeeding ones).

240 Elizabeth Beale was the daughter of Caleb Beale and Margaret Pim, earliest known owners of the stumpwork in FHLD.

On Silent Worship.

What tho' no Object strike upon the Sight,
Thy sacred Presence is an inward Light,
What tho' no Sound should penetrate the Ear,
To list'ning Faith the Voice of Truth is clear,
Sincere Devotion wants no outward Shrine,
The Centre of an humble Soul is thine.
Here may I worship and here may'st thou place
Thy Seat of Glory, and thy Throne of Grace,
Yea fix, if Christ mine advocate appear,
The strict Tribunal of thy Justice there,
Let each vain Thought and each impure Desire,
Meet in thy Wrath with a consuming Fire,
Whilst the kind Rigours of a righteous Doom,
All selfish Pride and filthy Lusts consume,
Thou too canst raise (tho' punishing for Sin,)
The Joys of peaceful penitence within.
Thy Justice and thy Mercy both are sweet,
Thou mak'st our Suff'rings and Salvation meet,
Befall me then whatever God shall please,
His Wounds are healing and his Griefs give ease,
He is the true Physician of the Soul,
Applies the Med'cine that can make it whole.
I'll do, I'll suffer, whatsoe'er he wills,
I see his aim thro' all these transient Ills,
'Tis to infuse a salutary Grief,
To fit the Mind for absolute Relief,
Till purg'd from every false and finite Love,
Dead to the World, alive to things above,
The Soul renew'd as in it's first form'd Youth,
Shall worship God in Spirit and in Truth. Eliza Pike

Eliza Pike sampler c.1790, 45cms x 25cms. (FHLD)

Long samplers

In the seventeenth century samplers were usually long and narrow, but in the eighteenth tended to become shorter and wider. However, the old-fashioned long format such as we find with the Fenns continued with some Quaker girls even into the nineteenth century. The work of elderly relatives or teachers may well have been used as models. We know for example that there were bags of old samplers hanging up in Molly Webster's dame school in Ballitore. Both Jane Pim and Eliza Pike made good use of the long shape for pieces of text. Apart from working three alphabets and a few simple divisions in soft red and green, Jane has fifteen lines of Penn's advice on simplicity of dress and regard for others. Eliza Pike's austere sampler has thirty lines of a poem *On Silent Worship*, stitched in black silk within a surround of two simple lines.[241]

The following long samplers executed between 1782 and 1837 give an idea of the variety that existed. They are not plain and, with one exception, are definitely colourful. None of them was made at schools under Quarterly Meetings; all are a little old-fashioned and the alphabets used are mostly the basic ones. Several also incorporate short pieces of verse.

Sarah Lovell's 1782 monochrome sampler is finely worked in dark blue silk and has a delicate eyelet alphabet. A feature that is not usually found with Irish Friends is the depiction of a scene. Standing in her garden is a lady wearing the fashionable white muslin or cambric apron of the time. On either side of a fine house is an urn supporting a flower and two facing birds (a vestige of the Tree of Life motif). A little curly-tailed dog stands stiff-legged and a rather dopey peacock contemplates the date.

also employed by Presbyterians and served as a mnemonic aid. A sampler from the Free School in Youghal dated 1828 has a brief rhyming version of the ten commandments, whilst another version of The Lord's Prayer in rhyming couplets was worked by Mary Jacob in 1781 and placed within a monochrome floral border so stylised as to be almost geometric.

[241] There are two possible Eliza Pikes. On the back of the frame is written 'Left by her mother to Maria Grubb nee Garrat'.

Jane Pim sampler, 1788-9, 54cms x 21cms.
(FHLD)

Sarah Lovell sampler, 1782, 55cms x 20cms.
(NMI)

Far more colourful is Ann White's work done at the age of six in 1786.[242] She used the convention of changing the colour after each pair of letters, a practice which can be seen on a number of other pieces This one is 54cms x 30cms, and contains a variety of different bands. Using worsted thread in a wide variety of colours, the designs are worked on a linen ground and seem at the same time to look back to old motifs and forward to alphabets with decorative divisions and pieces of text. The floral

arcaded frame is stylised, with an idiosyncratic but delightfully random choice of colours. Within this surround are various bands including two with moral poems and two with alphabets. The first alphabet is in eyelet stitch, as are the division lines above and below. The other alphabet and its divisions are also worked in a single stitch, in this case cross stitch.[243] Satin stitch is used on the flowers in the arcaded border and for the saw-toothed division.

---

[242] Ann White (1782-1869). She married Thomas Waring and their daughter Elizabeth married the grandson of Elizabeth Pim. Both Anne White's sampler and Elizabeth Pim's medallion sampler remained in the family until the 1990s when they were donated to FHLD.

[243] Crawford, 1989, p.26.

Ann White sampler, 1786, 54cms x 30cms.
(FHLD)

Bands from Ann White; seventeenth-century
English sampler; Azemmour work - all based on
a Renaissance design

One broad band has a pair of stylised trees with, between them, a distinctly plump bird sitting on a diminutive vase or urn, while another large bird is placed between two odd flowers. What is unexpected is a very credible stag, surprisingly similar to the one in the stumpwork already described, which almost certainly had its origins in earlier pattern books.[244] Another very old pattern is the repeating design of two birds and a flower (here a carnation) in the very narrow border above Ann White's name. Italian Renaissance in origin, this pattern can be found right across Europe from Dutch samplers to Hungarian household linen, and even in Azemmour, Morocco, where it was brought by Jewish refugees from Spain at end of the fifteenth century.[245]

Simplified bands are a feature of six-year-old Jane Simmons' sampler of 1788. Working on linen scrim, a loose-woven fabric, she too changed the colour of thread after every two letters when stitching her alphabets. Cross and eyelet are the main stitches, with double running to outline the leaves of the top strawberry border. Individual strawberries near the date are alternately reversed in a repeat pattern, such as can be found on upholstery. The strawberry, which often appears as a meadow plant in medieval paintings of the Virgin and Child, later continued as a much-loved sampler pattern and by the nineteenth century had become one of the most hackneyed and copied of border designs.[246]

An arcaded strawberry band, followed by alphabets and a poem extolling the virtues of a good homemaker, occupies the upper part of ten-year-old Jane Richardson's work of the 1790s

---

[244] As recently as 2003 this motif was still available as a design for a cushion in Austria. (See Erlbacher, 2003, Teil 3, p.42.)
[245] See Paine, 1990, p.31, no.86, and Goldenberg, 2000, p.8.
[246] Colby, 1964, pp.42-43.

Jane Simmons sampler, 1788, 54cms x 21cms.
(Private collection)

Huldah Bewley sampler, 1809, 44cms x 19.5cms.
(FHLD)

(the final figure of the date is illegible). The lower part includes three bands of different patterns employed in upholstery. A selection of abbreviated pieces of strawberry bands appears in Huldah Bewley's sampler of 1807, and she also has the divisions favoured by Irish Quaker schoolgirls in the nineteenth century.

The popular sixteenth-century honeysuckle arcaded band worked by Blessing Fenn in 1710 appears as late as 1812, on a long sampler by Elizabeth Mee.[247] The top of this piece is occupied

by a single alphabet and the same variation of the Greek meander pattern that appears on the work of Dorcas Haynes, a London Quaker, in1720.[248] Elizabeth Mee attended a school run by a Mrs Egan, probably not a Friend, but who may have employed a Quaker teacher who used old samplers as patterns. Mee's band of alternating tulips and carnations worked in satin and cross stitch is very similar to ones found on two samplers of 1734 and 1756 in the Royal Scottish Museum and on a 1782 Dutch one.[249] While Ann White had the classic pattern-book stag, the one on the Mee sampler

[247] Other examples can be seen in Colby 1964, pp.34, no.138 and 172, no.154.
[248] The V&A reference for the Caitlin sampler is T.22-1955. That for the Haynes one in the Fitzwilliam Museum is T.15-1950
[249] The Royal Scottish Museum references are 1962.1056 and 1922.543. and the V&A reference T.283-1960.

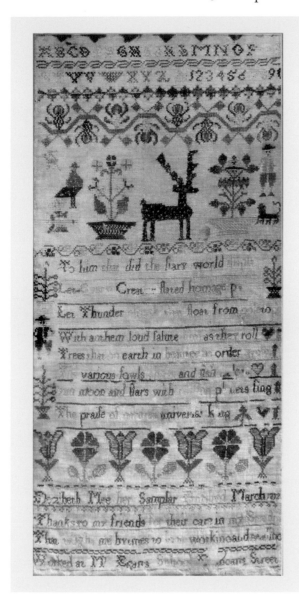

Elizabeth Mee sampler, 1812, 64cms x 30cms.
(Private collection)

M. Peat sampler, 1837, 42 x 21cms.
(Private collection)

is rather more schematic. Placed in the centre, it is flanked by two Tree of Life plants, but the framing device of a pair of birds has been reduced to a vestigial bird on the left. A little dog with a curly tail, that we find on some other samplers, provides a detail that possibly reflects the youthful enthusiasm of the maker. A curious feature is two little men in breeches and big hats. Such figures were unusual on a Quaker sampler but may have been picked up from a piece of Dutch or English work. In a centrally-placed poem, each word is in a different colour.

Some fifty years after Sarah Lovell's work, two highly stylised peacocks, guarding a basket of flowers or fruit, can be found at the base of

M. Peat's long sampler of 1837. This treatment of the peacocks with tails in pride, the feathers treated as sticks surmounted by a circle representing the 'eye', is often found in Scotland, as are the pairs of initials (possibly those of family members or friends). The Peats were a more southern family, but this does suggest some more direct connection with Scotland (possibly via Ulster). As well as alphabets the Peat sampler has the earlier classic band of arcaded carnations and there are single flowers, upholstery diamonds and a small curly-tailed dog scampering off.

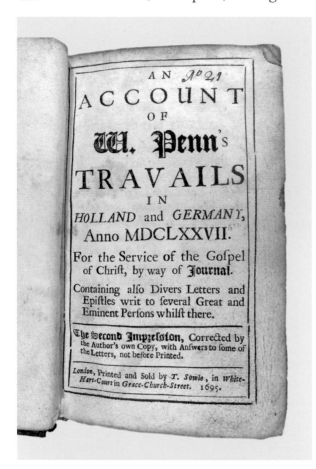

Title page, William Penn's *Travails*, 1695,
employing a large variety of typefaces.   (FHLD)

Anthony Benezet *Spelling book*, "Samplar letters",
1801 edition. (Swarthmore)

Alphabets and the development of scripts

After the establishment of the Friends' boarding schools, samplers developed certain more identifiable characteristics. In the Irish schools many of the girls obviously took a delight in producing a great variety of scripts and division designs. This emphasis on the execution of the lettering became a distinctive feature of the Irish Quaker schools, where a wider range of scripts was employed than was common in Friends' schools in England. To understand how this developed it is necessary to look briefly at the history of both handwriting and printing in Western Europe as well as the stitching techniques practised.

In the Roman Empire square capitals and rustic capitals were the scripts for specially valued books, with the uncial being favoured for Christian manuscripts. Other documents and letters used a quickly-written hand, the informal Roman cursive which, when mixed with the uncial, led to the development of the half-uncial. With the collapse of the Roman Empire Ireland became a centre of learning and the Irish half-uncial was used for the illuminated gospels of the Book of Kells, thought to have been written on the island of Iona. The liberal tradition of Celtic scholarship that went on to develop in Northumbria was brought by Alcuin of York to the court of Charlemagne, where the half-uncial evolved into the Caroline minuscule.[250]

In Italy, with the renaissance of learning, scholars (humanists) searched in libraries for forgotten Latin authors and copied the Caroline book-hand. This neo-Caroline script was then chosen for printing and formed the basis of the lower-case letters used today. The capital letters, on the other hand, were borrowed from inscriptions on ancient Roman monuments.[251] The Gothic script of the Middle Ages was a precise, angular, compressed version of the Caroline miniscule. In Germany, Gutenberg, who is said to have invented

---

[250] See Fairbank, 1949, p.10-11.
[251] Ibid, pp.8-13.

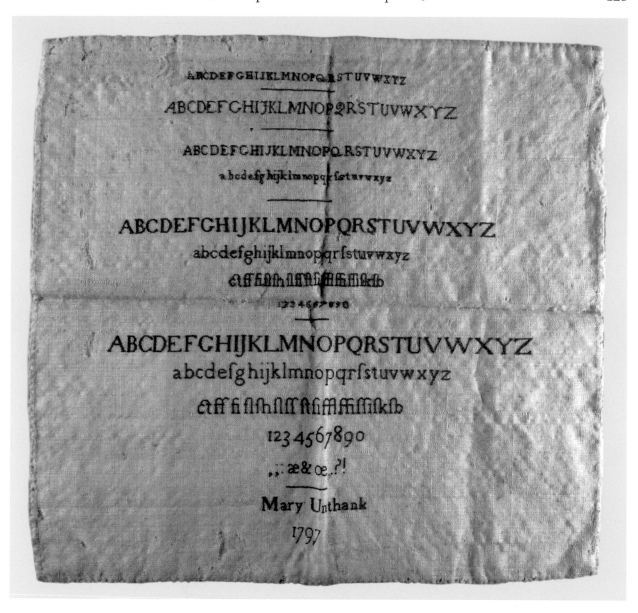

Mary Unthank sampler, 1797, 25.5cms x 26.5cms. (FHLD)

moveable type for printing around 1450, based his typeface on the Gothic book-hand.

The 1595 London printing of the Geneva Bible has Roman typeface for the introduction and the main text in Gothic, also known as Black Letter.[252] Gradually Roman type became standard, but Gothic continued into the eighteenth century for the titles of popular literature and can be found in such places as chapbooks, printed tracts and early editions of *Pilgrim's Progress*. In many cases a surprising variety of type-faces appears on title pages. A very wide range of scripts can be found on Irish samplers, whereas ones from Ackworth and York are generally limited to a combination of Roman capital letters with basic lower-case ones in cross stitch.

A slightly surprising source of lettering is Anthony Benezet's *Pennsylvania Spelling Book*. Benezet (1713-1784) came of a Huguenot family that emigrated to London in 1715 to avoid the persecution that followed the revocation of the Edict of Nantes, and then settled in Philadelphia, where he became a Quaker and an important educator. His spelling book was widely used in Ireland where a sixth edition was printed in Dublin in 1800 by John Gough, the son of the schoolmaster.

[252] A copy of this edition is held by FHLD. The Geneva Bible was also the first cheaply produced Bible in a portable format and consequently it would have been familiar to many early Friends.

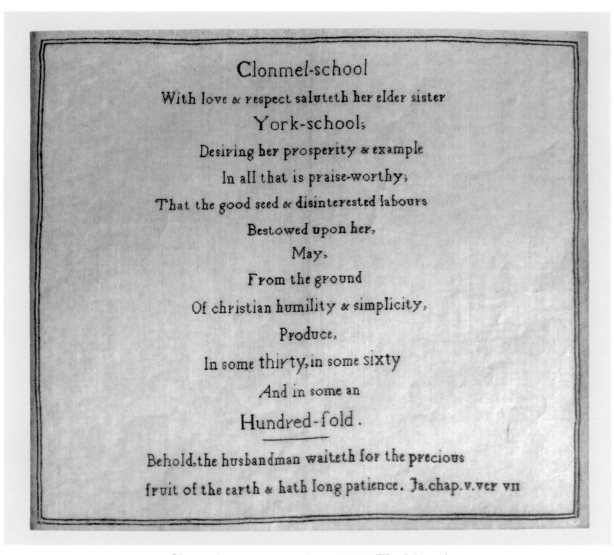

Clonmel greeting sampler, c.1789. (The Mount)

Benezet's 1782 (revised) edition, in addition to the standard Roman alphabet, contained a page of 'Samplar Letters' for embroidery and this served as a model for letters on samplers, both Quaker and non-Quaker.[253] This seems to have inspired what Naomi Tarrant saw as a particularly Irish type of lettering and Heather Crawford also noted that it was much more popular in Ireland than in the rest of the British Isles.[254] Crawford thought it was of German origin. It is possible that it may have come from Dutch and German settlers in Pennsylvania and been adopted by Benezet. The earliest example found by Crawford is dated 1813, but at Mountmellick it was already in use by 1790 and would later appear in the Kildare Place work.

Clonmel school and simplicity

Friends placed great emphasis on literacy, seriousness and plainness and this was a fundamental concern when Sarah Grubb, who had been one of the founders of York School, opened Clonmel School (Suir Island) in 1787. Initially both schools stressed the importance of plain sewing well-executed, without either material or time being wasted on the unnecessary. Their early alphabet samplers are remarkably elegant with a superb sense of lay-out. At Suir Island Mary Unthank worked hers in red silk, a colour also used for marking, and several other very similar samplers still exist. Heather Crawford notes that samplers stitched entirely in red thread were common in the Isle of Man, while Ackworth and York schools used black silk.

[253] Ring, 1993, p.287.
[254] Crawford, 1989, p.88.

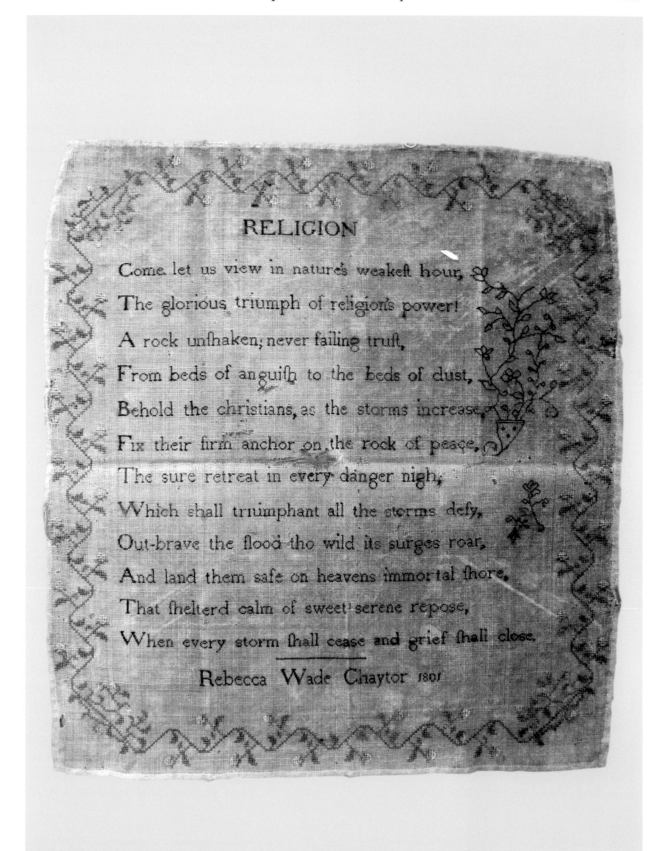

Rebecca Wade Chaytor, sampler, "Religion", 1801, 33cms x 30cms.

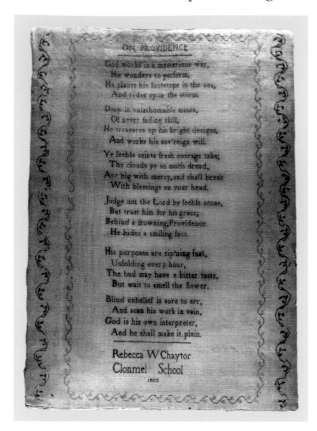

Rebecca Wade Chaytor, sampler,
"On Providence" 1803, 40cms x 26cms. (FHLD)

Black silk on cream linen was used for a
greeting sampler, unfortunately undated, made
at Suir Island and sent to York School (today's
Mount School) where it is still kept. The beauty
of this monochrome piece of work lies in its sheer
simplicity. The girls of York school in turn sent one
to Clonmel which read:

> Esther Tuke and her Children Salute Sarah
> Grubb and her helpers. The Girls of York School
> Who have the pleasure working this salutation
> For their valued friend S.R.Grubb   Love to her
> assistants and pupils at Clonmel School   York
> 4th month 1789.[255]

Rebecca Jones, who spent a week at Clonmel
School, where the pupils became much attached to
her, received a sampler and valued it enough to have

it framed and hung in her chamber. The wording in
this case was: 'Clonmell School To Rebecca Jones
of Philadelphia On her return from a long and
arduous visit to the Churches of the People called
Quakers In Europe: Sendeth greeting'.[256]

When the English Quaker schools used
divisions and borders, they favoured very simple
monochrome designs. A border with a campanula
or bellflower is found at Ackworth, at Westtown
School, Philadelphia, and also at York School. It
is therefore hardly surprising to find it copied at
Clonmel School where Anne Walpole, in 1792,
chose it to frame a religious poem.

The Clonmel school samplers were initially
distinguished by their extreme simplicity. In 1799
at the age of 14, Sarah Goodbody's working of the
poem *Religion* consisted entirely of lettering in
black silk and could not be plainer.[257] Six years later
in this school, Rebecca Wade Chaytor framed this
same poem in a delightfully light rosebud and leaf
border, even adding a bonus of a cornucopia and a
spare flower sprig. In 1799 Ann Newsom worked
Religion with a simple flower border and fitted it
into an oval, a popular shape at this period which
can be found at Clonmel school, Ackworth and
York. The oval shape suggests a piece made with
the intention of being framed. Rebecca Chaytor
was also responsible in 1803 for executing six verses
of Cowper's hymn *God works in a mysterious way*
with exceptionally delicate monochrome columns
of leaf-and-bud to set off the text.[258]

A rare case of a group of samplers from one
family is that of the five pieces worked by the
four Moore sisters in Clonmel. These illustrate
the development from plain to decorative work.
Their mother Susanna (1771-1805), a daughter
of the wealthy grocer Benjamin Grubb (1727-
1802), almost certainly attended Clonmel School.
She was extremely pious and, after a careful
upbringing, married James Moore, a prosperous
miller, by whom she had five daughters. In 1805,
on her deathbed, she expressed the desire that her

---

[255] FHLD, Portfolio 5a, no.11.

[256] Jones,1849, p.176. After the greeting the wording on the sampler continues: 'After a frequent and sympathetic conflict with
this her endeared friend and instructive companion, SARAH R. GRUBB, rejoices in HOPE that by the POWER OF
OMNIPOTENCE, and in the covenant of love and life, She is now restored to the bosom of the Church in AMERICA, and
to the precious society of her most beloved and constant friend, in the Tribulation and Consolation of the Gospel, Hannah
Catherall - Eleventh Month, 1788.'

[257] Reproduced in Feller, 2012, p.38.

[258] Five verses of Cowper's hymn were framed with a bellflower border by Hannah Wigham at Ackworth in 1786 (reproduced in
Humphrey, 2006, p.21).

Ann Newsom sampler, 'Religion', 1799, oval, 34cms x 31cms. (FHLD)

children should be 'educated in plainness'.[259] The small sampler stitched that year by the five-year-old Charlotte reflects this Quaker way of thinking.

Later, in 1816, Charlotte's name heads the signatures of twenty girls of Clonmel school who wrote to Lindley Murray expressing their indebtedness 'for his many useful publications, and particularly for his last one, entitled, *A Compendium of Religious Faith and Practice* [...] a section of the volume [...] they weekly commit to memory, and so doing feel much satisfaction, and a hope that it will conduce to their present benefit'.[260] Murray's charming reply is positive but also points out how privileged they are. Charlotte herself later assisted as an unpaid governess at Newtown in 1825, and her name crops up again as a helper in the Famine soup kitchen in Clonmel.

In 1802, at the age of seven, Charlotte's sister Anne worked a religious poem framed by a single cross-stitched line. The other three pieces by the Moore girls have all had their dates neatly cut out. This practice was not uncommon. As three of the sisters remained spinsters in Clonmel, they may not have wanted their ages known. Anne married Charles Frederick Wakefield of Moyallon in the north of Ireland and left her work behind with her sister

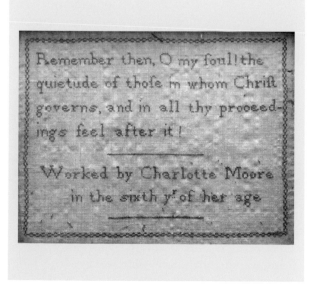

Charlotte Moore sampler, 16cms x 21cms, 1805. (Private collection)

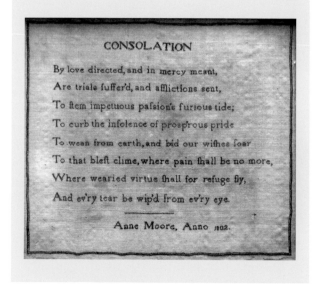

Anne Moore sampler, "Consolation", 21cms x 23cms, 1802. (Private collection)

[259] Ahern, 2009, p.218.
[260] FHLD, Portfolio 4, nos.38 and 39.

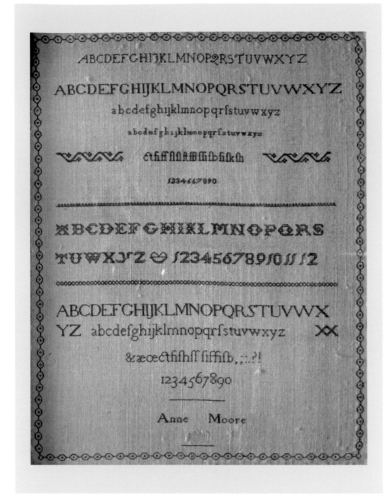

Anne Moore, monochrome alphabet sample in blue silk, 32cms x 24cms, date removed. (Private collection)

Susannah, who married William Fennell in 1814, and all these samplers are now with the Fennell descendants.

A second sampler by Anne is in monochrome with alphabets in blue silk thread. This has many of the hallmarks of the earlier Clonmel ones such as spacing, Roman alphabets in different sizes, ligatures, punctuation marks and numbers. However, Anne has added the fancy alphabet of Benezet. There also two short strips of the leaf-and-bud design.

Elizabeth Moore used only Roman lettering for her alphabets and has the usual ligatures etc. Her spacing is much more cramped, but the alphabets are now in different colours. There are

two short lengths of satin-stitched saw-tooth division, and a leaf-and-bud border frames everything. This alphabet sampler is half-way between Anne's monochrome one and Mary's comparatively crowded polychrome one.

Mary Moore's sampler is much nearer the earlier ones of Mountmellick School, being well-packed with seven alphabets, including the Benezet one. Of the eight divisions and borders one is leaf-and-bud and another is a strawberry arcade set within two lines of satin-stitched saw-tooth. A different strawberry arcaded border frames everything. The bottom section in blue monochrome harks back to the York samplers, with the exception of the letter 'Q' in a hand-writing script version resembling a '2' that was popular with Irish Friends. On closer examination it is possible to discern two dogs and two birds which are so miniscule that they look like punctuation marks.[261]

Stitches and lettering

Earlier Irish Quaker samplers tend to have only one type of lettering but are executed in a large variety of stitches and colours. Ann Wright's alphabets of 1765 are in a glorious range of colours with a number of different geometric borders. Chain stitch, eyelet, three-sided and half-cross stitches are used with cross stitch.[262] Other samplers have lettering in four-sided stitch or are decorated with Holbein stitch. Satin stitch could also be used for lettering, but, so far, no existing Quaker examples are known.

Throughout the eighteenth century and up to the mid-nineteenth, eyelet-stitched block capitals appear on many Quaker (alphabet) samplers in Ireland. The eyelet stitch most frequently used for this had a 16-pointed stitch forming one hole. As well as being worked decoratively for other aspects of embroidery, including whitework, eyelet holes were made to take the laces on corsets. A much less dense eyelet stitch of eight points, which looks

---

[261] Sarah Davis, at Clonmel school in 1824, made a polychrome sampler that has many points in common with Mary Moore's sampler. An additional element is an eyelet alphabet together with a floral band such as can be found on existing Mountmellick ones after 1808.

[262] Heather Crawford's analysis is in FHLD. See also Crawford 1989, pp.23 and 126.

Elizabeth Moore sampler,33cms x 24cms,
date removed. (Private collection)

both delicate and elegant can be found on certain
Quaker samplers, including Sarah Lovell's one.[263]

The four-sided stitch was sometimes employed
for lettering and geometric borders. Heather
Crawford noted its use among nineteenth-century
northern Irish girls, and FHLD has three Quaker
examples, one circa 1810 by Jane Green and those
of Anne Wethereld (1833) and Elizabeth Sinton
(1835), both pupils at Prospect Hill (Friends
School, Lisburn). This stitch can also be found
with Maria Reeves in Waterford and with Jane
Binyon (1815) whose monochrome sampler was
probably worked in England.

The commonest stitch for lower-case alphabets
was the cross stitch, which was also the one most
used for capitals of various different alphabets, such
as the classic Roman one and the Benezet one.
These alphabets were fairly standard, apart from
the way in which 's' was written, which sometimes
appeared in the older typographic form closer to
an 'f'. One letter that differs from the Benezet
'Samplar Letters' is the capital Y where the tail

263 NMI reference DT:1994.22.

Mary Moore sampler,41cms x 24cms,
date removed. (Private collection)

curves backwards (as with the lower-case letters)
rather than pointing straight down, perhaps to
avoid confusion with V.

The marvellous 'Holbein' capitals, worked
in cross stitch and fantastically decorated with
double-running, are like something out of a
fairy-tale. This lettering is found in Friesland and
Germany, in Scotland and in Ireland, where it
may have been introduced by Presbyterian settlers.
Holbein-decorated capital letters can be found on
three Lisburn samplers (Wethereld, Sinton and
Ann Frances Murray), on three Mountmellick
ones of 1808, and also on that of Maria Reeves.

Sarah Davis sampler, 1824. 34cms x 22cms. (FHLD)

Types of lettering: eyelet, four-sided stitch, secretary, Holbein.

Jane Marion Wakefield handkerchief with ornate lettering, c.1853. (FHLD)

In contrast to the highly decorative nature of the Holbein script is the lettering based on everyday handwriting. A form that appears frequently is the so-called 'secretary script', a small sloped hand

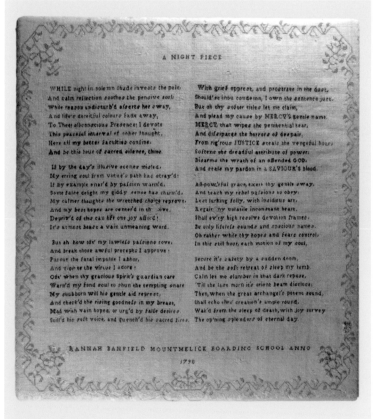

Hannah Banfield 'A night Piece', 1798, 34.5cms x 30cms. (FHLD)

used in Rome in the late sixteenth century. This was speedy to write and considered to be 'the only usual hand of England for dispatching of all manner of

business'.[264] Commercial activities required good but speedy hand-writing and this was essential for the boys, and for Quaker girls who might later run businesses or need it for record-keeping and correspondence, whether as ministers or privately.

In the late sixteenth century, with the change from engraved wood-block to copper-plate for the reproduction of manuals on hand-writing, the letter-forms became less angular. The secretary script version of capital letters sometimes appears on continental samplers as well as on those of some English charity schools, especially the Bristol Orphanages, and on Irish Quaker ones. In Irish schools this script was still being used in the copybooks of the 1950s. The special version of the letter 'Q', which looks like a '2' also dates back to the Italian secretary script and is often found both on samplers and in the writing in Friends' Minute Books, an obvious case here being the initial 'Q' of Ireland's Queen's County (today's Laois).

Gothic lettering became popular in the nineteenth century when there was a return to the 'medieval' in architecture and design. A. Wicklow, related to the Sintons, chose to sign her initials in Gothic letters, and she also worked the alphabet in this style, which is similar to what can be found in

[264] Fairbank, 1949, p.16.

Sarah Williams sampler, 1802 32cms x 25.5cms. (FHLD)

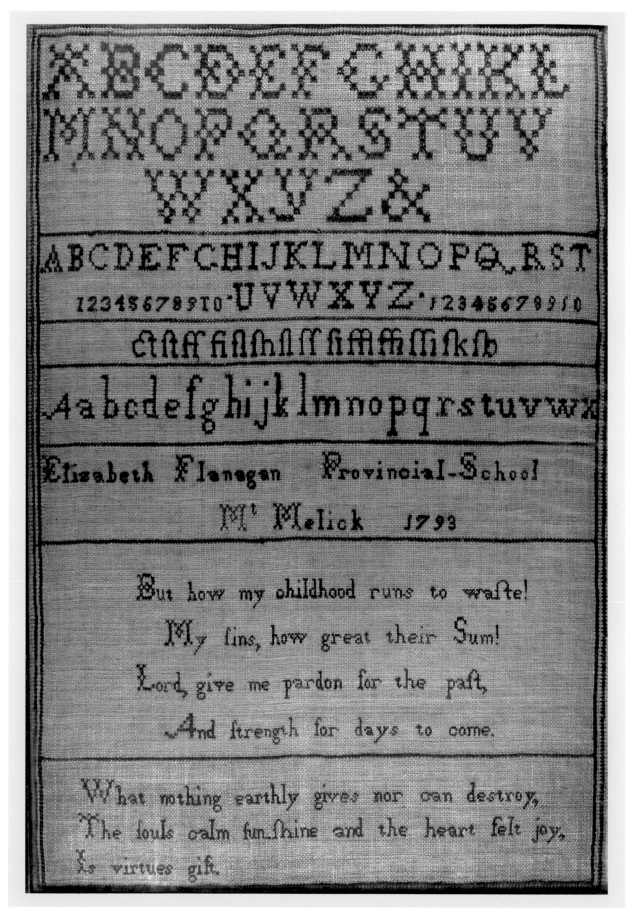

Elizabeth Flanagan monochrome sampler, 1793, 43cms x 29cms. (FHLD)

Hannah Thompson sampler, 1810, 52cms x 32cms. (Private collection)

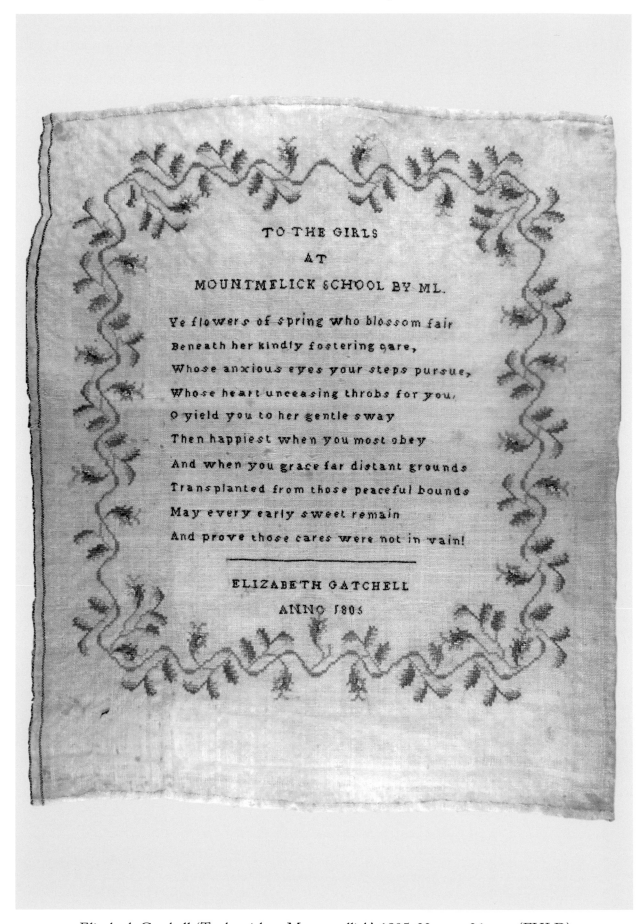

TO THE GIRLS
AT
MOUNTMELICK SCHOOL BY ML.

Ye flowers of spring who blossom fair
Beneath her kindly fostering care,
Whose anxious eyes your steps pursue,
Whose heart unceasing throbs for you,
O yield you to her gentle sway
Then happiest when you most obey
And when you grace far distant grounds
Transplanted from those peaceful bounds
May every early sweet remain
And prove those cares were not in vain!

ELIZABETH GATCHELL
ANNO 1805

Elizabeth Gatchell, 'To the girls at Mountmellick', 1805, 32cms x 26cms. (FHLD)

Sarah Walpole monochrome sampler, 1810,
41cms x 33cms. (FHLD)

Alphabets, borders and divisions
A look at the work known to have been executed at the Quarterly Meeting schools of Mountmellick and Lisburn may be useful in that it can reveal characteristics that sometimes act as indicators as to the provenance of the work. At Mountmellick, each girl is likely to have made more than one sampler, depending on how long she stayed there. Considering the hundreds of samplers made, only a very small number have survived and it is rare to find more than a single one from any girl.

Hannah Banfield's poem sampler of 1798 returned from England to Ireland in 1947, but only recently has it been discovered that in 1797 she had also made a polychrome alphabet sampler, which another relative took to South Africa. A very poor photograph shows that this piece of work is basically similar to one made by Sarah Williams five years later. One particularly interesting detail is the treatment of borders and divisions which, as Crawford pointed out, in Ireland tend to be either geometric or foliate.[267] Within a leaf-and-bud framing border the Banfield alphabet sampler contains about twelve divisions, one of which is a strawberry-arcaded band. Another is a Greek meander and wave pattern, variants of which were popular in Ireland, but here it is given greater importance by being placed between two lines of satin-stitched saw-tooth in a contrasting colour. Of the eight alphabets one is in eyelet stitch and another is of the Benezet type.

The Sarah Williams sampler, now in FHLD, is very like another Mountmellick sampler by Eliza Sparrow (1802) in NMI, and four similar ones are known to be now in England.[268] An earlier and simpler polychrome sampler worked by an

the DMC pattern books edited by Thérèse de Dillmont.[265] Ornate capital letters were used for marking initials on handkerchiefs and house linen such as napkins. Shortly before their marriage, John Grubb Richardson gave a set of twenty-four fine linen handkerchiefs to Jane Marion Wakefield with her initials in very fancy lettering.

The ligature is another typographic feature that can appear on samplers, in addition to punctuation marks. The first writing-manual, printed in Rome in 1501, shows such pairs of connected letters.[266] Five monochrome alphabet samplers worked in the 1780s at Ackworth School include lines of ligatures. In Ireland they can be found from the 1790s onwards and there is one as late as 1844, worked by Ann Green at Moira School, Co Down.

---

[265] Such an alphabet can be seen on an Austrian alphabet sampler of 1865 in Hänsel, 2003, p,27.
[266] Fairbank, 1949, p.14, pl.18.
[267] Crawford, 1989, p.19.
[268] Alicia Goodbody (1803) and Hannah Banfield (1797) are still in the possession of the families. Anne Murphy (1796) and Eliza Simmons (1800) are reproduced in Feller, 2012, pp.48 and 49.

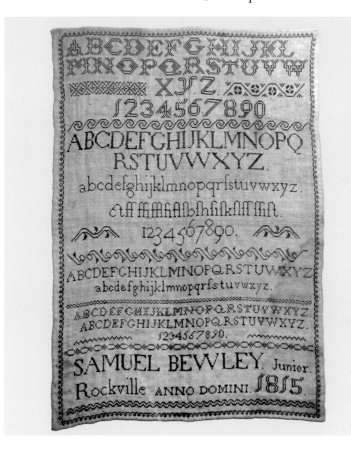

Samuel Bewley sampler, 1815 (Private collection)

Thompson in 1810. She uses nine other alphabets with a comparable number of different divisions, and includes four floral bands. The arcade structure can be seen on one, but is barely discernible on the others which are very free and fluid.

A couple of years earlier, in 1808, Margaret Watson had worked a sampler that was almost identical to the Thompson one. She re-utilised one floral band from this sampler as a surround for a poem, An address to the Deity, which she stitched the following year. This surround had been employed in 1805 by Elizabeth Boardman and Elizabeth Gatchell to frame the verse, *To the girls at Mountmellick School by ML.* (possibly Mary Leadbeater). The Boardman and Gatchell samplers are so similar that, given the sentimentality of the period, one can imagine the two girls sitting together as they sewed and chatted.

Elizabeth Hogg in 1790, uses only five alphabets, including an eyelet one and a Benezet one, all enclosed within a leaf-and-bud border.[269]

A complete contrast to the well-packed, colourful examples above is Elizabeth Flanagan's monochrome black silk on linen (1793) where the sense of spatial arrangement carries a hint that she might have seen a Clonmel sampler. She employs only three alphabets, of which one is eyelet, and divisions and framing are managed with simple lines of cross stitch. This leaves room for two pieces of moral thoughts in rhyme. A small touch of personal frivolity lies in her choice of fancy capital letters for names and in the poems.

It is around this time that yet another alphabet appears on some samplers that are gloriously extravagant in their colourfulness and length. This is a Holbein decorated alphabet and an example can be seen worked in blue silk by Hannah

In Belfast, Eliza Byrne, a Quaker girl, chose a floral band as a surround for her undated sampler which delighted Heather Crawford: 'Her foliate border stitched in silk thread almost dances around the joyful words of her poem.'[270] On a second sampler, Eliza used another of these designs, ostensibly as a frame for her secretary script and Benezet alphabets, but in this case the scrolling background of flowers forming the surround has become an integral part of the entire piece of work. Floral bands, whether as divisions or in the form of surrounds, are not exclusive to Quaker samplers and can also be found on non-Quaker pieces in Ulster.[271]

Not everyone chose to work in colour. In 1810 Sarah Walpole at Mountmellick used black silk thread on very fine wool to make her monochrome sampler. Apart from the leaf-and-bud frame, her eleven borders and divisions are geometric, and she also employs the secretary script in addition to eyelet, Benezet and Roman alphabets.

[269] The Elizabeth Hogg in question may have been the daughter of Hubert Hogg of Edenderry, but another Elizabeth Hogg is recorded amongst the pupils in 1792. A third Elizabeth Hogg is recorded at Anne Shannon's school in1791 and so could not have made it.
[270] Crawford, 1989, pp.33 and 49.
[271] Examples are Eliza Charles (1818), in Crawford ,1989, pl.5. and Catherine McNeill 183.[last digit missing], still with the family.

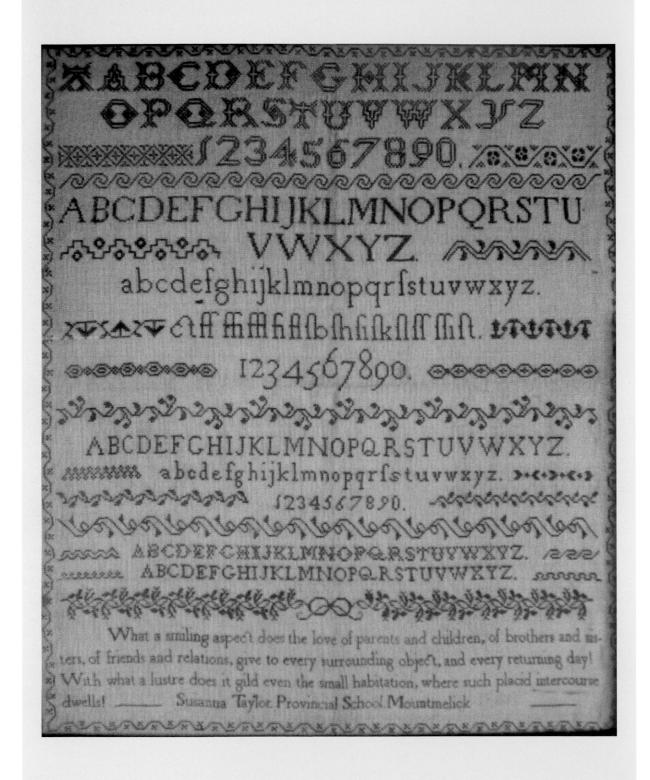

Susanna Taylor sampler, n.d. (Newtown)

Maria Reeves sampler, worked in blue silk, 181..(digit missing), 38.5cms x 33cms(Private collection)

elaborate and colourful.[273] Their father Samuel Bewley (1764-1837), one of the main movers in the setting up of the Kildare Place Society was a significant figure in early nineteenth-century Dublin business. He had his own ships and imported silk from the Levant and Italy. Through the Dublin Chamber of Commerce, he was amongst those who put pressure on parliament to end the East India Company's monopoly over the China tea trade, which was finally removed in 1833.

Virtually no samplers survive from Newtown school. To date the writer has been able to locate only one fully-authenticated piece. This is an alphabet sampler worked by Susan Hanks of Youghal, a pupil at Newtown from 1820 to 1826. Dated 1826, this sampler, still in the possession of the family but now in Amsterdam, is in the style of the colourful Mountmellick ones, and includes a fluid floral band, together with a Benezet alphabet and secretary script.

Maria Reeves is known to have been a pupil at Newtown from 1798-1803.[274] Coming from a Tipperary, family Maria may have finished her education at Clonmel School, and possibly made her sampler there, but unfortunately the last digit of the date has been unpicked, probably before her marriage in 1813. Her excellent composition and her use of monochrome in blue thread have much in common with the early alphabet samplers of Clonmel School. Unlike the latter, hers is longer than it is wide and this allowed her to insert a number of extra alphabets popular in Ireland. These include the Holbein decorated one, a Benezet one, secretary script, and block capital letters in four-sided stitch. Her divisions are patterned instead of being simple lines in cross stitch, such as were used in the early Clonmel work and at York School.

Susanna Taylor, who entered the school in 1810, also made a monochrome sampler in black and this included a floral band as well as twenty examples of geometric, leaf-and-bud and other divisions. In addition, the work contains seven alphabets, two sets of numbers, ligatures and a short piece on love within the family, but the carefully balanced spacing and use of a single colour prevent it from looking over-crowded.

Slightly simpler than Susanna's, but visually remarkable similar, is a rare example of a sampler stitched at his home in Dublin by a boy in 1815. The boy in question was the nine-year-old Samuel Bewley.[272] His sister Huldah's sampler was far more

---

[272] Samuel Bewley junior went on to become a much-respected member of the Dublin Quaker community and was particularly involved in the temperance movement.

[273] Their mother was Elizabeth Fayle (1771-1848) from Limerick, possibly related by marriage to the Mrs Fayle referred to in chapter three.

[274] Maria married Joseph John Fisher in 1813. Their daughter Margaret Hanks Fisher married Joshua Bewley, son of Samuel Bewley (senior), in 1845. In 1840 Joshua Bewley had opened the China Tea Company, later Charles Bewley & Co. Margaret was heavily involved in the business which eventually became Bewley's Oriental Cafes in 1926.

Elizabeth Sinton sampler, worked in black silk, 1835, 29.4cms x 23.75cms. (FHLD)

Anne Wethereld, sampler, worked in black silk, 1833,
29cms x 21cms. (FHLD)

Lisburn school, originally for poor Friends, like the other Committee schools, was co-educational, with the girls having needlework as an important part of their instruction. Hannah Morison's polychrome marking sampler of 1810 is now the proud possession of the Lisburn Linen museum, thanks to the generosity of an anonymous American donor. Its old-fashioned long format without a framing border contains six alphabets including the Benezet one and secretary script, as well as two lines of ligatures. In addition to three simple divisions there is a leaf-and-bud band and an example of the classic strawberry arcade band, which in this case is rigid and angular with a rather geometric appearance.

Elizabeth Sinton's monochrome sampler of 1835 has been analysed and described by Heather Crawford as 'the best example I have ever seen of Irish sampler work in any collection. A piece to be treasured!'[277] This is smaller than most, measuring only 25.5cms x 30.5cms and is worked on woollen tammy cloth of 48 threads to the inch with black silk. Sinton employed cross stitch (over one thread each way), four-sided stitch (over two threads each way) and eyelet stitch (over two threads each way). In the last alphabet the fantastic capitals are decorated using the double-running Holbein stitch (referred to by Crawford as the 'Scottish style alphabet').

Like Sinton, Anne Wethereld (1833) employed a greater variety of stitches than many girls, and a larger number of alphabets, as well as many examples of the different divisions favoured by Quaker girls. The bottom division of the Sinton sampler appears here as a framing border. This very simple design had already appeared in 1792 at Clonmel, but in Lisburn a stylised carnation head occupies the central position earlier held by a bellflower. Both girls use a Greek meander and wave pattern, which can also be found with Ann Murray, another Lisburn pupil around the same

In 1831, also in Waterford, although not at Newtown, Sarah Hutchinson worked an alphabet sampler in monochrome using blue silk and this is very similar to the Reeves one.[275] In the same year her younger sister, Jane, who was not at Newtown either, made a sampler which looks like a simpler version of that of Susan Hanks, but the quality of her work is not nearly as fine as her older sister's.[276] Sarah and Jane's mother was Jane Blain, originally from Cumberland, who had married the Waterford merchant Thomas Hutchinson in 1819. A pupil at Ackworth from 1801-1803, in her last year she made both a small text sampler and a medallion piece with octagons and half octagons. The text piece is still in the Ackworth collection, while the other is now in the Ulster Folk museum. It is unusual to know of four samplers from the one family, and all are surprisingly different.

[275] The Sarah Hutchinson sampler is now in America.
[276] Jane Hutchinson's sampler is now in NMI, ref. DT: 1995. 242.
[277] A full analysis of this sampler has been deposited at FHLD by Heather Crawford.

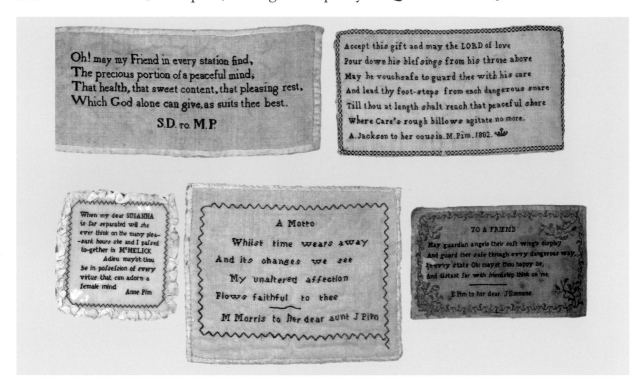

Token of love samplers. (FHLD)

time. This serves both as a framing device and, in a couple of cases, as a division. Murray separates her ten alphabets from a poem and there is a strongly marked border of black leaves, producing a monochrome working of the glorious technicolour floral band used at Mountmellick by Watson (1808) and Thompson (1810).

Tokens of love

The sampler sent from the girls of Clonmel to York school has already been mentioned. Some pieces of this type carry the words 'a token of love' and their function was broadly similar to a hand-made greeting card. There is a little group of such friendship samplers in the FHLD collection. Mostly quite small, they range from 7cms x 11cms to 23cms x 12cms. The names or the initials of the maker and the recipient are accompanied by an expression of friendship or love, and maybe a very short poem. Usually done in cross stitch, these seem to have been popular little gifts made by girls, especially in the late eighteenth century and early nineteenth, a period of much sentimental affection or 'sensibility'. They used their skills to make something special for their friends and the few materials needed were easily available. By the 1840s a popular development was the commercially-produced punched-card book mark mounted on satin ribbon. This had to be overstitched, but required little skill. Producing

Sarah Grubb sampler, c.1790, 17cms x 11cms. (FHLD)

an effect similar to that of the 'token of love', the girls worked the sentiments expressed in cross stitch. Several examples of these dating from the 1860s can be found in FHLD. In the twentieth century girls no longer learnt embroidery, and a new fashion was the autograph albums in which they inscribed verses.

The Ackworth samplers sometimes include a token of love motif, or a simpler dedication, as in a 1796 sampler where 'EW to A TUKE' has been worked, in this case without any surround.[278] In the Sarah Harris sampler there are two attempts at working out a token of love design. One reads 'Love for love' and is surrounded by flowers, the other, 'A token of love to E G 1788', has birds, hearts and flowers.

Mary Creeth remembered the play hours at Lisburn School:

> We worked lines of poetry on 'Bolton' [bolting] as presents for friends. We also knitted pin cushions (for friends) in sampler patterns, and some of these which I still have in my possession attest to the endurance of the colours of the worsted of those days. I very much enjoyed knitting them, and for one girl - Jane Bell - I made 19! I was favoured too by Sarah (née Dickenson) Douglas with permission to knit one, oval in shape, for her to present to Sarah Lynes Grubb (now a well-known Quaker minister). The pin cushions were always washed after being knit, then when still a little damp were stretched on a ball before being stitched into shape. So devoted were some of us for a while to this work that we often sat up in our beds to knit while the others were asleep.[279]

Pincushions were useful gifts, and, as dresses were commonly fastened with pins, could provide a daily reminder of the sentiments of the maker. Decorative little pincushions are known to have been made in the early eighteenth century. Besides being presented as gifts, they could be sold as fancy work. Hannah Robinson, who attended Ackworth from 1807-1809, records that 'the amusements were chiefly knitting pincushions in silk and beads, and skipping'.[280] An Ackworth girl's pincushion, now in Auckland Museum New Zealand has a

medallion design earlier used by Elizabeth Pim.[281] In Lisburn, Mary Creeth copied patterns from samplers, knitting in fine worsted of various colours. The skill to knit clocks on stockings could be turned to good account for patterned pincushions and purses.

A very small number of these pincushions has survived. Even rarer are knitted Friendship samplers. One that carries the legend 'a Token of Love from Sarah Grubb to Hannah Grubb' dates from about 1790 and would have been made in or around Clonmel where the Grubb family had mills.[282] Initially, identification of the maker seemed simple, but, as it then transpired that there were five Sarahs and four Hannahs in the immediate family group at the time, this has proved impossible. One Hannah Grubb was a great friend of Sarah Lynes Grubb, but a letter in FHLD shows that this Sarah was most unenthusiastic about knitting.

Worked in stocking stitch, the Grubb sampler employs the same technique as for knitting clocked stockings. Despite being hung carefully out of direct light it has faded over the years. The Token of Love inscription is knitted in white on a pale-yellow ground. The white silk used for lettering and parts of the motifs only became visible after the frame had been removed. A different silk used for much of the design has retained something of its original colour, which may have been a darkish brown. On very close examination it is possible to distinguish a number of classic motifs enclosed within a framing border.

The central, highly stylised Tree of Life motif, much faded, is barely recognisable as such. It is just possible to make out five white flowers, a tulip, two roses (?) and two carnations symmetrically arranged. Two peacocks, similar to those on the Elizabeth Pim sampler, flank the central tree motif. On either side of this there are, alternately in brown or white, five fleurs-de-lis, a motif that can be found on samplers from the sixteenth to the nineteenth century (including the 1761 Lisburn one).

---

278 Reproduced in Humphrey, 2006, p.149.
279 JFHS 18, no.2, 1922, p.53. Probably this was in summer when there was daylight till late.
280 Humphrey, 2006, p.16.
281 Ibid, p.167.
282 This sampler has been given to FHLD by the Grubb family in Tipperary.

Versions of Tree of Life motif: Sarah Grubb;
Russian ritual cloth.

Slovak border repeat design.

The significance of the Tree of Life has already been discussed, but the Grubb sampler provides an excellent example of how designs can modify over the years as they are copied and reinterpreted in different contexts. The centrally-placed vase has now become a container with a heart in it and the lower part or base seems to have morphed into a simplified triangular plant root. The motif of a vase/heart/tree with an uneven number of flowers, and flanking birds is relatively common in Germany and Eastern Europe.[283] A Russian ritual cloth has a Tree with roots and above them a heart from which spring the flowers.[284] A large heart, supported by a vase out of which grow two pomegranates, and which is framed by pair of flowers and is surmounted by a large carnation appears on the highly stylised border of a nineteenth-century embroidered cloth from Slovakia[285], whilst the central element of the design on the border of a Hungarian linen funeral sheet of 1766 is an ornate column that looks like iron work, starting with a vase and ending with a huge carnation.[286] It would be interesting to know how some of these variants of traditional motifs came into the Irish Quaker repertoire, but one cannot discount the possibility of pieces being seen when Quakers travelled abroad on ministry.

Dresden Whitework
Friends denounced extravagant fashions such as lace, which, apart from being a superfluous adornment, was extremely expensive. The few extant portraits of wealthy Quaker women do not show lace or ruffles, but they do show large triangular handkerchiefs of very fine quality covering the neck and shoulders. A form of needlework known as Dresden whitework was a kind of delicate, fine, pulled work that evolved in Germany and Friends may have found it more acceptable in that it was all-white and therefore less likely to attract disapproval. A good example, although not of Quaker provenance, is a white muslin handkerchief in Gawthorpe Hall. This has a border of leaves, each one with a different needlework filling, and some of these are the same as ones practised on the Irish Quaker Dresden samplers.[287]

---

[283] The Tree of Life as a vase of flowers flanked by birds was among patterns from European books introduced in Ramallah from the late nineteenth century when Quakers founded the school there and also promoted embroidery (Paine, 1990, pl.91). At Ramallah School, as a teacher from 1927 to 1935, and later in Amman, Phyllis Sutton, studied and encouraged the using of ancient Palestinian embroidery motifs. (Gostelow, 1975 p. 157).

[284] Paine, 1990, Pl.87.

[285] Danglova, 2011, p.44. This is worked in red thread, There is just one pair of peacocks but a number of goats are also included.

[286] Hofer and Fel, 1994, no.235. This is embroidered in brown crewel and is also extremely stylised. Arranged amongst the carnations of various sizes are three pairs of peacocks and two pelicans.

[287] In Philadelphia in 1771 Jane Humphreys, a Quaker girl of eleven, used this technique on her sampler. Her basket of flowers includes the rose, carnation and tulip, which like the leaves, have different forms of pulled work to give them interest. This sampler is now in the Philadelphia Museum of Art. See Gostelow, 1975, p.278.

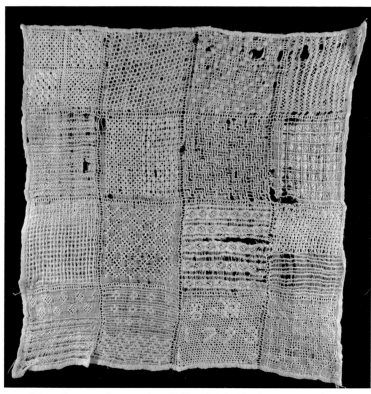

Dresden work sampler, B.R. 1793, 27.5cms x 28.5cms.
(Private collection)

Three Dresden whitework samplers of Irish Quaker provenance are known. These are fairly similar, almost square, and made of a loosely woven fabric. Marked into sixteen squares, each compartment shows different patterns of pulled work, stitched with white thread, and suitable for embellishing clothing. Often combined with drawn- and cut-work or embroidery in white thread it could produce the effect of lace, but was far less costly. By 1750 Dresden work was taught in many schools for young ladies, and the celebrated Mrs Delany is known to have used this technique to make a set of ruffles in 1769.[289] In 1769 MB (Beale?), a Quaker, worked her sampler on a linen ground and this is now in NMI. Eliza Pike made her sampler in 1792, while another by 'BR' in 1793 belongs to descendants of the Goff family in Wexford.

The making of Dresden work began with the drawing of designs onto a piece of coloured card or stiff paper. These might include exotic flowers (another outlet for artistic skills). The muslin or fine linen cambric was stretched over the card and tacked onto it. The outlines of the design would be visible through the fine fabric and could then be worked in running, chain or stem stitch. Using a blunt needle and regular counted-thread stitches pulled very tight, the weave was distorted to form holes to imitate lace. This might be further embellished with added needlework. Another method was to draw the design directly onto the fabric and put it in an embroidery hoop for working. Standards were frequently very high, even amongst amateurs. The white 'laced' aprons worn when visiting were most probably made in this way. Dorothea Herbert, when calling on the landed Roe family in Rockwell (Co Tipperary) in 1790, found the daughters involved in making 'laced' aprons.[288] The apron that was offered to Sarah Dillwyn when she came to Friends Yearly Meeting in London in 1784 was regarded as a necessary costume accessory, but probably would not have been laced.

The ready availability of fine cottons, linens and muslins was ideal for the very simple white chemise dresses popular in the 1790s, and Dresden work, being subtle, was an obvious form of decoration for the gay Quaker.

Darning samplers

Darning is basically a way of repairing a piece of clothing by weaving threads across the hole, and in modern times is best known for mending socks. The mending and maintenance of fabric was an essential part of the running of any household and extended to such things as strengthening worn areas of sheets, towels and clothing. Darning exercises were taught and sometimes added to alphabet samplers, but towards the end of the eighteenth century whole samplers begin to appear showing the different types of darn needed according to the type of fabric. The earliest darning samplers are thought to have been made in the Netherlands, Germany and Denmark.

Rebecca Goff, was painted wearing a fashionable dress of fine white muslin. By the age of ten, at a private boarding school in Cork, she had already learnt the skills for mending such a flimsy fabric. Rebecca's own darning sampler of white thread on a very fine, firm, white linen gauze shows that

288 Herbert, 1988, p.281.
289 Marsh, 2006, p.111.

Eliza Pike, Dresden work sampler, 1793.
(Photo in FHLD)

executed in plain darning with added accents of button-holed eyelets for the flower centres, fine chain-stitched outlining, and the veins of leaves in Bokhara couching. A very similar one, most probably from the same private school, was made by Ann Murphy of Cork (1803), who, at the age of five in 1796, had worked an alphabet sampler in Mountmellick Boarding School.[290] Two other similar darning samplers, probably from the same school in Cork, are those of Catherine Kent (1802) and Ann Kent (1811).[291]

Darns, whether plain, twill or damask, required a high degree of skill so as to be virtually invisible. In school a contrasting coloured thread was used for practice, allowing the workmanship to appear more distinctly. Sarah Gatchell (1796) chose blue, while Sarah Ridgeway's sampler, also stitched at Clonmel School, is in red on white linen; each shows five different damask darns. All these girls were from prosperous families and received a superior education, but they also had to learn thrift and know to repair the household linen as well as the clothing.

she was competent in needle-weaving and would have been capable of mending any tear in a piece of delicate fabric such as muslin. On her sampler, surrounded by specimens of different darns, there is a central motif of an attractive basket of flowers

Rebecca Goff, white sampler of darning/needle-weaving on fine gauze, 1795, 38cms x 36cms.
(Private collection).

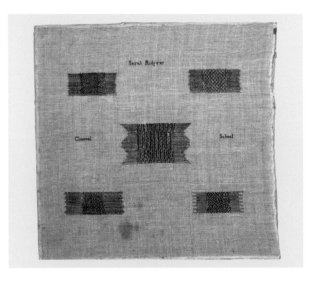

Sarah Ridgeway, Darning sampler, Clonmel school, no date, 28cms x 28cms. (FHLD)

[290] Feller, 2012, Vol. II, pp.45 and.48. Ann Murphy was the daughter of Samuel Murphy and his wife Margaret (née Malcolmson).
[291] NMI. Ref, DT:1983.9 and DT:1983.10. Kent occurs as a Quaker name but so far it has not been possible to identify these girls.

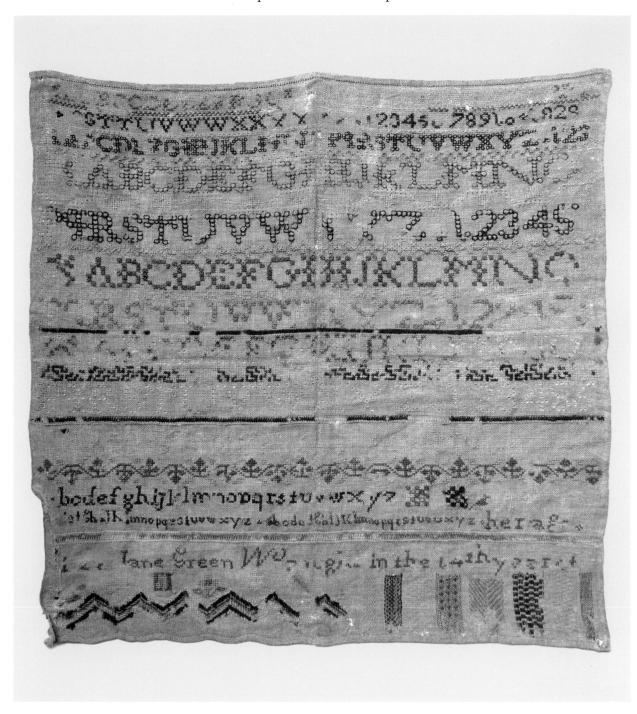

Jane Green sampler, age 13 , n.d., 43cms x 43cms. (FHLD)

In Lisburn school the girls' standards were such that they were often given paid work by better-off Friends. Mary Creeth, who had been taught to sew with great neatness by Mary Dickenson, received half a crown for darning a damask tablecloth for Lucia Richardson. Best of all, Mary enjoyed darning stockings for John Conran, an elderly Quaker minister.[292]

None of the Lisburn School darning exercises are known to have survived. However, in some cases, a lettering sampler might also include a number of types of darns. Such is the case with an early nineteenth century one by a Jane Green whose work is a hybrid, with six different darns across the bottom, as well as various borders and alphabets, including two full ones in four-sided

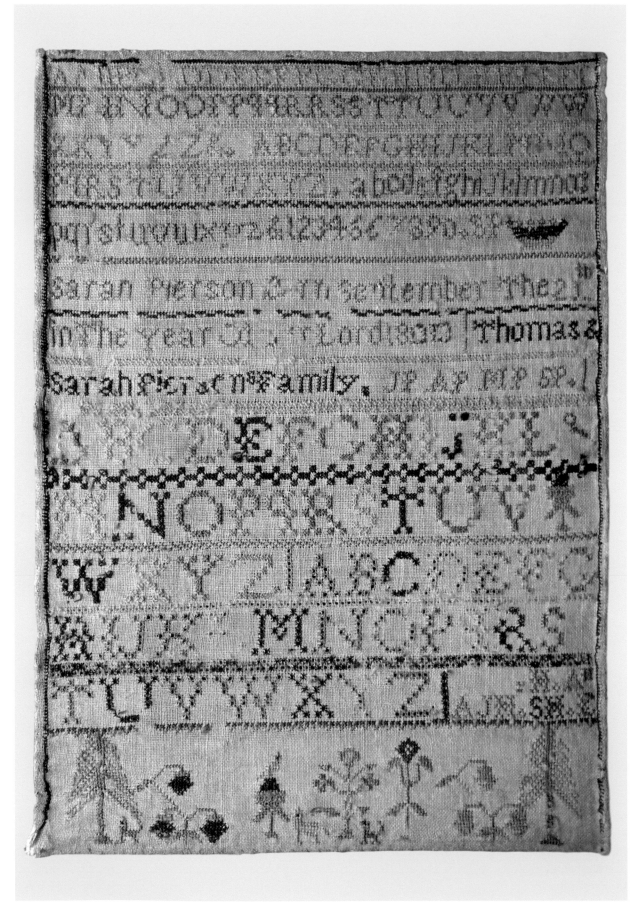

Sarah Pierson sampler, 1800, 43cms x 31cms. (Private collection)

Jane Flanagan sampler. (Private collection)

stitch.[293] At the bottom, next to the darns, is a polychrome Florentine style zigzag pattern, executed in worsted and possibly for upholstery work. Although little is known about her, it is similar to two other samplers worked in the north of Ireland in 1799 and 1817.[294]

Pictorial motifs

Pictorial motifs are relatively scarce on extant Irish Friends' samplers. In Sarah Pierson's work of 1800 a panel beneath the alphabets is filled with a variety of motifs including plants, a bird on a strawberry and three dogs. The two strawberry patterns next to the pair of framing pine trees evoke a seventeenth-century overall design. This alphabet sampler with geometric divisions employs a range of colours comparable to that of Jane Green with an emphasis on maroon, plum and purple – colours frequently found on Ulster girls' samplers.[295]

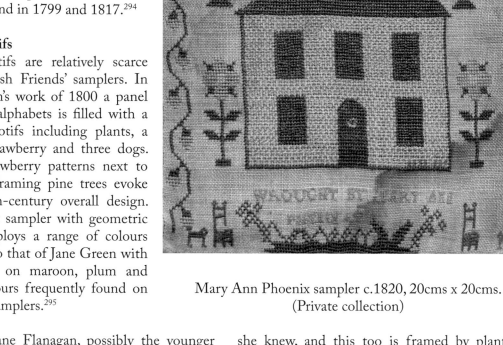

Mary Ann Phoenix sampler c.1820, 20cms x 20cms.
(Private collection)

In 1803 Jane Flanagan, possibly the younger sister of Elizabeth, divided her space with a top section of capital alphabets and, below, a panel in which she groups a number of individual motifs, reworked to compose a complete scene. Central to it is an exuberant plant growing from a vase and sporting flowers of various botanic species and a very large bird perched on a branch. Below, two dogs bound merrily over the grass from which sprout two further plants. The whole picture is framed with a strawberry border. To date no similar samplers have been found amongst Irish Quakers, although many girls in nineteenth-century England stitched scenes within floral borders, often combining them with poems.

Sarah Lovell's sampler of 1782 has a band with an early depiction of an elegant mansion framed by its garden. In Ulster a large plain square farmhouse fills Mary Ann Phoenix's small piece of c.1820 and may well be a representation of a dwelling

she knew, and this too is framed by plants. A detail that is unusual on Irish samplers, although sometimes worked in Europe, is a pair of upright chairs. Crawford found two examples of this motif on Ulster pieces of c.1816 and 1841 and gives patterns for them.[296]

Quite different from all the samplers already examined is Elizabeth Andrews' piece of 1838 in which she depicts a large building, possibly an institution. Above this are angels flying with birds and a butterfly underneath the stars. An unusual detail is two post-mills (windmills that could rotate on a central post to face the wind). By the end of the seventeenth century post-mills had been superseded by water-power in Ireland, but they continued in use in Britain and Europe and are depicted in the English samplers of Elizabeth Cridland (1752) and Mary Ann Body (1789). Elizabeth Andrews also introduces Adam and Eve, together with many motifs arranged symmetrically

---

[293] This sampler is in poor condition. At the end it is possible to read 'Jane Green Wrought in the 14th year of', but the year is illegible. It belonged to the Australian Don Finley whose mother was a Malcolmson of Waterford. In the north of Ireland, the Malcolmsons had intermarried with the Greens. A Witney Antiques catalogue describes a sampler of 1817 in two parts, one of which contained alphabets and the other a number of different darns, and describes this type of mixture as typical of northern Europe (Witney, 2006, no.10).

[294] Crawford, 1989, pp.40-41.

[295] Crawford, 1989, p.19.

[296] Ibid, p.105.

Elizabeth Andrews sampler, 1838. (Glorney)

end of the century Berlin wool work had descended into a form of painting by numbers and was frequently in garish colours. At Brookfield School in 1865, Sarah Ann Baird worked her neatly stitched sampler which includes a house motif that is reminiscent of Berlin work, and the sampler itself may have been made as a teaching aid.

Map samplers

As part of the teaching of geography, the making of map samplers was encouraged at Quaker schools. Between 1770 and the early 1800s, such samplers were popular across Europe and in the Americas.[298] At first they were drawn by hand on linen, silk or cotton, but very quickly publishers realised that the printing of these opened up a new market. Irish girls favoured couching the outlines with polychrome silks and putting their names in a floral cartouche. Sometimes the map had an oval border of free-flowing flowers worked in long and short stitch, running, chain and stem stitch.

To date, the earliest known Irish Quaker map sampler was made in 1791 at Mountmellick School by Susanna Harvey. Entitled 'A Map of Ireland', it

in pairs, and the whole is framed in a reversed flower arcaded border. Like many nineteenth-century decorative pieces of this type, the alphabet is omitted. Much about this sampler evokes a model that was current in England. Although its exact provenance is uncertain, this sampler, together with one from Mountmellick, hung for many years in the Dublin office of a Quaker business.[297]

A. Wicklow's minuscule treatment of a two-storey house with a red roof was worked in 1836, probably in Northern Ireland. In this case the house and all the other motifs, including little figures and flowers in garlands, were most likely chosen from hand-coloured printed patterns on squared paper. Pioneered by a Berlin printer c.1804 these patterns became immensely popular in Victorian Britain and specially dyed wool was sold together with the design. Initially an interesting development, by the

Sarah Ann Baird sampler,1865 27cms x 27 cms. (FHLD)

---

297 It is not known whether Elizabeth Andrews was a Friend. Another sampler hung in the same office and was made by Susanna Corlett at Mountmellick School in 1815.
298 Colby, 1964, p.125.

A. Wicklow sampler, 1836. (Private collection)

Hannah McCann, map of Ireland, 1829, 49.5cms x 44cms (Private collection)

Mary White, map of Europe, 1813, 62cms x 54cms. (FHLD)

is worked on printed cloth. Three other pupils, an Elizabeth Pim in 1794 and Anna Watson and Jane Shaw in 1799, all used this same version.[299] As the school was originally for less well-off Friends it ran on a tight budget, so it is possible that a stock of this printed map was bought by a benefactor for the girls to enjoy working in the evening. One of the charges on Anne Shannon's account for the Elizabeth Hogg at her school was for a 'Map of Ireland' at four shillings and ten pence together with 'Tape and paper for ditto'.

At Mountmellick School each girl worked the floral cartouche differently. On the map itself, scales in both Irish miles and English miles are included, and there is a pointer to the North. Lines of longitude and latitude are marked, as are county boundaries, but few towns.

When looking at Irish map samplers it is necessary to take into account names that may have changed, such as the counties of Offaly and Laois, which appear as Queen's County (after Mary I of England) and King's County (after Philip of Spain), names which they received in 1556 when Mary dispatched settlers to establish plantations there with a view to the more complete subjugation of Ireland.

Marked on the map are the castles of Maryborough and Philipstown, later to become today's towns of Portlaoise and the rather less important Daingean. In the north of Ireland, Londonderry appears, but the newly founded Belfast is not marked on all maps.[300]

In 1814 Mary White in Waterford stitched 'A New Map of Ireland'. A harp cartouche adorned with Kathleen Mavourneen and shamrocks gives this work a flavour of nascent Irish nationalism. A later edition dated 20 July, 1820, was published by R.H.Laurie of 53 Fleet St. London. This now indicates that the scale is in Irish miles, and the printer has added a border of free-flowing flowers tied with a ribbon bow, plus four large shamrocks. In

Killileagh, Co. Down, in 1829, a Hannah McCann embroidered a version of this with polychrome silk thread on linen.[301]

On maps of Europe, names and even the borders of countries were rather different from today. When Mary White worked her map of Europe in 1813, towards the end of the Napoleonic Wars, the Turks ruled Rumania, Bulgaria and the Balkans including Greece. Buda (later to be linked with Pest as Budapest) was the capital of Hungary. The kingdom of Sweden includes Finland, but this is already out-of-date, as Finland had been ceded by the Swedes to Russia by 1809. Åbo (Turku) is indicated as the capital, which it remained until a disastrous fire in 1837 destroyed much of this elegant city of wooden buildings. Germany and Italy are marked as countries, but were still collections of independent small states. On Mary White's oval sampler, the outlines are couched in silk and the whole is framed by a cartouche-garland of leaves and flowers with an embroidered bow.[302]

Hannah Davis, worked a map of Europe in 1805, and gave it to her niece Margaret, who married Joseph Beale, a wealthy Mountmellick businessman. Beale emigrated to Australia 1852, and his family followed two years later.[303] This map has recently returned from Australia after more than 150 years, having been found rolled-up amongst family papers. Descendants of Margaret Beale have generously given it to Mountmellick Museum.

In the 1700s Britain and other nations sought new lands to colonise and exploit. This resulted in an interest in other countries. Travel books became best sellers and, as a consequence of this, maps of the world were also printed for embroidering. *An outline map of the World for Ladies Needlework and Young Students in Geography* was published in 1798 by R. Laurie & J. Whittle. Printed on a rectangular piece of cloth, this shows the Western and Eastern hemispheres, complete with longitude and latitude.

---

[299] Humphrey, 2006, p,156, and Feller, 2012, p.228. Feller noted that satin, running, couching and chain stitches were employed by Jane Shaw.

[300] The City of London's companies received the County of Coleraine in 1613. They developed the small settlement of Derry, whose name means oak, and turned it into a walled city.

[301] It is not certain whether Hannah was a Quaker, but the sampler has been handed down in a Quaker family.

[302] Two other map of Europe samplers are that of Susanna Abbott (1800-1844), Mountmellick School (1813, still with family members) and one by Jenepher Fisher, age 18, Clonmel School 1809, which is worked with polychrome silks in an oval enclosed by freely drawn flowers.

[303] O'Keefe, 1994, pp.31-34.

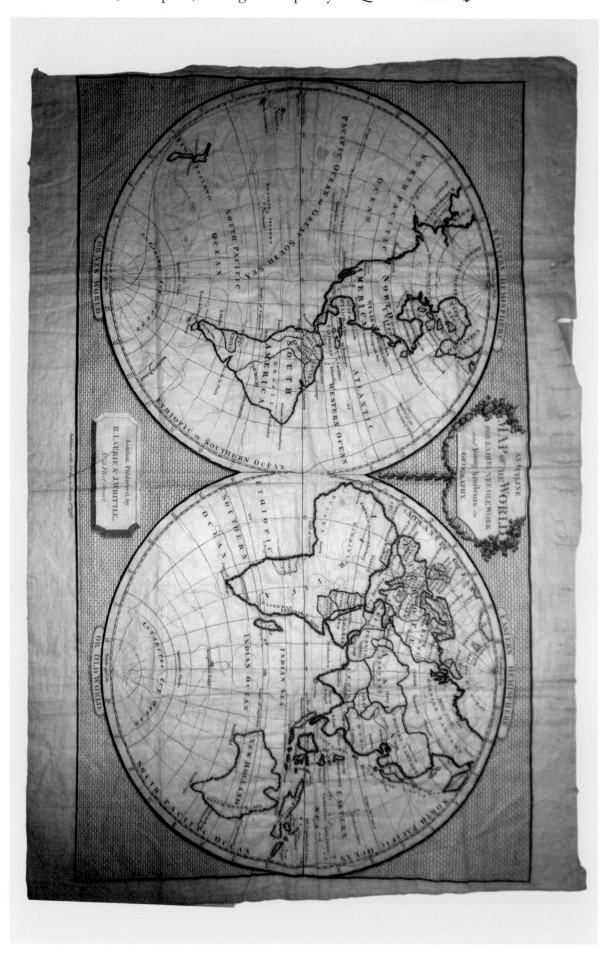

Map of the world, no date. (Private collection)

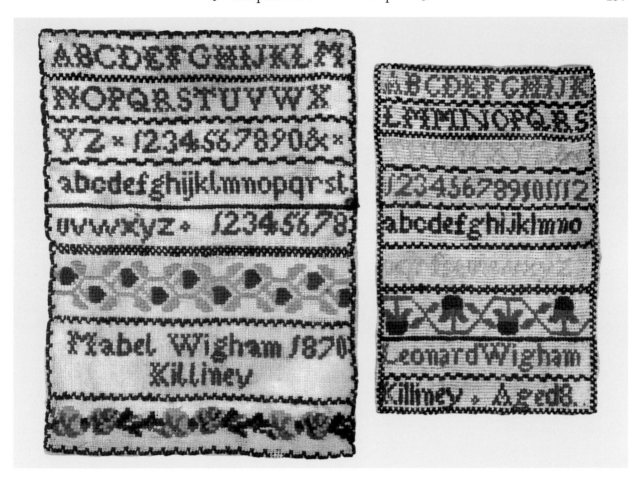

Mabel Wigham sampler, 1870, 33cms x 24cms; Leonard Wigham sampler, 27cms x 17cms.(FHLD)

In North America, early settlement was mainly on the eastern seaboard where Pennsylvania would have been of special interest to Irish Friends, as many had settled in the democratic Quaker colony created by William Penn in 1681.[304] The centre of North America, which at this period remained little known to Europeans apart from French and other fur trappers, is empty.[305] The North of Canada remains vague despite unsuccessful attempts to find the North-West Passage, including one by Captain James Cook (1728-79), whose earlier charting of the St. Lawrence river had made it possible for Wolfe to capture Quebec from the French in 1759.

Maps drawn at this period owe a great deal to Cook who, as an apprentice seaman to the elderly Walker brothers, Quaker ship-owners in Whitby, lived in their house in winter working on boat repairs and studying navigation. Aged twenty-seven he joined the Royal Navy and on his three epic voyages of 1768, 1772 and 1776 he explored the Pacific down to the Antarctic Circle. The Dutch had already charted the coast of Western Australia and called it New Holland, under which name it appears on this map. In 1770 Cook surveyed the east coast, as a result of which Port Jackson and Botany Bay are marked, but Tasmania is not yet included. The map also includes the Sandwich Islands (Hawaii) where Cook met his death in 1779. Egypt is marked but most of the interior of Africa remains blank, still unknown to Europeans, as is the case of the Arctic and Antarctic.

---

[304] In North America the British had settled along the Atlantic seaboard during the seventeenth century. In 1681, Charles II, who was heavily in debt to Admiral Penn, granted land to William Penn who founded Pennsylvania and made peace treaties with the Native Americans.

[305] Margaret Boyle Harvey met her future husband when he visited America in connection with his trade in beaver-fur hats.

Decline of samplers

In the nineteenth century, surviving samplers tend to be predominantly lettering ones. One reason for the comparative scarcity of more decorative samplers may be that these were more likely to be acquired by collectors abroad.[306] As a marking exercise such samplers continued to be made up to the end of the century. Many were rather simplistic and as the century progressed the verve and variety of the alphabet samplers, whether in colour or black thread declined to just a few basic alphabets with some simple divisions.

The wave of Evangelicalism in the nineteenth century led to a renewed and literal emphasis and dependence on the words of the Holy Scriptures. Its impact on the working of samplers often meant a focus on text only, neatly executed but with little artistic appeal. Abigail Wright's minute sampler of 1832 manages to fit seventeen lines of text extolling the Bible into a space of 10cms x 7cms, while Mary Elizabeth Walpole's much later working of *Lead Kindly Light* in brown thread with gold capitals occupies 28 lines.[307]

Epilogue for samplers but not for sewing.

Julia Goff of Horetown, in a diary of the1860s, mentions using the sewing machine she had bought. By this time the sewing-machine was used both in factories and middle-class homes. Large Department stores such as Pim's, Arnott's and Clery's were opening in Dublin, Cork, Limerick and Belfast. These sold quality readymade clothing. The less well-off might buy fabric and make it up by hand-sewing at home, and some might use the services of a local dressmaker with her machine. The embroidered sampler which has been the central focus of this book had virtually disappeared by the end of the century. What continued to survive was one showing plain-sewing techniques. Between the 1880s and the 1920s plain-sewing samplers were made in colleges of Domestic Science and girls' secondary schools. A rather basic example of such work was made by Hilda Barclay

between 1894 and 1896, at The Mount School. Some fifteen years later, Caroline (Carrie) Pim of Mountmellick also attended The Mount, but her notebook shows that by this time sewing was just one amongst other subjects of a more academic curriculum. Caroline Pim's 'Needlework Notes', made between April and November 1911, when she was eighteen, are carefully written into a hardcover exercise book and provide a useful document of the plain sewing needed for the making and repair of clothes, curtains and blinds for the house. In addition, the book contains beautifully-worked specimens of the different techniques described.[308]

As sewing lost its central place in a school curriculum which now offered many more possibilities than had previously been conceivable, Quaker women who had grown up with a belief in equality between the sexes were quick to avail of the opening up of higher education. Anna Haslam (1829 -1922), educated at Newtown and then Ackworth, was part of the founding group of The Irish Society for Promoting the Training and Employment of Educated Women.[309] Described as, 'one of the giants of the women's cause' in the report of the Irish Women's Suffrage and Poor Law Association for 1917, she lived long enough to vote in the election of November 1918.

An early demonstration for women's suffrage in Ireland occurred in 1910 in Greystones, Co Wicklow, on the occasion of an official visit from the Chief Secretary for Ireland, Augustine Birrell, to examine the poor condition of the pier. He was accosted by a leading figure in the movement, Hannah Sheehy Skeffington, accompanied by Hilda Barclay, now the wife of the Dublin Quaker lawyer Leonard Webb.[310]

Their daughter Stella Webb (1910-1994) entered the law school of Trinity College Dublin in 1928, and later took over her father's law practice. After the end of the Second World War, her strong sense of social justice led her to joining the

---

[306] The author has known one Irishman who, in the 1960s, collected up samplers for his American girlfriend to sell in the USA.

[307] Mary Elizabeth (1859-1945) was a daughter of Joseph and Elizabeth Walpole of Mountmellick.

[308] FHLD. Caroline Alberta Pim, later returned to the family home near Mountmellick and helped her sister-in-law run the house. According to her nephew Alan Pim, apart from her ability to run the kitchen, she had considerable sewing skills.

[309] Anna Haslam came from the Quaker Fisher family of Youghal which had been involved in the anti-slavery and temperance movements. She married Thomas Haslam of Mountmellick who was also educated at Newtown and already interested in the women's question. Besides education she was active in promoting women's property rights. (See 'Anna Haslam' in Cullen and Luddy, 1995.)

[310] FHLD has examples of plain sewing worked by Hilda Barclay (later Webb), who made them at the Mount School, York, in the mid-1890s.

British Friends Service Council, with which she served from 1945 to 1948. She was sent to Greece and seconded to the United Nations Relief and Rehabilitation Association (UNRRA) and here her skills as a lawyer were of special value in dealing with the legal problems of displaced persons, who often had little or inadequate documentation.[311]

As professional training became more available for women, their artistic abilities now began to find new outlets. Lydia Shackleton (1828-1914) studied botanical art at the Royal Dublin Society Schools in 1850 and in the 1880s was appointed to record the extensive collection of orchids at the Botanic Gardens, Glasnevin where she executed some 1,400 botanical portraits of which over 1000 were orchids. This work is now kept in Glasnevin.[312]

Between 1908 and 1919 Shackleton's work at the Botanic Gardens was continued by Alice Jacob (1862-1921).[313] Also coming from a Quaker family, she studied at the Dublin Metropolitan School of Art (DMSA), and would play a significant role in the Arts and Crafts movement. A prize-winner in the Art Industries competition at the Royal Dublin Society Horse Show in 1890, her work went on to be shown regularly in London and featured at the Art de la Femme exhibitions in Paris between 1891 and 1893, and in1898 it was selected by the Hungarian Government for the new Museum of Industrial Art in Budapest. She taught at the Cork School of Art and the Rathmines Technical School, and in 1898 was appointed teacher of Design and Ornament at DMSA. Primarily a lace designer, she incorporated elements based on her botanical studies in her patterns for lace, floral damask, embroidery, crochet, and painted silk and she also supplied various linen firms with designs

Quality of craftsmanship has always been important with Quakers. The strong practical sense that was inculcated from an early age could make some women extremely suitable for the running of a business, and this often coincided with their own natural interests or talents in the artistic field. Pauline Clotworthy (née Keohler, later Keller, 1912-2004), attended Alexandra College, and then DMSA (1931-1933). Her real interest was fashion but she realized that the ability to draw was not enough, as she needed to understand the technicalities of pattern-making, cutting, and garment construction. She therefore went to London, to the British Institute of Dress Designers, for training in the practical skills that underlie dress-designing. In May 1938, having completed the course, and recognising the need for an equivalent training in Dublin, with her father's help, she leased rooms at 6 St Stephen's Green, in Dublin city centre. There she established the Grafton Academy of Dress Designing and Millinery with a first enrolment of 15 students. Rather unusually for the period, she continued to work professionally, even when married and with a family. Designers who have established Ireland's reputation in international fashion studied under Clotworthy, and her pioneering Academy also provided skills which enabled hundreds of less celebrated people to earn their living as dressmakers and tailors throughout the country. Some seventy years later her work at the Academy was described as the 'backbone of the Irish clothing trade'.[314]

The ability to sew is obviously no longer essential for every woman, but many Quakers take an unashamed delight in such activities as embroidery, patchwork, quilting, knitting and lace-making. Materials do not have to cost a lot or take up much space, and such activity has now become a form of recreation that some have brought to a very high artistic level. It can be a solo occupation or enjoyed as a social occasion, whether informal or more organised. Various groups such as those doing Mountmellick work and lacemaking, the Irish Patchwork Society and the Ross Tapestry in Wexford, led to a renaissance of knowledge and skills by the end of the twentieth century in Ireland.

---

[311] Webb's regular letters home (now in FHLD) describe conditions in refugee camps and the almost total lack of clothing of some of the inmates. Two leaflets in FHLD describing Quaker efforts to overcome this describe the acquiring of sewing machines, bags of old clothes and fabric (even rags) and giving desperately-needed employment to those with skills. One leaflet is from Bad Pyrmont, one of the earliest Quaker settlements in Germany.

[312] Butler, 2000, p.30.

[313] Ibid, p.29. In addition to her work for the Botanic Gardens, between 1908 and 1919, Jacob painted some 150 illustrations of Sir Frederick Moore's collection of orchids.

[314] *Irish Times*, 5 April 2008.

An interesting cross-community project in Northern Ireland in 2008 was the making of the Peace Quilt by thirty-two women from across the sectarian divide. A mixture of Loyalists, Nationalists, Republicans and Unionists, they met regularly in Quaker House, Belfast, where working together and talking they came to understand more about the others' community. Each expressed her hopes for the future and worked a square. Put together these squares became a quilt which now carries the title of 'Shared Visions'.

Long live creativity and hope.

Shared Visions quilt. 200cms x 203cms
(Conflict Textiles. Photographer Christopher Keenan)

BIBLIOGRAPHY

Anon
A Collection of Approved Recipes (by Quakers),
FHLD, eighteenth century.

Anon
One Hundred Years of Mountmellick School, Dublin,
Webb, 1886.

Ahern, Michael
Threads in a Clonmel Tapestry, Clonmel, Ardo,
2012.

Ahern, Michael
The Grubbs of Clonmel, M.A. Thesis (unpublished)
University College, Cork, 1998.

Ahern, Michael
The Quakers of Tipperary, Clonmel, Ardo, 2009.

Alexander, Hannah
A Book of Cookery, Deirdre Nuttall (ed.), Cathair
na Mart, Evertype, 2014.

Allott, Stephen
Quaker Pioneers, London, Bannisdale, 1963.

Arnold, Janet
Perukes & Periwigs, London, Her Majesty's
Stationery Office, 1970.

Arnold, Janet
*Patterns of Fashion 1 English Women's Dresses
and their Construction c.1660-1860,* London,
Macmillan, 1972.

Arnold, Janet
*Patterns of Fashion 2 English Women's Dresses
and their Construction, c.1860-1940,* London,
Macmillan, 1977 (first edition 1966).

Arnold, Janet
*Patterns of Fashion 3 The Cut and Construction of
Clothes for Men and Women c.1560–1620,* London,
Macmillan, 1985.

Arnold, Janet
*Patterns of Fashion 4 The Cut and Construction
of linen Shirts, Smocks, Neckwear, Headwear and
Accessories for Men and Women c.1540-1660.*
London, Macmillan, 2008.

Arrizzoli-Clémentel, Pierre
Le Musée des Tissus de Lyon, Lyon, Fondation
Paribas, 1990.

Ashton, John
Chapbooks of the Eighteenth Century, London,
Chatto and Windus, 1882. (Reprint: London,
Skoob Books, n.d.)

Aslanapa, Oktay
One Thousand Years of Turkish Carpets, Istanbul,
Eren, 1988.

Avi-Yonah, Michael
Ancient Mosaics, London, Cassell, 1975.

Barker, Nicholas
*The Oxford University Press and the Spread
of Learning, an illustrated History,* Oxford,
Clarendon Press, 1978.

Beckett, J. C.
The Making of Modern Ireland 1603-1923,
London, Faber,1966.

Bell, S. Hilda
'Notes on Friends' Education in Ireland',
typescript, Portfolio 5, FHLD, 1919.

Bennett, Ian
Oriental Carpet Identifier, London, Arlington,
1989.

Bielenberg, Andy (ed.)
Irish Flour Milling a history 600-2000, Dublin,
Lilliput Press, 2003.

Bovini, Giuseppe
Ravenna: Art and history, Ravenna, Longo, 1991.

Bradfield, Nancy
Costume in Detail 1730-1930, London, Harrap, 1981.

Braithwaite, William C.
The Second Period of Quakerism, London, Macmillan, 1919.

Brannigan Cyril G.
Quaker Education in Ireland 1680-1840, unpublished M.Ed. thesis, Saint Patrick's College, Maynooth, 1982.

Brayshaw, A. Neave
The Quakers, London. R. Davis, 1921.

Browne, Clare and Wearden, Jennifer
Samplers, London, Victoria and Albert Museum, 2010.

Butler, Patricia
Irish botanical Illustrators & Flower Painters, Suffolk, Antique Collectors' Club, 2000.

Chapman, Arthur G.
History of The Religious Society of Friends in Lurgan, Lurgan, Lurgan Friends Meeting, 1997.

Chapman Arthur G.
History of Friends in Portadown 1655-2005, Lurgan, 2005.

Chapman, Arthur G.
Quakers in Lisburn, Lisburn, Ulster Friends Home Mission, 2009.

Chatzidakis, Manolis
Byzantine Athens, Athens, M. Pechlivanides, 1960.

Clabburn, Pamela
Masterpieces of Embroidery, Oxford, Phaidon, 1981.

Clabburn, Pamela
Patchwork, London, Shire Publications, 1990.

Clabburn, Pamela
Samplers, London, Shire Publications, 1998 (2nd edition).

Colby, Averil
Samplers, London, Batsford, 1964.

Colby, Averil
Quilting, London, Batsford 1972.

Coleman, Evelyn, Elizabeth and Dorothy
The Age of Dolls, Washington DC, self- published, 1965.

Coolahan, John
Irish Education: its History and Structure 1605-1923, Dublin: Institute of Public Administration, 1981.

Corrigan, Mario Kavanagh, Michael and Kiely, Karel (eds.) Mary Leadbeater
Annals of Ballitore and Betsy Shackleton *Ballitore and its Inhabitants seventy Years ago*, Kildare County Library, 2009.

Coutts, Peter J.
Towards a history of the Quaker Meeting at Newgarden, County Carlow 1650-1730 including some New methods for analyzing Quaker records, n.p., self-published, 2016.

Crawford, Heather M.
Needlework Samplers of Northern Ireland, Crawfordsburn, Allingham, 1969.

Creeth, Mary
'Reminiscences of Lisburn School' in *Journal of the Friends Historical Society*, 18, no.2, London, Friends' Book Centre, 1921.

Cullen, Mary and Luddy, Maria (eds.)
Women, Power and Consciousness in the nineteenth Century, Dublin, Attic Press,1995.

Curtis, E.
A *History of Ireland*. London, Methuen, 1936.

Danglova, Olga
Embroidery in Slovakia, Bratislava, Institute of Ethnology 2009.

Davis, Mildred J.
The Art of Crewel Embroidery, NY & London 1962.

de Breffny, Brian and ffolliott, Rosemary
The Houses of Ireland, London, Thames and Hudson, 1975.

De Dillmont, Thérèse (ed.) *Alphabet de la Brodeuse*, Mulhouse, D.M.C, n.d.

Djelloul, Néji
Sousse Ancient Hadrumetum, Sousse, Contraste, 2006.

Douglas, John M.
The Beginnings of Quakerism in 17ᵗʰ-Century Ireland, Dublin, FHLD, 2004.

Du Mortier, Bianca. M.
'Costumes in Gabriel Metsu's Paintings: Modes and Manners in the Mid-Seventeenth Century' in Adriaan E. Waiboer, *Gabriel Metsu*, Dublin, National Gallery of Ireland, 2010.

Duke, Dennis and Harding, Deborah (eds.)
America's Glorious Quilts, New York, Park Lane, 1987.

Dunlevy, Mairead
Dress in Ireland, London, Batsford, 1989.

Dunlevy, Mairead
Pomp and Poverty, a History of Silk in Ireland, Yale University Press, 2011.

Ellis, Marianne and Weardon, Jennifer
Ottoman Embroidery, London, Victoria and Albert Museum, 2001.

Elton, G. R.
Reformation Europe 1517-1559, London & Glasgow, Fontana, 1963.

Evans, E. Estyn
Irish Folkways, London, Routledge and Kegan Paul, 1957.

Fairbank, Alfred
A Book of Scripts, London, Penguin, 1949.

Feller, Micheál and Elizabeth
The Needlework Collection vols. I and II, UK, Needleprint, 2011-12

Fox, George
The Journal of George Fox, revised by Norman Penney, London 1924.

Fraser, Antonia
Marie Antoinette – The Journey, London, Phoenix, 2002.

Gambin, Kenneth
The Prison Experience at the Inquisitor's Palace Vittoriosa, Malta, Heritage Books, 2004.

Gantzhorn, Volkmar
The Christian Oriental Carpet, Cologne, Taschen, 1991.

George, Dorothy
England in Transition, Middlesex, Routledge, 1931 (reprint 1962).

Ginsburg, Madeleine (ed.)
The Illustrated History of Textiles, London, Studio, 1991.

Gittinger, Mattiebelle
Master Dyers to the World, Washington D C, Textile Museum, 1982.

Gloag, John
2000 Years of England, London, Cassell, 1952.

Gloag, John
A Short Dictionary of Furniture, London, Allen and Unwin, 1969 (revised edition, first edition 1952).

Goldenberg, André
Bestiaire de la culture populaire musulmane et juive au Maroc, Aix-en-Provence, Édisud, 2000.

Goodbody, Michael
The Goodbodys: Millers, Merchants and Manufacturers: the Story of an Irish Quaker Family 1630-1950, Dublin, Ashfield, 2011.

Goodbody, Olive
'Quaker Inventories', in *The Irish. Ancestor* 3, no.1, Dublin, Mount Salus Press, 1971.

Goodbody, Olive
'Inventories of five Dublin Quaker merchants in the late Seventeenth century', in *The Irish Ancestor* 10, no.1, Dublin, Mount Salus Press, 1978.

Hampden, Gordon
Old English Furniture, A simple Guide, London, John Murray, 1948.

Gostelow, Mary
A World of Embroidery, London, Mills & Boon, 1975.

Gough, John
Practical Arithmetick in four Books, Dublin, R. Jackson (printer), 1792.

Grant, Elizabeth
Highland Lady in Ireland, Edinburgh, Cannongate, 1991.

Grant, Elizabeth
Memoirs of a Highland Lady, Edinburgh, Cannongate, 1992.

Greer Mrs.
Quakerism or the Story of My Life, Dublin, S.B. Oldham, 1852.

Grubb, Clodagh
Quaker Girl, Anne Grubb 1815, story & paper-doll, Dublin, FHLD 2015.

Grubb, Geoffrey
The Grubbs of Tipperary, Cork, Mercier, 1972.

Grubb, Isabel
Quakers in Ireland 1654- 1900, London, Swarthmore, 1927.

Grubb, Isabel
Quakerism and Industry Before 1800, London, Williams and Norgate, 1930.

Grubb, Isabel
Quaker Homespuns 1655-1833, London, H.R. Allenson, 1932.

Grubb, Isabel
'Irish Quaker records: some items of interest in the Dublin collection', in *Journal of the Friends Historical Society*, 34, London, 1937.

Grubb, Isabel
Irish Quakers: Social Conditions in Ireland in the seventeenth and eighteenth Centuries as illustrated by early Quaker Records, Cork, published privately, 2018.

Grubb, Sarah (Tuke)
Some Account of the Life and religious Labours of Sarah Grubb, ed. Lindley Murray, Dublin, Jackson, 1792.

Grubb, Sarah
A Selection from the Letters of Sarah Grubb (formerly Sarah Lynes), Sudbury, J. Wright, 1848.

Gummere, Amelia Mott
The Quaker: A Study in Costume, Philadelphia, Ferris and Leach, 1901.

Hänsel, Volker (ed.)
Kreuzstichmuster, Landschaftsmuseum im Schloss Trautenfels, Trautenfels, Schloss Trautenfels, pt. 1, 2002, pt.2, 1987, pt.3, 2003, pt.4, 1997.

Harrison, Richard S.
Cork City Quakers 1665-1939, Cork, privately published, 1991.

Harrison, Richard S.
Merchants, Mystics and Philanthropists, 350 Years of Cork Quakers, Cork, Cork Monthly Meeting, 2006.

Harrison, Richard S.
A Biographical Dictionary of Irish Quakers, Dublin, Four Courts Press, 2nd (revised) edition 2008 (original edition 1997).

Harrison, Richard S.
Dublin Quakers 1650-1900, Cork, privately published, 2018.

Harvey, Margaret Boyle
Journal of Margaret Boyle on a Visit to Ireland, 1809-1812, ms copy in FHLD (ref. Diaries and Journals).

Herbert, Dorothea
Retrospections of 1770-1806, G.F. Mandeville (ed.), Dublin, Town House, 1988 (original edition, London, Gerald Howe, 1929-30.).

Hodgkin, Lucy V.
Gulielma: Wife of William Penn, London, New York, Longmans Green, 1947.

Hofer, Tamás and Fél, Edit
Hungarian Folk Art, Budapest, Corvina, 1994.

Hole, Helen G.
Westtown through the Years, Westtown Alumni Association, 1942.

Holland, Vyvyan
Hand-coloured Fashion Plates, 1770-1899, London, Batsford, 1955.

Houston-Almquist, Jane
Mountmellick Work – Irish white Embroidery, Mountrath, Dolmen Press, 1985.

Hughes, Kathryn
The Victorian Governess, London, Hambledon, 2001.

Humphrey, Carol
'Canvas Work' in *The Royal School of Needlework Book of Needlework and Embroidery* Lanto Synge (ed.), London, Collins, 1986.

Humphrey, Carol
Samplers, Cambridge University Press, 1997.

Humphrey, Carol
Quaker School Girl Samplers from Ackworth, n.p., Needleprint, 2006.

Humphrey, Carol
Sampled Lives, Cambridge, Fitzwilliam Museum, 2017.

J.M.R.
Six Generations in Ireland 1655-1890, London, Edward Hicks, 1893.

Jackson, Bill
Ringing True, The Bells of Trummery and beyond: 350 Years of an Irish Quaker Family, York, Sessions, 2005.

Jackson, Bill
Them Wild Woods, The Transatlantic Letters of an Irish Quaker Family 1818-1877, Belfast, Ulster Historical Foundation, 2011.

Jarrett, Joy and Stephen and Scott, Rebecca
Stitched in Adversity Samplers of the Poor, Witney, Witney Antiques, 2006.

Jenkins, James
Records and Recollections of James Jenkins, Lewiston, Edwin Mellen Press, 1984.

Jones, Laura and Meldrum, Alex
Irish Patchwork, Kilkenny, Design Workshops, 1979.

Jones, Rebecca
Memorials of, William Allinson (ed.), Philadelphia & London, Longstreth, 1849.

Jones, Rufus, *Spiritual Reformers of the Sixteenth and Seventeenth Centuries*, London, Macmillan, 1928. (Reprint of 1914 edition).

Jorns, Auguste
Quakers as Pioneers in social Work, N.Y. Macmillan, 1931.

Joy, E.T.
'Furniture' in *The Late Georgian Period 1760-1810*, Ralph Edwards and L.G.G. Ramsey (eds.), London, Connoisseur 1956.

Kay-Williams, Susan, *The Story of Colour in Textiles*, London, Bloomsbury, 2013.

Kendall, Joan 'The Development of a Distinctive Form of Quaker Dress', in *Costume*, No. 19, Edinburgh, The Costume Society of Great Britain, 1985.

Kilroy, Phil *Protestant Dissent and Controversy in Ireland (1660-1714)*, Cork University Press, 1994.

King, Donald 'Textiles', in *The Late Georgian Period 1760-1810*, Ralph Edwards and L.G.G. Ramsey (eds.), London, Connoisseur 1956.

King-Hall, Magdalen
The Story of the Nursery, London, Routledge and Kegan Paul, 1958.

Kingsmill Moore, Henry *An Unwritten Chapter in the History of Education : Being the History of the Society for the Education, of the Poor of Ireland, Generally Known, as the Kildare Place Society 1811-1831*, London, MacMillan, 1904

Kinmonth, Claudia
Irish Country Furniture 1700-1950, United States, Yale University Press, 1993.

Kitson, Michael
Frans Hals, London, Knowledge Publications, 1965.

Köhler, Carl
A History of Costume, London, Harrap, 1928. (reprint, Dover, 1963).

Kybalova, Ludmilla, Herbenova, Olga and Lamarova, Milena
Encyclopédie illustrée du Costume, Paris, Gründ, 1976 (second edition).

Lampson, Mrs Godfrey Locker (ed.)
A Quaker Post-bag: Letters to Sir John Rodes and John Graton 1693-1742, London, Longmans Green, 1910.

Laver, James
A Concise History of Costume, London, Thames and Hudson, 1969.

Leadbeater, Mary
Anecdotes taken from Real Life for the Improvement of Children, Dublin, printed and sold by John Shea, 1809.

Leadbeater, Mary
'Annals of Ballitore' in Corrigan et al. (eds.) *The Annals of Ballitore*, Kildare County Library, 2009.

Leadbeater, Mary
Cottage Dialogues among the Irish Peasantry, London, printed for J. Johnson, 1811.

Leadbeater, Mary
The Leadbeater Papers, London, Bell and Daldy, 1862.

Lloyd, Arnold
Quaker social History 1669-1738, New York, Longmans Green, 1950.

Lockett, Alison
The Wool Trade, London, Methuen, 1974.

Longfield, Ada
Guide to the Collection of Lace, National Museum of Ireland, 1982.

Longfield, Ada
Irish Lace, Dublin, Eason, 1978.

Ludvíková, Miroslava
Moravská lidová vyšivka, Brno, Moravian Museum,1986.

MacCurtain, Margaret
Tudor and Stuart Ireland, Dublin, Gill and Macmillan, 1972.

Maracco, Ezio
Grado, a Guide to the City, Trieste, Fachin, 2000.

Marsh, Gail *18th Century Embroidery Techniques*, East Sussex, Guild of Master Craftsmen, 2006.

McLoughlin, Riana
The sober Duties of Life: The domestic and religious Lives of six Quaker Women in Ireland and England 1780-1820, M.A. Thesis, University College, Galway, 1993.

McManus, Antonia
The Irish Hedge School and its Books 1695-1831, Dublin, Four Courts Press, 2002.

Meldrum, Alex
Irish Patchwork, Kilkenny Design Workshops, 1979.

Miller, Kerby A.
Irish Immigrants in the Land of Canaan, Oxford, The University Press, 2003.

Moody, T.W., and Martin, F.X. (eds.)
The Course of Irish History, Cork University Press, 1967.

Murray, Lindley (ed.)
Some Account of the Life and religious Labours of Sarah Grubb, Dublin, 1792.

Murray, Lindley *An English Grammar* (Fourth edition improved, 2 vols), York, Longman et. al., 1819.

Murray, Lindley
The English Reader, York, Longman, 1799.

Murray, Peter
The Cooper Penrose Collection, Cork, Crawford Art Gallery, 2008.

Myers, Albert Cook
Immigration of Irish Quakers into Pennsylvania 1682-1750, Maryland, Heritage Books, 2006 (original edition, Philadelphia, Ferris and Leach , 1902).

Nevinson, John
The Dress of the Citizens of London 1540-1640, London, Museum of London, 1978.

Newhouse, Neville
Friends School Lisburn, Lisburn, Friends School, 1974.

O'Connor, Anne V.
'Anne Jellicoe' in Mary Cullen and Maria Luddy (eds.) *Women, Power and Consciousness in the nineteenth Century*, Dublin, Attic Press,1995.

O'Dowd, Anne
Straw, Hay and Rushes, in Irish folk Tradition, Newbridge, Irish Academic Press, 2015.

Ogg, David
Europe of the Ancien Regime 1715-1783, London and Glasgow, Collins, 1965.

O'Keefe, Regina (ed.)
The Quakers of Mountmellick 1650-1900, Mountmellick, n.p,, n.d.

O'Neill, Timothy P.
Life and Tradition in rural Ireland, London, J. M. Dent, 1977.

Orme, Nicholas
From Childhood to Chivalry; The education of the English Kings and Aristocracy 1066-1530, London, Routledge, 1984.

Paine, Sheila
Embroidered Textiles, Traditional Patterns from Five Continents, London, Thames and Hudson, 1990.

Parker, Rozsika
The Subversive Stitch: Embroidery and the Making of the Feminine, London, Bloomsbury, 1984.

Parkes, Susan M.
Kildare Place: The History of the Church of Ireland Training College and College of Education 1811-2010, Dublin, Church of Ireland College of Education, 2011.

Pekin, Ersu
Turkish flat Weaves and Carpets, Istanbul, Galeri Minyatur, 1990.

Penn, William
The Peace of Europe, The Fruits of Solitude and other Writings, Edwin B. Bronner (ed.), London, Everyman, 1993.

Penney, Norman (ed)
Journal of George Fox, Cambridge University Press, 1911.

Penney, Norman (ed.)
The Household Account Book of Sarah Fell, Cambridge University Press, 1920.

Pickvance, T. Joseph
George Fox and the Purefeys, London, Friends Historical Society, 1970.

Pike, Joseph
Some Account of the Life of Joseph Pike of Cork, in Ireland, who Died in the Year 1729, John Barclay (ed.), London, Darton and Harvey, 1837.

Piotrovsky, Mikhail and Vrieze, John (eds.)
Earthly Beauty, Heavenly Art, Amsterdam, Lund Humphries, 1999.

Prichard, Sue (ed.)
Quilts 1700- 2010, Hidden Histories, Untold Stories, London, Victoria and Albert Museum, 2010.

Pryde, George S.
Scotland from 1603 to the present Day, London/Edinburgh, Nelson, 1962.

Punshon, John
Portrait in Grey A short History of the Quakers, London, Quaker Home Service, 1984.

Raftery, Deirdre and Parkes, Susan M.
Female Education in Ireland 1700-1900, Dublin, Irish Academic Press, 2007.

Reynolds, Mairead
Some Irish Fashions and Fabrics c.1775-1928, Dublin, National Museum of Ireland, 1984.

Ring, Betty
Girlhood Embroidery American Samplers & Pictorial Needlework 1650-1850, New York, Knopf, 1993.

Roberts, Abigail
The Cottage Fireside, Dublin, Kildare Place Society, 1821.

Ross, Isabel
Margaret Fell, London, Longmans, Green, 1949.

Rothstein, Natalie (ed.)
Four hundred years of Fashion, London, V&A, 1984.

Rutty, John
A History of the Rise and Progress of the People called Quakers in Ireland from the Year 1653 to 1700 by Thomas Wight of Cork. Now revised, enlarged, a Continuation to 1751, Dublin, I. Jackson (printer), 1751.

Savery, William
A Journal of the Life, Travels, & religious Labours of, Jonathan Evans (ed.), London,1844.

Sefton, Henry R.
John Knox. Edinburgh, Saint Andrew Press, 1993.

Sethom, Samira
Signes & symboles dans l'art populaire tunisien, Tunis, 1976.

Seymour, St. John D.
The Puritans in Ireland (1647- 1661), Oxford, Clarendon Press, 1921.

Shackleton, Betsy
'Ballitore and its Inhabitants Seventy Years Ago' in *The Annals of Ballitore,* Corrigan et al. (eds.), Kildare County Library, 2009.

Shackleton, Richard and Elizabeth
Memoirs and Letters, Mary Leadbeater (ed.), London, Harvey and Darton, 1822.

Smellie, Alexander
Men of the Covenant, London, Banner of Truth Trust, (10th edition) 1960.

Smith, Carol
Quaker Dress in Ireland in the nineteenth Century, unpublished M.A. thesis, Dublin, National College of Art and Design, 2013.

Somerville-Large, Peter
The Irish Country House – a social History, London, Sinclair-Stevenson, 1995.

Staniland, Kay
Medieval Craftsmen: Embroiderers, London, British Museum, 1991.

Stankova, Jitka and Baran, Ludvik
Lidove, Umeni z Cech, Moravy a Slezska, Prague, Panorama, 1987.

Sturge, H. Winifred and Clark, Theodora
The Mount School York. 1785-1814, 1831-1931, London and Toronto, J. M. Dent, 1931.

Swain, Margaret
Ayrshire and other Whitework, Oxford, Shire, 1982.

Sylvester, David W.
Captain Cook and the Pacific. London, Longman, 1971.

Synge, Lanto (ed.)
The Royal School of Needlework Book of Needlework & Embroidery, London, Collins, 1986.

Tarrant, Naomi
'Remember now thy Creator' Scottish Girls' Samplers, 1700—1872, Edinburgh, Society of Antiquaries of Scotland, 2014.

Tarrant, Naomi
The Royal Scottish Museum Samplers, Edinburgh, Royal Scottish Museum, 1978.

Thomas, Mary
Mary Thomas's Embroidery Book, London, Hodder & Stoughton, 1936.

Toller, Jane
British Samplers, Chichester, Phillimore, 1980.

Trevelyan, G. M.
Illustrated History of England London, Longmans Green, 1956.

Van Hemert, Maria
The Needlework of the Island of Marken, Arnhem, Netherlands Open-air Museum, 1978.

Van Thienen, Frithjof
The Great Age of Holland 1600-60 (Series: Costume of the Western World), London, Harrap, 1951.

Waiboer, Adriaan E. (ed.)
Gabriel Metsu, Dublin, National Gallery of Ireland, 2010.

Waiboer, Adriaan E.
Vermeer and the Masters of Genre Painting Inspiration and Rivalry, Dublin, National Gallery of Ireland, 2017.

Wall, Maureen
'The Age of the Penal laws, 1691-1778', in T.W Moody and F.X. Martin, *The Course of Irish History*, Cork University Press, 1967.

Waterer, J. W.
Leather, Boston and London, Ginn, 1959.

Waugh, Norah
Corsets and Crinolines, London, Batsford, 1987.

Webb, Maria
The Fells of Swarthmoor Hall, London and Dublin, A.W. Bennett and J. Robertson, 1865.

Webb, Maria
The Penns & Peningtons of the seventeenth Century in their domestic and religious Life, London, Kitto, 1867.

Whatman, Susanna
The Housekeeping Book of Susanna Whatman 1776-1800, Christina Hardyment (ed.), London, National Trust, 1987.

Wichert, Sabine and O'Dowd, Mary (eds.)
Chattel, Servant or Citizen: Women's Status in Church, State and Society, Belfast, Institute of Irish Studies, Queen's University, 1995.

Wigham, Maurice
Newtown School, Waterford, Newtown School, 1998.

Wigham, Maurice
The Irish Quakers A short History, Dublin, Historical Committee of the Religious Society of Friends in Ireland, 1992.

Willoughby, Karen
Slates UP!; Schools and Schooling in the Nineteenth Century, Dublin, Church of Ireland College of Education, 2005.

Witney Antiques
Samplers, Town and Country (catalogue), The Classic Press, 1997.

Yacoub, Mohamed
Stone Paintings the Mosaics of the Bardo Museum, Sousse, Contraste, 2003.

Yardwood, Doreen
The Encyclopaedia of World Costume, London, Batsford, 1978.

GLOSSARY

Over the centuries many words have changed their primary meaning with usage, and some have become obsolete or dropped out of use altogether. There may also be differences between British and American usage. Measurements and money have changed with the shift from imperial to metric. Technical terms relating to sewing may vary from one writer to another.

Baize
Coarse, woollen cloth with a long nap. Various colours but now mainly green.

Bolting/Bolton
Coarse cloth for sieving flour, sometimes used as a sampler base.

Broadcloth
Good quality wide woollen cloth. Chiefly used for men's clothes.

Brocade
Silk fabric with raised pattern.

Calico
Plain white cotton cloth, in USA refers to printed cotton. (Name derives from Calcutta/Kolkata, India).

Camlet /Camelot/Camblet
Various combinations of wool, silk, mohair, and linen or cotton.

Cambric
Very fine white linen.

Cassimere
A thin fine twilled woollen cloth used for men's clothing.

Closed robe
A gown of joined bodice and skirt with no front opening.

Corduroy
Coarse thick-ribbed fabric.

Crepe
Lightweight worsted. Thin plain weave gauze (of highly twisted silk- crape.

Damask
Monochrome silk fabric woven with designs, also damask linen

Dimity
Cotton cloth woven with stripes and patterns, for bed curtains and garments.

Drab from French *drap* (cloth)
A dull light brown or yellowish brown cloth.

Drugget
Formerly a lightweight fabric of pure wool, or a union of wool and silk or wool and linen used for clothing. Later a coarse woollen material often used for floor covering.

Duroy
A coarse woollen fabric (not corduroy).

Flannel
An open woollen material.

Frieze
Coarse, hard woollen cloth, heavily felted with a nap. A speciality of Ireland.

Fulling
The process of felting woollen cloth by pummelling it in water to shrink it and make it firm.

Fustian
Coarse thick twilled cloth of cotton and linen, with a nap, often dyed a dark colour.

Gauze
Sheer transparent silk first made in Gaza. Also made of cotton or linen.

Jean
A strong cotton cloth. The name derives from Genoa where it originated (French *toile de Gênes*).

Harebine
Thin rather stiff woollen material for women's wear.

Kersey
Coarse, narrow woollen cloth, usually ribbed. (Name derives from the English village of Kersey).

Kerseymere/Cassimere
A soft, lightweight woollen cloth, often twilled.

Lawn
Very fine white linen resembling cambric. (Name derives from Laon, France).

Levantine
A strong, twilled silk first made in the Levant.

Lutestring
A glossy silk fabric.

Muslin
1 (Britain and Ireland) A very fine transparent cotton material originally from Mosul, Iraq.
2 (USA) Heavier cotton goods used for bedding and shirts etc.

Poplin
A mixed fabric of silk warp and a worsted weft with a corded surface, developed in late seventeenth-century Dublin. Can be plain or watered, brocaded or plaid.

Plush
Cloth of silk, cotton, wool etc., with a nap softer and longer than velvet.

Say
Fine, twilled cloth of wool, or of wool and silk.

Sarsenet/Sarcenet
A fine soft silk, possibly of Saracen origin.

Satin
Silk fabric of close texture with a glossy face and dull back.

Serge
A twilled worsted.

Stuff
Thin worsted without nap or pile.

Tabinet
A watered fabric of silk and wool resembling poplin; a speciality of Irish weavers. (Name attributed to a Huguenot weaver with this name).

Tabby
Watered silk taffeta. Striped appearance.

Taffeta
Light-weight, glossy silk.

Tammy
Very fine worsted of good quality, often with a glazed finish. Often used as a base for samplers.

Thickset
Coarse fustian with a dense close-grained nap.

Vandyke
Edging for a collar or a garment with V-shaped points. (Named after the painter).

Worsted
A fine smooth yarn spun from combed long staple wool. Term also used for the fabric woven from this.

INDEX